NEW ENGLAND IN THE AMERICAN REVOLUTION

Stories of Starvation, Disease and Determination

ROBERT A. GEAKE

Published by The History Press
An imprint of Arcadia Publishing
Charleston, SC
www.historypress.com

First published 2025

Manufactured in the United States

ISBN 9781467170222
Hardcover ISBN 9781540299802

Library of Congress Control Number: 2025941119

Notice: The information in this book is true and complete to the best of our knowledge. It is offered without guarantee on the part of the author or The History Press. The author and The History Press disclaim all liability in connection with the use of this book.

CONTENTS

PREFACE

During the course of the Revolutionary War, the skirmishes, battles, naval confrontations and covert missions conducted in the colonies brought British, French, German and American troops together both on the field and in encampments—where foot soldiers, artillerymen and officers from all forces often found themselves battling an enemy that could be more lethal than any wound suffered in war. As U.S. Army medical historian Dr. Mary C. Gillett notes,

> *It has been estimated that, during the American Revolution, 90 percent of the deaths occurring among the inexperienced, poorly clothed, poorly fed soldiers of the Continental Army, most of them country boys without previous exposure to communicable diseases, and 84 percent of those among the seasoned, disciplined British regulars were from disease.*[1]

Add to this astonishing number the prisoners of war who died of cold and hunger. In terms of human loss, the American Revolutionary War was more fatal to its participants off the field of battle than the wars to come, until those of the twentieth century.

This volume examines the battles fought by communities to gather and continually provide provisions and men for the American army—and by the soldiers themselves, who faced disease, hunger, imprisonment and death throughout the course of the War of Independence. It is an account of the often brutal, impoverished and threadbare existence of the Continental army and the difficulties faced in providing medical care for thousands of troops who were scattered in encampments throughout the rebellious colonies. It also takes a straightforward look at the treatment of prisoners of war by both sides, a complex war in itself within the boundaries of the greater conflict between Great Britain and the United States.

My hope in writing this book has been to illuminate for the reader a chapter in the history of the War of Independence that is sometimes overlooked, though I credit those historians who have written stellar books on the subjects covered here. I hope mine can stand among them and offer the reader a compelling narrative equal to the stories of these brave soldiers of the revolution who faced those risks and who perhaps feared them even more than death by musket fire or the fatal flight of an unseen cannon ball.

The resilience of young Americans willing to face these consequences again and yet again through the eight years of the conflict, as well as the resolution of American officers under General Washington, would ultimately win the war—but the fight would continue for many suffering from the aftereffects of the grueling years of service, from the commander in chief to the humblest conscript in a small-town militia. This work is a tribute to both the great and humble among those who believed and fought in the American Revolution.

CHAPTER 1

STATE OF WAR

The Call to Arms in the New England Colonies

One hundred and fifty years after the first Europeans settled on the continent of British North America, few Americans, as the British called them, could read the tea leaves, so to speak, and foresee the coming separation between the mother country and the colonies. Even as tensions simmered over constrictions on American manufacturing and fees and taxes on all manner of goods, few could imagine the coming war. Americans had loyally taken up arms for Great Britain in the conflicts with Spain and France and their Indigenous allies. A few brought those British-made weapons home, but by 1770, there were fewer guns in American homes than during those troubled times of generations past.

In those years preceding the American Revolution, most men who did own guns in the colonies carried at least a fowling gun, an early, long-barreled predecessor of the rifle used for hunting fowl, as the name implies, or smaller game. Those in remote or wilderness regions might also own a "buck and ball" rifle for hunting deer or moose or to protect their livestock from larger predators.

The fowlers manufactured in colonial New England became distinctly American, compared to the long-utilized guns of European manufacture. As arms historian Merrill Lindsey explains, "The long fowlers themselves took on a New England look. They were no longer English, Dutch, or French. They were in a class by themselves—heavy yet graceful."[2] The New England fowler featured a long barrel of fifty inches or more and was fitted with a stock made of cherry, curly maple or walnut. The stock was carved in a graceful "roman nose" design, which made the fowler less cumbersome to carry and handle in the forest. The gun's hardware was almost always imported, though by the beginning of the revolution, local manufacturers were producing locks, trigger guards, side plates and butt plates of their own design. In addition, singular touches of the maker's hand—the decorative relief carving around the breech and moldings between the barrel and ramrod as well as around the lock—gave the weapon a subtle elegance.

The generations passed into the pre-revolutionary era, and forested regions shrank as the colonies became more enveloped in the widening world of goods and commerce. Even rural communities had little by way of woodlands left. By 1770, a coach carrying visitors through the region from one town to another would have seen mills along every river and, beyond the towns, a horizon of pasture and orchards, laid quilt-like upon the land. It was only beyond these pastures, in the woodlands leading into the hills and mountains, that one could see what wilderness remained.

Aside from those left over from the early and mid-eighteenth-century empirical wars that were kept by families, muskets were now used mainly by sportsmen and, as such, produced by gunsmiths throughout New England. Dedicated hunters traveled up to northern New England, as they still do today, to hunt deer, moose and bear. A hunter of the colonial era would have seen all these without concern for the population of the species, though within a few generations, the once thriving herds of caribou in Maine and Vermont had become extinct. In southern New England, the owners of large estates in Connecticut and Rhode Island adopted foxhunting as a sporting passion in the eighteenth century. The estates being smaller than those in England, such "hunts" would set out on foot, following the hounds.

The New England rifle crafted then was, as historian Lindsey describes it, "a practical and conservative tool for everyday use. The small amount of embellishment is executed in good taste. The New England gunsmith placed his emphasis on fine workmanship and the careful fit of wood to metal."[3] Those made for heavier game had a barrel of at least forty inches, with a heavy stock to absorb the recoil of a .45 caliber load of shot or a single ball. The straight-cut rifling of the barrel allowed for accuracy up to one hundred yards. Such rifles became the weapon of choice as militia units formed and practiced their marksmanship, but these were usually brought from home. Gun manufacturing was still in its artisan state. While there were several small factories in a few Massachusetts and Connecticut towns, gunsmithing was still largely an individual occupation, and few thought of expanding into large-scale manufacturing.[4]

Historian Michael Bellesiles caused a stir with his 2000 book *Arming America*, in which he claimed to have explored the probate records of northern New

Flintlock rifle and pistol. *Wikipedia Commons.*

Blacksmith shop in Hoover, Massachusetts. *Wikipedia Commons.*

England and western Pennsylvania in the years before the Revolutionary War and found that only 10 percent of families owned guns in these regions of the colonies.[5] These claims were almost immediately disputed, but the book was embraced by those espousing gun control in America, as did the author himself. Much of the skepticism about *Arming America* focused on data from probate records that Bellesiles claimed to have examined, and indeed, those numbers were greatly changed in the paperback version, published in 2003. The percentage of colonists who owned guns was adjusted to 21 percent. This is still a low figure—and one also disputed by some historians, as were Bellesiles's readings of journals and diaries outside of New England, where guns and hunting were more prevalent. However, previously published inventories of rural New England communities between the years 1750 and 1775 seem to bear his argument out, showing that of forty-one selected households, just sixteen held firearms.

A small survey, Abbot Lowell Cumming's *Rural Household Inventories, Establishing the Names, Uses, and Furnishings of Rooms in the Colonial New England Home 1650–1775*, gives a glimpse into the wider network of households in rural communities. Several held multiple firearms. Captain Richard Bracket of Braintree, Massachusetts, held "a gun and brass bullet mold" as well as "a pair of pistols."[6] Aaron Davis Jr. of Roxbury held "1 gun, sword and sash" in his household and "4 old guns" in his shop behind his house. A case could be made that many of the inventories selected were those of wealthy merchants, judges and justices of the colony and that one might expect to find more arms in the households of tradesmen and shopkeepers, but that seems not to have been the case:

Samuel Payson, a tanner in Roxbury, held just "one old musket, sword, &,…"—clearly treasured relics of his service with Great Britain. Payson was a man of modest means, owning, beyond his house and barn, "fifteen acres mowing land adjoining the north side of the road in Reversion," an additional fifteen acres for pasturing his animals and twenty acres of woodland on "clapboard hill."[7] On the other hand, cordwainer Consider Leeds's firearms were among the most valuable possessions in his modest Dartmouth home. His inventory shows an apparently widowed man whose house contained four beds, a chest of drawers and a minimal number of chairs or other furniture. Leeds's kitchen was full of the usual kettles, skillets and iron pots but shared space with "sundry axes, hoes, and beetle wedges." These findings may be said to be corroborated by surveys in Providence, Rhode Island, as we will see. What cannot be disputed is that, however many guns in their varied forms were in the hands of individuals, the stores of

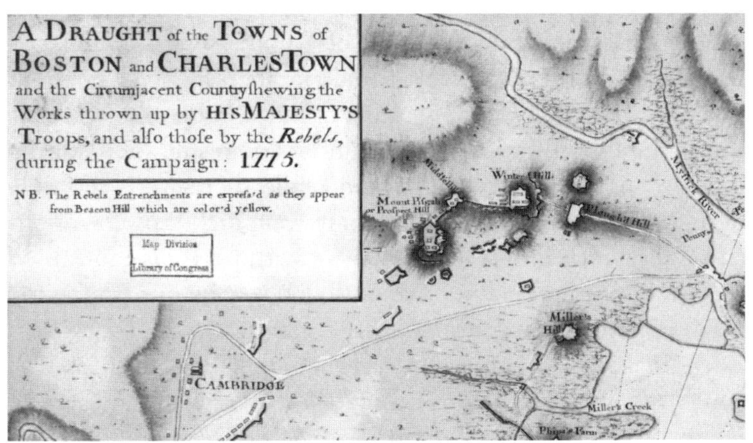

Map of Boston circa 1775. *Wikipedia Commons.*

ammunition, firearms and cannon were all in a neglected state at the start of the American Revolution.

Each community had its own armory or "powder magazine" to store the town's arsenal and gunpowder, though these had been neglected during the years of peace after 1763. The town of Boston, Massachusetts, had issued its last contract for weapons for the defense of the colony in 1745. Connecticut's stores of arms were apparently so low that the colony issued a proclamation that men of the militia were required to furnish their own weapons. This, I believe, was key: the lack of guns in households was partly due to the populace's belief that the town had sufficient arms and powder should they be needed in an emergency, while this was hardly the reality.

Guns were not readily available either in Indigenous communities or within the widely sprawled communities of free Black Americans in New England. The Indigenous peoples of the region with whom seventeenth-century investors, eager to profit from beaver and other pelts in New England, had eagerly traded guns, were subsequently severely marginalized in the colonies by laws passed against their buying liquor and visiting Whites' homes after dark and the attempted indoctrination of Indigenous children into English language, writing, religion and culture, which ultimately led to the armed conflict known today as King Philip's War. The resulting devastation to Indigenous nations and the wholesale distribution of male captives to planters in the West Indies, some in trade for enslaved Africans, marginalized Indigenous survivors even further.

By 1700, the Nipmuc and other remnants of Massachusetts tribes had abandoned their lands to be placed in "Christian" Indian towns. The Pokanoket briefly held oversight of these lands and, though scattered, held together as a nation. The Narragansett people of Rhode Island were placed on a reservation in 1700, though there were tribal members living throughout the colony and beyond. By the 1750s, a significant number had departed for Christian communities away from their homeland.[8] The result, then, for the remaining Native Americans was poverty, and while there were certainly skilled Indigenous blacksmiths who could repair weapons, those weapons must have been scarce indeed. It is more likely that those Indigenous men who hunted for sustenance and ceremony continued to practice traditional and time-honored methods of hunting.

When it came to African Americans, those free and especially the enslaved, reports of uprisings, rebellion and acts of revenge had been published in New England newspapers since the Great Stono River Slave Rebellion of 1739, and by the 1770s, local governments were still deeply divided on the issue of allowing Black men, free or enslaved; Indigenous men; and indentured servants of mixed race into local militias.[9] While a significant number of African American and Indigenous men did serve in southern New England militias, especially in support of British troops during Queen Anne's and the Seven Years' Wars, it may be argued that in preparing for the War of Independence, little was done to place guns in the hands of people of color before Lord Dunmore's proclamation of November 1775.

The issue of a lack of weapons became acute as tensions with Great Britain continued to mount in the colonies. The inhabitants of the smallest of these, Rhode Island, displayed a fierce independence in burning a British revenue schooner, the HMS *Gaspee*, in 1772, when it ran aground on Namquid Point, a long sand barrier that stretches nearly three-quarters of the way across the entrance to the Providence River as the tide retreats into Narragansett Bay. The resultant legal wrangling and the British authorities' failure to hold Rhode Island's rebels to account was partly responsible for Parliament's ban on the export of firearms, gunpowder and other military stores to the colonies in 1774.[10]

In June 1774, the Rhode Island General Assembly passed an act establishing the Providence Light Infantry.[11] The general assembly placed the independent militias under one body, the Cadet Company, and assigned a colonel who would take command under supervision of the governor. That same year, Rhode Island blacksmith Jeremiah Hopkins, brother of Governor Stephen Hopkins, moved from Scituate to Coventry, and he soon petitioned the state, along with his son Elisha, to conduct a lottery, which would earn them the sum of $200—enough to outfit his workshop "so as to make guns and smaller arms with advantage to myself and others at this

Waters off Gaspee Point. *Photo by author.*

time when guns are so much wanted and not to be had from England."[12] Such lotteries were often used as a quick method of raising cash and to get subscribers to improve roads or help to build a needed mill or waterworks.

New England communities responded in other ways to the rising crisis in the region. When Boston ports were closed by the British in June 1774, support from the colonies began pouring into the city.[13] The citizens of East Greenwich took up subscriptions to come to the aid of their neighbors to the north. Not all citizens of the town agreed, and after a loyalist mob nearly burned the town at the close of summer, forty-nine male citizens signed a pact to form the first independent company of militia in the colony. The proliferation of militia units, both regenerated and formed anew in the following months, including independent companies throughout the colonies, made the manufacture and procurement of arms of critical importance.

Within the colonies, Pennsylvania and New York held a greater advantage than those in New England, as foundries and gunsmiths were already established there in significant numbers. These men produced the long, smooth-bored rifles that became popular among the enlistees of the famed riflemen units that fought with such deadly accuracy against the British officer corps.

Connecticut militiaman with a Brown Bess. *Courtesy of Jack Bullock.*

Early muskets for New England's militias would have been based on the 1765 British model of the "Brown Bess" musket.[14] While individual gunsmiths imparted details in scrollwork and, sometimes, in the stock, the muskets were generally of the same design.

By January 1775, Rhode Island blacksmith Stephen Jenks, whose family operated carpentry, blacksmithing and forge shops on the property they owned just below the Pawtucket Falls, had begun supplying New England militias with muskets of his own manufacture.[15] That year, he sold an unrecorded quantity of muskets, including twenty gun barrels with ramrods and bayonets, to the Town of Providence.[16] So fine was Jenks's work that a committee led by John Brown of Providence purchased from him what is believed to have been an intricately designed fowler rifle as Rhode Island's first presentation arm, given to a visiting Oneida sachem the following year.

An attempted raid on the magazines of Massachusetts met stiff opposition, particularly in Salem, where British regulars, or "lobsterbacks," under the command of Colonel Alexander Leslie were thwarted by civilians who pulled up the drawbridge over the river and a gathering armed mob shouting threats across the water, resulting in a British withdrawal.[17] The skirmishes at Lexington and Concord just a week later, on April 19, only exacerbated the need for armaments, both for militias and home defense.

In the majority of the colonies, committees of safety were formed, the first in Boston on October 27, 1774, its members three men from the city and six others from the surrounding counties.[18] These took charge of procuring the needed weapons for militia and citizens alike. Even as the militia companies marched with their own weapons to Boston that spring, Rhode Island resisted forming a committee of safety. Governor Joseph Wanton still sided with Great Britain, and that inclination led to a tug-of-war with the legislature until he was removed from office. On June 12, 1775, Nicholas Cooke, the newly appointed governor, acted on the Rhode Island General Assembly's request that "every man in the Colony, able to bear Arms…equip himself with Arms and Ammunition, according to law."[19] Those men joined with the militia of their towns and rural villages in the march to Cambridge and would then be conscripted into the Continental army to lay siege to Boston.

Privateer Nathaniel Fanning recorded the recollections of a British officer of the gathering rebel forces:

> *I recollect, said he, a person who arrived in Boston about the time that the rebels were collecting their forces near this town…who told me that the main road leading from New York to Boston was covered with men…to join the rebel forces under the command of the rebel general Washington. Those men, thus on their march were what they called the militia; some of whom were clothed in rags, with a knapsack, or something like it, on their backs, and each* [had] *an old rusty mu*[s]*cket up upon their shoulders some of which the gentleman observed, had no locks to them.*[20]

Image of early Providence, circa 1776. *Courtesy of the Rhode Island Historical Society.*

The committees of safety throughout the colonies surveyed towns for preparedness. Individual towns then procured their own gunsmiths for the manufacture of arms, to be stored in magazines or warehouses at a central location. The town of Providence, Rhode Island, assigned Benjamin Thurber the task of supervising "the repair & assembly of muskets" for the town. Thurber also acted as an agent for a network of gun manufacturers, as well as blacksmiths and woodworkers, who could supply the necessary components to assemble a musket.[21]

By 1750, longtime Providence blacksmith and shopkeeper Jacob Whitman had mounted a ship's figurehead of an Ottoman warrior on his house alongside the Providence River as a navigational marker.[22] The 1774 census shows that Whitman's household consisted of fourteen people, including six people of color and one Indigenous servant. In a family history, his granddaughter Jane Keeley recalled, "He had a large forge near the cove. I think it was worked by a large number of hands. He was the owner of a number of slaves, the most trusty one was Baine, he had the care of the forge."[23] Keeley lists his enslaved people as "Primmy No Nose…Cato, Pomp, Sisser, Card, Amy, Tullis, Nancy, and Dorcas." Primmy and a "Temp" No Nose appear as former servants of Cyrus Butler in a 1768 survey that listed 184 Black men in Providence. Primmy may well have been a paid laborer by this time, along with others in the house who worked in the blacksmith shop.[24] Keeley recalled that the enslaved "lived in a row of houses near [Whitman's] own that faced Westminster Street."

There were seemingly many apprentices and enslaved workers involved in blacksmith shops, gunsmith shops and forges. There was a wealth of artisans in the harbor town.[25] Some, such as Paul Allen, Amos Atwell and Josiah Greene, each of whom advertised in the *Providence Gazette*, provided gunlocks and gun barrels in those crucial early months.

Providence blacksmith Prince Keene manufactured ten gun barrels and thirty bayonets for the town. The war thrust upon them soon became a boon to Keene and craftsmen like him. Keene himself was born, raised and married in Plymouth County, Massachusetts. Sometime before 1773, he and his family removed to Providence, as by the time of his contract with the town, his family included a two-year-old son to support. Atwell and Greene, in the meantime, had forged a partnership to better meet the demand.

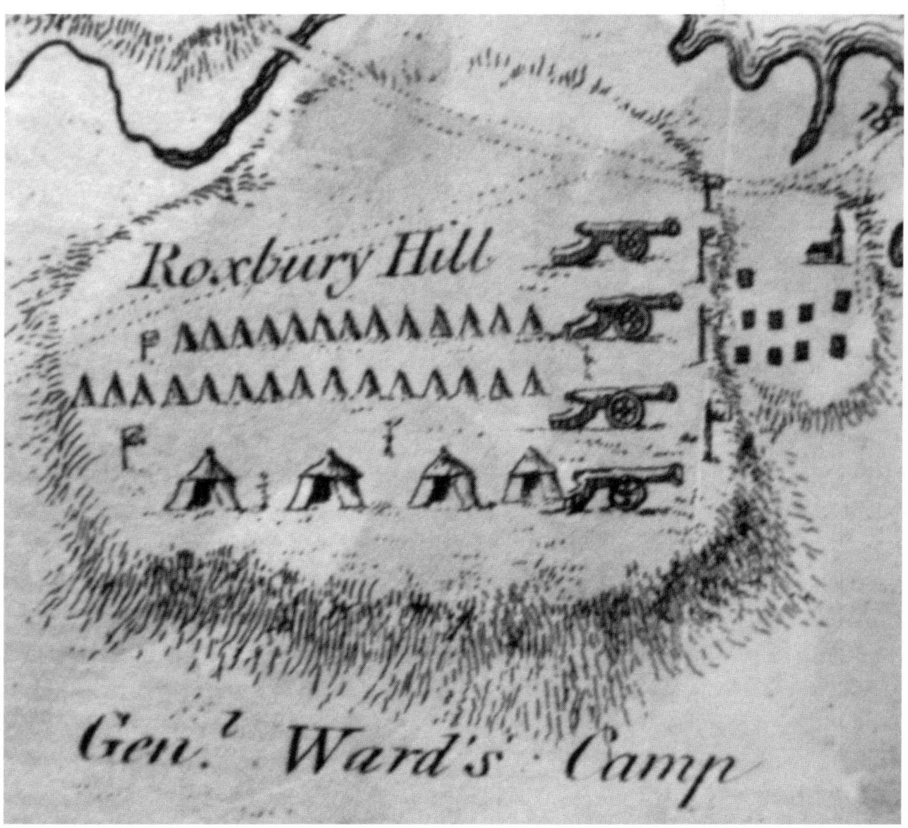

Detail of a map showing the encampment on Roxbury Hill during the siege of Boston. *Courtesy of the RI Archives.*

During the summer of 1775, as the siege of Boston occupied the colonies' forces, Thurber continued procuring the necessary stocks and hardware for needed arms. William Potter sold the town of Providence twenty guns outright. Gunsmith Thomas Bicknell produced ten gun barrels.[26] Edward Martin manufactured and sold to the town "fifty-four sets of gun trimmings, eighty-eight rods of swivels, and one hundred and nineteen sets of scabbard hooks and plates." Tanner Martin Thurber manufactured cartridge boxes, bayonet belts, scabbards and gun trimmings for the town. One bill alone accounted for fifty-one cartridge boxes and 102 bayonet belts.[27] Christopher Barney also produced "twenty-six sets of gun trimmings" at his Providence shop.

The Jenks family continued producing guns. John Jenks, who by then had opened his own shop in Gloucester, manufactured and sold some twenty-seven gun barrels with ramrods to Providence in November 1775, twenty-two of which came with semi-completed stocks, making the woodworkers' job in completing the muskets easy and efficient.[28]

Outside of occupied Boston, Massachusetts, gunsmiths were kept occupied producing arms for the troops laying siege to the town. Most had brought their firearms from home. Hugh Orr, a long-established gunsmith from Bridgewater who had produced five hundred stands of arms for Massachusetts Bay's magazine on Castel Island in 1745, now saw his guns confiscated by the British. Orr erected a cannon foundry and produced iron and brass cannon in sizes ranging from three-pounders to forty-two-pounders for the siege of the town.

Thomas Barret and his son Samuel were already operating a gunsmith shop in Concord before the battle at Concord Bridge. A fellow gunsmith named Isaac Davis was commander of the supporting Ashton Militia that day and, while leading his company, was felled by the first British volley. "Deacon" Barret contracted to provide muskets for the Massachusetts Committee of Safety in 1775. A report to the committee commented on Barret's "fine laboratory for gun making…where every branch of the business is carried on." The shop being located near a stream, the tasks of boring, grinding and polishing could be accomplished with machines powered by water.

Gunsmith Jonathan Blaisedale was appointed armorer to the Colony of Massachusetts Bay on May 15, 1775. Like his contemporaries, he cast far and wide across the colony to secure adequate arms. One early musket maker for the Committee of Safety was Eliphalet Leonard, of Easton, Massachusetts. Leonard was reputedly one of the first steelmakers in the colonies and proudly marked his Brown Bess–modeled muskets "E. Leonard in Easton 1776." His son Jonathan had cofounded a gun forge in Stoughton, Massachusetts, by 1778. All told, the Massachusetts Committee of Safety contracted with some thirty-seven musket makers, scattered from Attleboro to Bridgewater to North Brookfield and Sutton.

In November 1775, the Continental Congress encouraged the colonies to "keep their gunsmiths at work" and specified the weapon they desired: "good flintlocks with bayonets" for the army.

> *Each flintlock to be made with a good bridle lock, ¾ of an inch bore, and of good substance at the breech, the barrel to be 3 ft. 8 inches in length, the bayonet to be eight inches in the blade, with a steel ramrod, the upper loop thereof to be trumpeted.*[29]

The congress required that each musket manufactured for troops of the Continental line be stamped with the letters "C-R." Desiring to control and ensure quality, some states required the manufacturer to account for their origin. Some of the earliest Massachusetts Bay gunsmiths stamped "M.B." on the barrel near the lock. Connecticut required the name or initials of the gunmaker to be stamped on the gun. The state also took the step of impounding guns, stamping the owner's initials with the promise of payment in due time. Rhode Island required that all guns manufactured in the state be stamped with the state coat of arms.[30]

Some legislators deviated slightly from congressional orders. The Massachusetts House of Representatives decreed on November 3, 1775:

> *Every effective and substantial Fire Arm…manufactured in this Colony* [requires] *a barrel of three feet and nine inches in length that will carry an ounce ball, a good bayonet with a blade not less than eighteen inches in length, a steel ramrod with a spring to retain same, two loops for gun strings and the makers name stamped or engraved on the lock.*

The demand for longer bayonets grew as the war continued. Some manufacturers produced actual swords that, with a brass mount, could be slid and locked into place on the barrel.

Local artisans throughout the colonies soon adapted to the need for guns and took advantage of the opportunity. Cabinetmaker Ambrose Peck of Swansea, Massachusetts, turned to furnishing stocks and repairing guns. He would come to produce guns of extraordinary quality. One such musket, featured in historian Lindsey's *The New England Gun*, displays

Peck's skills in carving bas-relief and inscribing. The long top barrel, created with patriotic fervor, is inscribed with large, elegant letters that read "TO DEFEND CONSTITUTIONAL LIBERTY AND PROPERTY." Further engraving on the brass wrist escutcheon portrays a scene of a heron and an eagle fighting, around which is inscribed the Latin phrase "EXITUS IN DUBIOUS" and the name "A. CARPENTER."[31] The fowler-like stock is equipped with an unusual feature: a slit in the butt plate in which to sheath the bayonet.

Carpenter Elihu Peck of Providence also turned to stocking guns, and Thomas Tew of Newport repaired the hardware on small armaments. He would later briefly serve as a captain in the infantry and be appointed keeper of the Newport Jail, a post he held until his death in 1821.[32] Blacksmith Amos Atwater left his own shop and contributed greatly to the production of fine cast cannons manufactured at Hope Furnace in Scituate.

Such artisans became valued in these communities struggling to support the war. Nathan Miller of East Greenwich, Rhode Island, was exempted from enlistment in exchange for his service as "an excellent bayonet maker." Miller was a longtime silversmith in town, having worked out of a shop at the rear of his house on the corner of Pierce and Division Streets since 1755. By 1775, his son James was working in the shop as well, having apprenticed with his father since 1767. The senior Miller went on to serve as a captain in the Rhode Island Militia. In South Kingstown, gunsmith Jeremiah Sheffield was active in the Kingston Reds but was exempted that year, along with George Tefft of the same company, for the express purpose of manufacturing and stocking guns.

As the war neared its second year, the Continental army was better armed beyond the fowling pieces and ball and buck muskets brought by citizen soldiers to battle. Still, the need for armaments to supply Continental troops and militia as well as citizens continued.

In the winter of 1775, Timothy Pickering of Salem, Massachusetts, found that of the 618 men mustered into the town militia, each one owned a firearm. Neighboring communities reported 90 percent gun ownership among the enlisted militia.[33] Ordinary civilians, however, remained largely unarmed.

In February 1776, Martin Seamans surveyed the east and west sides of the Providence River to assess the number of guns in preparedness for the defense of the town. He found even fowling pieces woefully lacking. On the town's wealthy east side, he listed 419 men with 305 guns among them. On the more pedestrian west side, 307 men held but 192 guns. Most of the 229 men who did not have a gun received one, and many of the wealthy merchants and government officials received several weapons, presumably for men working for them as well as their own use.

In the town of Warwick, Rhode Island, that same month, the town council voted to authorize James Arnold, Colonel John Waterman and Captain Samuel Aborn to procure "twenty-five arms well equipped with bayonets and cartridge boxes" at the expense of the town. In response to the need for arms, Rhode Island's General Assembly passed an act in the March 1776 session for the procurement of "two thousand stand[s] of good firearms, with bayonets, iron ramrods, and cartouche boxes."[34] Gunmakers like Caleb Harris of Providence produced "twenty-five stand of small arms with bayonets," some with hardware procured from other artisans by Benjamin Thurber. Harris also provided the town with twenty-four cartridge boxes in 1776.

Jenks, Sheffield and Tefft continued to produce "C-R" muskets. Individual rifles and fowlers made in Rhode Island by men like part-time gunmaker Jeremiah Smith of Limerock have also been noted by arms historians. Smith was a lime maker by trade, and while he occasionally produced guns, his principal work was in barrel making and rifling during the winter months. Fowling pieces and muskets manufactured by John Matthewson of Burriville have also been noted and praised for the exceptional skill with which they were crafted. Mathewson's son George would continue the family business and its reputation well into the nineteenth century.

Repairs, when needed, seem to have been maintained between gunmaker Caleb Harris, Thomas Tew and Isaac Tuckerman of Providence, who, in 1776, repaired "forty-seven arms belonging to the town."

Other, lesser skilled artisans contributed to the war effort as well. Richard Mathewson, who operated a saltpeter mill in East Greenwich, also made cartridges for the colony's arsenal. In Providence, John Wells and Waterman Williams also produced paper cartridges as late as 1777.

In the years before the alliance with and purchase of weapons from France placed European weapons once again in American hands, communities of craftsman kept the Continental army, militias and citizens well-armed.[35] Many of these weapons were taken into skirmishes and battles against the British, and a good number of foot soldiers and officers continued to use customized muskets and rifles brought from their own hometowns.

Gunsmiths and artisans had developed skills they "never knew they had, under the emergency" of the call to arms and the American Revolution.[36] These skills allowed for the development of mass quantities of arms under contract for the first time in the nation, and more importantly, the craftsmen's skills and ingenuity led to the development of the machine tool industry, which changed the local agrarian economy with its expansion up and down the Connecticut River valley.

By the close of the eighteenth century, Rhode Island gunsmiths such as Thomas Bicknell, Stephen Jenks and Welcome Mathewson had been joined by Elisha Brown; Hosea Humphry, who partnered with Jenks; and merchant partners William Rhodes and William Tyler—evidence of a well-established cottage community.[37] These artisans would adapt yet again, as the imported French muskets were .69 caliber and featured three iron bands fastened to the stock—both of which, according to historian Harold Peterson, were "important design factors, for they permitted a lighter weapon than the .75 caliber Brown Bess, which needed a fore stock heavy enough support the barrel-fastening pins."[38] The French muskets' hardware was also stronger and more reliable than the British design. These muskets, made at the royal manufactories of Charleville, St. Etienne and Maubeuge, became the standard for the Continental army.[39]

Of equal importance was the manufacture of cannons and mounted guns for the defensive forts and groundworks constructed along the shoreline of New England, as well as for the fledgling Continental navy. Two types of iron manufacturing were important for the war effort. Cast iron, which was molded into ingots called pig iron, was heavy on carbon and too hard to hammer into shape. It was melted instead in a blast furnace and then cast in molds to make frying pans, kettles and tools. Wrought iron, a much softer metal, was easily hammered into horseshoes, wheel rims and rods for nails.[40] For efficiency, ironworks in New England generally consisted of a compound that included a blacksmith shop, a foundry, bloomeries, a charcoal kiln and a lime kiln.

In Rhode Island, John and Nicholas Brown partnered with Stephen Hopkins to found an iron forge in the town of Scituate. As shipbuilders and slave traders, the Browns had use of a complex that could include a blast furnace, a forge and a blacksmith shop. The men established the Hope Furnace shortly after the discovery of pig iron in 1765. Initially, the forge produced goods for the Browns' shipping concerns as well as household goods, from teakettles to nails, hinges and iron hoops. At the onset of the war, the forge began producing cannon and guns for the revolution. The Hope Furnace would produce some seventy-six cannon for the Continental navy as well as shoreline defense.

The old Saugus Iron Works of Connecticut was reopened for use during the war. The reconstructed ironworks—the oldest known forge in

Iron furnace, Kent, Connecticut. *Photo by author.*

the country—became one of the primary sources of manufactured tools, weapons and hardware for the Continental army during the war.

Elisha and Samuel Forbes established several forges in the years leading up to the war. Having established two forges in East Canaan, Connecticut, Samuel Forbes was enticed to establish another ironworks there by Norfolk leaders, who offered him a 999-year lease in 1760. Forbes established the forge and eventually sold it to Thomas Day Sr., who agreed that he would contract with Forbes for all the iron ore needed for production.

Among his holdings, Samuel Forbes owned two iron ore beds in Salisbury, Connecticut. These allowed him to supply his brother's forges as well as the forge in Norfolk. He partnered with Ethan Allen of Lakeville to establish a blast furnace in 1762 and went on to purchase several blast furnaces in Norfolk as well as a nail mill in Washington, Connecticut. The brothers' partnership came to an untimely end when Elisha "died from the kick of a horse" in Williston, Vermont. Soon after, Samuel became the sole proprietor of the family's ironworks.

During the war, Forbes was persuaded to return to the Lakeville blast furnace, where he oversaw the production of a significant number of "heavy and light cannon, cannon balls, grapeshot, huge cast iron kettles for soldiers' meals, pig iron, and other cast iron products."[41] He also increased production at the East Canaan forges, producing iron rods that were used by swordsmiths to make bayonets, daggers, knives, sabers and swords.

The Salisbury Forge in Salisbury, Connecticut, had also been established by the Forbeses in 1762. The forge was sold to Richard Smith of Hartford, Connecticut, in 1768. Smith was a loyalist and had relocated to Boston at the outset of the Revolution. As a result, the Connecticut Committee of Safety ordered on January 17, 1776, that "the foundry, furnace lands and ore beds on the estate of Richard Smith, late of Boston, now gone to the enemy, be taken over."

Within a few weeks, the Committee of Safety had appointed Lemuel Bryant as cannon founder; David Carver, David Oldham and Zebulon White were hired as molders. By March, under the supervision of Colonel Porter, production of cannon—three-, four-, six-, nine- and eighteen-pounders—had begun. Perhaps the most important contributions to the war from this forge were the improvements that, by 1778, allowed the casting of thirty-two-pounders. The forge also provided cannon shot and produced hand grenades. In 1777, the forge was given the contract to produce swivel shot and grenades for the ship *Oliver Cromwell.* The forge was also part of a contract to supply all the guns for the American vessels *Alliance* and *Confederacy*.[42] Local historians have called the Salisbury forge the "Arsenal of the Revolution" and claim that 80 percent of the cannons used in the Revolution were produced at the forge.

In Massachusetts, John Adam Sr. and his son established a forge in Taunton in 1777. By the closing year of the war, the Springfield Arsenal in Western Massachusetts had evolved from making cartridges and accoutrements to casting bronze cannons and building carriages for the four-pound guns that the French had given for the American cause.

CHAPTER 2

FACING KNOWN AND UNKNOWN ENEMIES

A Scourge of Ailments for the Army

When General George Washington took command of American forces in Cambridge on July 2, 1775, the whole of New England was in the throes of a smallpox epidemic. As a result, one of his first acts as commander in chief was to ask Congress to establish a Department of Medicine for the Continental army. Once the department was formed, physicians were recruited to serve as surgeons, both embedded with the troops and in occupied houses and buildings converted into hospitals throughout the colonies. The department would face many challenges during the war, chief among them the following:

> *The colonial physicians who formed the American Army's Medical Department in 1775 were all civilian practitioners, many without any military experience. A small percentage had earned M.D. degrees, but most were either apprenticed or self-trained, and few made any attempt to specialize in the manner customary in Europe, where a choice was usually made among medicine, surgery, and pharmacy.*[43]

In the face of the physicians' inexperience, Washington attempted to reinforce the importance of general cleanliness and encamping in "healthy areas" uphill from swamps and the "miasmas," fogs of noxious odors that infected the air during the humid days of summer. Despite Washington's best efforts, smallpox continued to be the scourge of the army. In the spring of 1776, it became widespread among the troops, and it ultimately killed more soldiers than fell in battle that year. In February the following year,

Washington ordered the inoculation of all soldiers in the Continental army, writing to medical director Dr. William S. Shippen that if such measures were not taken against the disease, "We should have more to dread from it than the sword of the enemy."[44]

Such measures had remained controversial for more than sixty years, despite the recurrence of epidemics during that same span of decades. New England's population retained the greatest distrust of inoculation during the mid-eighteenth century, but the outbreak of 1764, which affected 700 of Boston's inhabitants and killed at least 124 citizens, prompted many, including John Adams, to be inoculated for the first time. Those inoculated could expect to come down with a mild case of the disease, but some patients contracted a more virulent strain and faced serious illness or even death. Patients were usually "prepared" for inoculation for a week prior to the visit to the doctor: given a purgative, usually of mercury, and instructed to abstain from eating meat and other foods.

Adams's doctor's instructions consisted of "a diet of milk and a course of mercurial preparations."[45] Adams, in his account of his own and his brother's inoculation, recalled:

> *Dr. Perkins demanded my left arm and Dr. Warren my brother's. They took their lancets and with their points divided the skin for about a quarter of an inch and just suffering the blood to appear, buried a thread about a quarter of an inch long in the channel. A little lint was laid over the scratch and a Piece of Ragg pressed on, and then a bandage bound over all.*[46]

The commander of the army also shared his concern about the spread of the illness with one of his most trusted advisors, General Horatio Gates. Worried that the movement of troops through infected areas would affect troops at encampments, Washington wrote to Gates that he had heard from Philadelphia: "Dr. Shippen wrote me that he intended to Inoculate the Troops as they came in, but that never can safely be done, except Inoculation goes thro the whole Army."[47]

On Washington's orders, thousands of troops would be inoculated. At the onset, however, there was evidently insubordination within the ranks. Dr. Lewis Beebe, assigned as surgeon to the troops on General Benedict Arnold's 1776 Canadian campaign, recorded that on Thursday, May 16,

> *General orders were given by Gen. Arnold for Inoculation, accordingly Col. Porters Reg. was inoculated. On fryday Gen. Thomas arrived at head*

> *Quarters from Quebeck and gave Counter orders that it should be death for any person to inoculate, and that every person inoculated should be sent immediately to Montreal.*[48]

Most of the regiments in the Northeast encampments were inoculated over the winter and into the spring, when hospitals established in newly taken Trenton and Princeton allowed for mass inoculations. Although some three thousand to four thousand troops never received inoculations, the vast majority of the American army underwent the procedure, so that ultimately, Washington's order was, in the opinion of historian Elizabeth Pell, "one of the most important decisions of the war."

Private Joseph Plumb Martin enlisted on July 6, 1776, in Samuel Peck's Third Company of Douglas's Fifth Battalion from New Haven, Connecticut. His wartime journal described the inoculation process he experienced while encamped with troops at Peekskill, New York, in the spring of 1777.

> *I was soon…ordered off, in company with about four hundred others of the Connecticut forces* [to] *a set of old barracks, a mile or two distant in the Highlands, to be inoculated with the smallpox. We arrived at and cleaned*

Guard at barracks and hospital, Trenton, New Jersey. *Courtesy of Old Barracks Museum, Trenton, New Jersey.*

> *out the barracks, and after two or three days received the infection, which was on the last day of May. We had a guard of Massachusetts troops to attend us. Our hospital stores were deposited in a farmer's barn in the vicinity of our quarters.*[49]

As expected, Martin and the others came down with a mild case of the pox. And like others, Martin remained skeptical about the preventative effects of inoculation, writing, "We lost none, but it was more by good luck, or rather a kind Providence interfering, than by my good conduct that I escaped with life." That "kind Providence" was a large rivulet that ran by the encampment, deepening in places where a species of fish called suckers was abundant. The young private recorded,

> *One of my roommates, with myself, went off one day, the very day on which the pock began to turn upon me. We went up the brook until we were out of sight of the people at the barracks, when we undressed ourselves and went into the water, where it was often to our shoulders, to catch suckers by means of a fishhook fastened to the end of a rod. We continued at this business three or four hours, and when we came out of the water the pustules of the smallpox were well cleansed.*[50]

Contrast this intuitive method of cleansing with what French artillery officer Jean-François-Louis, Comte de Clermont-Crèvecoeur recorded of his experience with Americans and their bathing practices:

> *It is dangerous to go bathing in this country. One sees few Americans indulge in this pastime. They maintain that the water loosens their bowels and causes fevers, and that one can bathe only before dawn or after sundown and stay in the water but a short time.*[51]

The suspicious attitude toward inoculation persisted in parts of New England well into the war. Minister Peleg Burroughs of Tiverton, Rhode Island, preached against inoculation in February 1778 and recorded later that he had "delivered a testimony against many practices in things civil and religious (especially inoculation for the small pox) as being not merely inventions of man, but foolish and sinful inventions."

Between his parishioners, "the perishing state of my neighbors and the abounding iniquities of this land," the minister found almost constant disappointment. Worse still, "My brother William has sent his 3 children to be inoculated…and sister Mary Smith has gone in to tend upon them; notwithstanding our Savior has said 'the whole need not a physician, but that they are sick.'"[52] One begins to see why epidemics raged for so long throughout the region.

As it turned out, the inoculation brought on an unexpected side effect the following spring: what Private Martin described as "the itch," an exasperating condition that flared up on the skin where the sores from the illness had sprouted. "We had no opportunity," he explains, while encamped at a small town between Philadelphia and Lancaster, Pennsylvania, "or at least nothing to cure ourselves with during the whole season. All who had the smallpox at Peekskill had it. We often applied to our officers for assistance to clear ourselves from it, but all we could get was 'Bear it as patiently as you can, when we get into winter quarters you will have leisure and means to rid yourself of it."

The situation for the affected men worsened, but still they had to wait until they reached winter quarters to find relief. Some of the men had acquaintances in the artillery and procured enough sulfur to effect a cure.

> *The first night one half of the party commenced the action by mixing a sufficient quantity of brimstone and tallow, which was the only grease we could get, at the same time not forgetting to mix plenty of hot whiskey toddy, making up a hot blazing fire and laying down an oxhide upon the hearth.… We began the operation by plying each other's outsides with brimstone and tallow and the inside with hot whiskey sling… Two of the assailants were so overcome…by their too great exertions in the action, that they lay all night naked upon the field. The rest of us got to our berths somehow, as well as we could: but we had killed the itch and we were satisfied, for it had almost killed us.*[53]

The British and Hessian troops were aware of the disease as well. Hessian Private Johann Conrad Döhla recorded in his diary in December 1778 from British-occupied Aquidneck Island:

> *Below the city of Newport on Rhode Island, a small island lies in the middle of the river, called Pest, or Smallpox Island, or in German; "Blaterinsel." The people and children who have smallpox are sent there because this is considered a contagious and most dirty disease.*[54]

The following year, Döhla recorded that the men were sent to cut down bushes on the island to fence in their encampment with an abatis, a field fortification made of felled trees to act as a blockade.

> *This Pest Island, lying between Conanicut (Jamestown) and Rhode Island (Aquidneck Island), is a small, narrow island surrounded by water, about a German mile in circumference, and thickly over grown with bushes. Only a single house stands on the entire island, to which those individuals are brought who are suffering from smallpox.*[55]

The united colonies also strove to combat the spread of smallpox and to provide better treatment. In the early summer of 1776, the Rhode Island General Assembly decreed, "One hospital may be established for inoculating the smallpox, in each county in this colony, in such town as the majority of the deputies in the county, in a meeting duly warned, shall agree upon."[56] Said "hospitals" for smallpox victims were to maintain a two-hundred-yard perimeter around the building as well as "set and maintain a sufficient guard, to prevent all persons in the hospital from going beyond those limits, and all persons without, from passing within one hundred yards of them without the permission of the directors of the hospital."[57]

Guards were charged with arresting and jailing any transgressors, and heavy fines were imposed on anyone transporting bedding, linen or clothing from the hospital. Fines were also imposed on recovered victims who traveled "without a certificate of his being thoroughly cleansed therefrom" on their person.

While smallpox was perhaps the most prevalent disease during the war, it was far from the only contagion soldiers would have to battle. Poorly clothed, ill fed and often marched under inhospitable conditions, those in the Continental army and militias on the home front faced a formidable array of illnesses during the eight years of conflict. Historian Jeanne Abrams notes that even as the harsh and deadly winters in New England came to an end, "Spring saw a rise in throat and respiratory infections, including diphtheria, scarlet fever, pleurisy, and pneumonia, and summer brought another host of diseases that thrive in the heat, such as malaria and dysentery.[58]

Private Döhla's journal gives a unique view of the conditions of the British encampment on Staten Island, where, in the summer of 1777, he recorded, "The climate here on Staten Island and in the northern regions of America in general is rather different from ours." The sun rose later and set earlier than in the region of Germany where the young private was from, and while

Map of Rhode Island circa 1777. *Library of Congress.*

the days during the months of July and August were shorter than he was accustomed to, he wrote,

> *In the day the great heat causes suffocation and death....Above all, the air, because of the frequent fogs from the nearby ocean and the foul fumes on Staten Island, is highly unhealthy. Therefore, sicknesses such as putrid fever, diarrhea, and dysentery, often spread through our regiment, and half the men were ill.*

Döhla's regiment, with others, was eventually ordered to Rhode Island, where British forces, who had occupied Aquidneck Island since December 1776, anticipated a coming attack from rebel troops gathering in Tiverton. In March 1779, an epidemic of scurvy swept through the troops on the island. Döhla recorded:

> *Many troops had to go to the hospital. The English doctors and medics prescribed bathing frequently with sea water and keeping the feet warm; also rinsing the mouth out with sea water or, better yet, with good vinegar to clean and stimulate the gums. This scurvy caused red and blue spots on the legs, and the gums became black, foul and swollen. The teeth loosened and they could be pulled out easily with the fingers, so that nothing hard could be chewed.*[59]

Döhla himself was quarantined with others in the "English hospital," and he returned to his company on June 14, 1779, "after having lain there eleven weeks and two days."

When French troops arrived to occupy the island the spring following the British departure, the young Comte de Clermont-Crèvecoeur, a first lieutenant in the Auxonne Regiment of the Royal Corps of Artillery, wrote of their journey:

> *We had aboard a large number of men suffering from scurvy, including some who were seriously ill. I had a touch of it myself—with bad food and poor sleeping quarters in contaminated air, how can one remain healthy?*[60]

Crowded encampments also fostered disease, especially typhus, spread by infected lice. Outbreaks of measles, influenza and dysentery were common in camps. The condition of the encampments and the clothing and hygiene of the men was critical in the field.

In fact, dysentery rivaled smallpox: there were widespread epidemics in heavily settled areas. An old adage from Galen's time stated the simple fact that "where soldiers go, plague will follow," and dysentery proved to be the plague of the eighteenth century. Fever, uncontrollable stomach cramps and bloody diarrhea were all symptoms heralding the disease. An outbreak in Boston in 1775 killed hundreds of people and affected thousands more. The disease spread quickly through both American encampments and the occupying British barracks and went beyond, into the outskirts of the city.

Abigail Adams wrote from her farm in Braintree, "Such is the distress of the neighborhood that I can scarcely find a well person to assist me in looking after the sick....So sickly and mortal a time the oldest man does not remember." Mrs. Adams knew at least the rudimentary practice of disinfecting the house by "cleaning with hot vinegar," a preventative prescribed by Dr. William Buchanan in his popular title *Domestic Medicine*.

Regimental surgeon Dr. Lewis Beebe, with Arnold's campaign in Canada in June 1776, recorded that amid his constant attendance to patients suffering from smallpox, "For 10 days past I have been greatly troubled with the dysentery, and for three days it has been very severe, took Physick in the morning. Hope for some relief."[61]

Reenactor Dan Newman as a regimental surgeon of HM Fifty-Fourth Regiment of Foot, circa 1777. *Courtesy of Dan Newman.*

For foreign troops who had crossed the Atlantic to wage war on Great Britain's behalf, the exposure to illnesses in a place long thought to have pure air and water caused great alarm. Hessian Private Johann Conrad Döhla, unaccustomed to the virulent strain of dysentery on North America's shores, wrote with understandable alarm about suffering from "astonishing diarrhea, the likes of which I had never had in my life, and I was so weak I could not get out of bed." This bout of dysentery laid him up for fourteen days in April 1779.[62]

The noted physician Dr. Craik (whom Washington would consult as president) concocted a cure for dysentery that consisted of "Tinct, Huxam and Tiner, Japon of equal parts, of this mixture one of two spoonfulls were given every morning before breakfast, and again before dinner."[63] Treatment was often purges that left one weaker. A popular medicine called Dr. James Fever Powder included laudanum, a drug used to treat a myriad of eighteenth-century diseases. This bottled form of liquid opium was prescribed for nearly every ailment from insomnia to diarrhea—as well as pain, perhaps the use for which it was most popularly prescribed. So dependent were Americans on laudanum that one noted practitioner quipped that the art of medicine itself "would be a cripple without it."[64]

Most soldiers suffered from some ailment or other much of their time on duty. Unless they were seriously ill, those ailments would need to be treated with whatever available cures could be found. In such a state, weakened soldiers marched from encampment to encampment, often ill clothed and ill provisioned, and if your company had to march through miles of woodlands and swamp, then brush huts for shelter were the best you could do.

Most of the soldiers who had left New England households were familiar with some form of homeopathic medicine, using remedies that had been passed down through generations of families, often recorded as "simples" in diaries, Bibles, ledgers and "medical" books, which gained in popularity during the eighteenth century. Colonial gardens held a host of plants that could be used in potions, tonics, "blisters" and teas, which were often healthier and more successful than the dubious medicines marketed at the time. This homeopathy was also practiced by early physicians and would prove to provide relevant discoveries by surgeons during the war.

Dr. Dutee Jerauld was one such early physician, having moved from his hometown of Medfield, Massachusetts, in 1742 and opened a practice in Warwick, Rhode Island, where he initially confined his practice to the six to eight miles surrounding his home. Dr. Jerauld became well known for his treatments for fevers and chronic diseases. He prepared infusions, syrups and decoctions from indigenous roots and herbs, particularly favoring prickly ash, which he used to treat rheumatic afflictions.[65]

As mothers and daughters were the sole practitioners of the art of grinding, mixing and concocting simples, those fathers, sons and brothers who once relied on such remedies had to procure what treatment they could once far away from home. Both surgeon and common soldier knew those natural plants that could supply diverse remedies: the leaves of the mullein plant, for example, to brew as a tea and clear congestion. The larger, fuzzy soft leaves of the mullein plant were also a good insert for a day's march in worn boots. Lamb's-ear could stem bleeding from small cuts or blisters. Even the common headache could be cured by a brew of chamomile or by grinding basil leaves and mixing them with snuff.[66]

If a researcher were to survey the accounts of Revolutionary War veterans, from surgeons to the common soldier, they would be struck by the diversity of flora and fauna through New England. Such experiments and the uses of these natural medicines were catalogued and categorized by an eighteenth-century American physician. The *Theraputic-Alphabet or a Pocket Dictionary of Medicine, Midwifery, and Surgery* (1787) by Matthew Wilson, doctor of medicine and theology, was the culmination of twenty-nine years of practice as a physician in Delaware. The work provides unmatched insight into colonial medicine, and while it was never published in the doctor's lifetime, some eighteen representative pages were printed in Dr. Maurice Bear Gordon's 1949 history *Aesculapius Comes to the Colonies: The Story of the Early Days of Medicine in the Original Thirteen Colonies*.

Dr. Wilson listed all diseases, ailments and complaints known during his years of practice, in Latin, with vivid descriptions of symptoms and stages of each illness as well as the treatments and cures known to be successful. The doctor identified "Catarrh" as "the most common Disease in our County, yet the least examined or understood. When People are taken with it, they only say they are very poorly, & have catched a bad Cold, & no further Notice is taken of it, till it frequently ends in dangerous Pleurisies, Peripnemonias, Consumption, &etc."[67]

Known remedies for catarrh included "Drinking large draughts of Hydromel," a kind of mead-like drink, drunk warm; a potion called 'Tissots Elder Flowers,' Balsam Traumatic, Vomits, Blisters, Anodynes wt Camphor...Flannel Shirts, smoking tobacco...etc." If these failed to bring about the desired recovery, Dr. Wilson notes, "It will be necessary to give gentle purges."[68] "Recipes" are provided for these "gentle purges," and Dr. Wilson further suggests a "gentle anodyne," to be taken with "large draughts of rosemary or bran tea," for the patient's anxiety. He includes concoctions for effective cough syrups and for maintaining patients' health after recovery.

Alcohol was viewed as a medicinal treatment and even a preventative. Home remedies included hot toddies to ward off colds and congestion. Washington believed rum to be a restorative for the soldiers. A gill (four ounces) was given for guard duty and "fatigue duty" (the tedious labor and noncombat tasks given a soldier), as well as on special occasions. Washington's own preference for a flask of homemade cherry brandy aside, the commander in chief struggled throughout the war to provide rum for the troops, even going so far as to deplete hospital stores and to instruct his officers to confiscate whatever rum might be in the vicinity of encampments, though as historian Joshua Shepherd notes, "It was a two-edged sword….Regimental orderly books are replete with a plethora of infractions—desertion, assault, insubordination, theft—which frequently stemmed from a soldier being inebriated in the first place."[69] As Shepherd explains, "Young soldiers, away from the watchful eyes of parents and family for the first time in their lives, were prone to get into far too much mischief, the results of which were by no means harmless."

Beyond those illnesses curable by household remedies, others required different forms of protection. Malaria was known to visit encampments during those months when mosquitoes, rather than "miasmas," threatened the lives of the troops. As malaria was a mosquito-borne disease (but not known as such until the late eighteenth century), the only preventative was to stay clear of woods and swamplands—not always an easy task when on the march.

There was a well-known treatment for malaria, discovered by Jesuit missionaries in Peru, who encountered both the illness and treatment among an Indigenous tribe. The missionaries introduced alkaloid quinine, a liquid derived from the bark of the cinchona tree, to Europe as early as 1630. It soon became a staple at apothecaries. The drug had no preventative effect against contracting malaria, but it could kill the parasite that caused the disease and thus minimize outbreaks, if not prevent the disease from spreading. Exact doses were difficult to measure, however, and the diagnosis of malaria itself was often subject to question, as it shared symptoms such as "virulent fever" with other illnesses, such as yellow fever. Like laudanum, quinine became extremely popular; it was widely used for a myriad of ailments and heralded as a kind of cure-all by the end of the eighteenth century.

Venereal disease was also widespread in military encampments, where young, inexperienced enlistees were having their first sexual encounters with women far from the staid villages where they grew up. For example, during the late summer of 1777, the general hospital in Providence held twelve soldiers afflicted with the disease: one was a prisoner, at least five were soldiers from Eliot's Regiment and the others belonged to the First and Second Rhode Island Regiments under Colonels Greene and Angell.

Those in militia encampments, if they were without a surgeon in their ranks, had to rely on local physicians or the medications procured by fellow soldiers on leave. Such was the case with nineteen-year-old Noah Robinson, a private in Colonel Caleb Richardson's Company of Daggett's Regiment of the Attleborough militia, which found itself, in late September 1777, stationed in Warren as part of the Kickemuit guard, patrolling the length of the river to its opening at Mount Hope Bay. In the early fall, provisions seem to have been plentiful: the soldiers easily obtained milk, poultry, roast beef and "cyder" in Bristol and Warren. As Private Robinson was the scribe for Captain Richardson, he often joined in the entertainment afforded the officers. On Thanksgiving Day 1777, he recorded:

> *I went to Bristol after provisions and though some fatigue got it on board a boat and set off for Warren with Capt. Richardson and Mr. Goff and*

View of the Kickemuit River. *Photo by author.*

> *got in to Warren before night....Sergt. Tiffany had a genteel supper cooked and Capt. Richardson and Lt. Jones went to supper with us, in the evening went down to Capt. Richardson's quarters and though we had not Polly to kiss, we had Black Bettey, and home to bed.*

Just a few days later, symptoms appeared. On Sunday, November 23, Private Robinson learned that in his encounter, "something of a carnal disease passed on." That night, he and Sergeant Tiffany were both "anointed" with an ointment procured by a Lieutenant Fuller from town, which likely contained mercury or lead.

Daggett's militia from Attleboro, Massachusetts, spent three lengthy terms of service in neighboring Rhode Island, including encampments at Warren, Warwick Neck, Tiverton and Little Compton. The return or accounting of the "hospital" in Warwick of the sick in Daggett's Regiment on February 5, 1778, shows two patients diagnosed with pleurisy, two men from Captain Hicks's company with measles and another with "bilious colick." Other militia companies found themselves under the care of a physician's apprentice, as many legitimate physicians had joined local companies as surgeons and were away on campaigns.

Another illness, thought to be the result of being ordered away on campaigns for lengthy periods of time, was recorded by Surgeon James Thacher. The young doctor was from Barnstable, Massachusetts, and had apprenticed under Abner Hersey, a local physician. He enlisted in the Sixteenth Continental Regiment of Massachusetts, whose men were encamped at Morristown, New Jersey, in July 1780. "Our troops in camp are in general healthy," Thacher recorded, "but we are troubled with many perplexing instances of indisposition occasioned by absence from home, called by Dr. Cullen *Nostalgia*, or 'home sickness.' This complaint is frequent among the militia, and recruits from New England. They become dull and melancholy, with loss of appetite, restless nights, and great weakness." Thacher noted that the affected soldiers' lethargy was sometimes cured by the efforts of older veterans, who rallied the less experienced recruits, but was more generally "suspended by a constant and active engagement of the mind, as by the drill exercises, camp discipline, and by uncommon anxiety, occasioned by the prospect of a battle."[70]

Such stress before battle and the resultant stress and anxiety after a battle was not yet recognized as a precursor of what we know today as post-traumatic stress disorder, or PTSD. If a man fled the scene of battle in horror, he was dishonored, court-martialed and perhaps even executed.

Then as today, however, the scenes of battle and bloodshed such soldiers witnessed would often affect them for their entire life.

One such case of the disorder came to light just a few years ago in the archives of the General James Mitchell Varnum Museum in East Greenwich, Rhode Island, when curator and current president Patrick Donovan came across a handwritten letter from one of the Black soldiers of the First Rhode Island Regiment addressed to his former master and mistress, written in January 1781. Thomas Nichols did not pen the letter to his former masters in his own hand; that was done by someone willing to help his case, for Thomas could not read or write, except for the *N* with which he signed the letter.

Nichols enlisted at the forming of the so-called Black Regiment and took up training before the Battle of Rhode Island put the new regiment to the test in its first engagement with British and Hessian troops. He was assigned to Captain Thomas Cole's company and appears on the muster rolls of August 23, 1778, six days before the battle. As Nichols enlisted in May, he did not undergo the rigorous training at Valley Forge that others of his regiment had been given under the Prussian-bred General Von Steuben. This may have left him, along with the others who had learned to use their weapons and tactics only in the past few months, unprepared for what was to come.

Whatever injuries or illness Nichols suffered occurred during this time. He may have been ill on the day of the battle, as an outbreak of illness had spread among the troops even before heavy rains soaked the encampment for three days during an unexpected gale. On the next month's muster roll, Nichols was listed as "sick, in hospital." He remained there through the following May, but by November 3, 1779, he was with the regiment when it landed on Newport after the British evacuation of the island. Nichols was assigned guard duty in Newport, among the mostly Black and Indigenous detachment of the Rhode Island regiment. The winter that year, 1779–80, was extremely harsh and included several deep snowfalls. Men seeking wood and provisions from Howland's Ferry were driven back by the depth of the snowdrifts. On January 14, 1780, Colonel Greene wrote to Governor William Greene:

> *The Uncommon severity of the weather has caused me to reduce the garrison to one hundred and eighty, officers included; as well as artillery and infantry....Our wood is within three or four days of being out, and being well assured there is not the least probability of being supplied from the main, I have this day ordered the racks belonging to Col. Wanton cut up and carried into the wood-yard, to be dealt out to the troops.*

Windham January ye 18th D 1781
Onered Master & Mistress I take this oppertunity
to inform you of my citiation att this time & Desire your
ade= after I Drove ye waggon as far a Windham ye Head
waggoner took away my Bath of Driving & orderd me to gard
ye waggons which I Refusd & turned Back to Conoal Green
att Covintree & ye wagoner Sente Back two men after me
ye Colonal Did Not Blame me But told ye men & me to goe
again & that I should take my waggon again But Beeing
over woried with this tramps I got But 3 mild further
then where I Left ye waggons in Sd Windham att ye House
of one Dan Murdock where I have Been confind with my
old fits But have good Car taken of me But I have a Desire
to Return to you Not having any money Nor Shows
fit to wair & all Strangers to me makes it Sumthing Dif:
:ficult for me I have had a Docter & a Surgans mate to me
which advise me to go to ye corps of invileds at Boston
where I may Bee under half pay During Life Remaining
in this poor State of Body But I ante able to go thether
Neither Do I incline to without advice from you But
I have a Desire that master or mistress would go to
Colonel Green & See if you cont git me Dischange from
ye War it Beeing very Disagreabell to my minde
as well as Destructive to my helth I suppose I Coldn
Ride on a horce or att Least in a Slay if you Could obtain
a Dischange for me So that I may Return to my
master & his family again During ye will of God in
your pleasure So No more att this time But I Remain
Your humble & Dutifull Thomas N His mark
December ye 31 D 1780 these Lines I Recd from ye
Surgans mate where as Thomas Nichols a Soldier
Belonging to ye first Ridgiment in Rhode Island
State hath Been for some time attended with fits
in this place & Still Like to Reman unfit for a
military Lif

Letter of Thomas Nichols. *Courtesy of the James Mitchell Varnum Armory & Museum.*

Two companies of the regiment were dispatched to Providence for the winter. The remainder of the detachment had a harsh and troublesome winter but greeted Rochambeau and his contingent of French officers, engineers and troops the following summer. In July 1780, the remainder of the regiment at Newport was mustered as the Rhode Island Six Months Continental Battalion. These men reinforced the works at Butts Hill and engaged in a "mock battle" with French troops before their departure.

In October 1780, Colonel Greene wrote to Washington requesting a discharge of the battalion. There is evidence that some detachment of troops remained into December. A team of four French officers and engineers was sent from Newport in November to survey the route chosen for the Continental army to pass along on its march to the Connecticut River and then to West Point. They would bring with them a handful of men drafted from the First Rhode Island regiment to serve as wagoners.

On November 11, 1780, the Marquis de Chastellux recorded in his journal,

> *I left Newport this day with M. Lynch, and M. de Montesquieu each of whom had a servant. I myself had three, one of whom led an extra horse, and another drove a small cart which I was advised to take to convey my portmanteaus, and thus avoid hurting my riding horses.*

The French major general traveled with his entourage along the route later taken by Continental officers. As he recorded, the roads along the route chosen were not always easily navigated. It was also meant to be a kind of reconnaissance mission, and the marquis seemed always to have a keen eye on the landscape as to where encampments might be made.

Making his way to Scituate, Rhode Island, the marquis stayed with other officers at Angell's Tavern. He moved on to a comfortable night at Governor Jabez Bowen's house in Providence and recorded at the conclusion of the following day's journey, on November 13, 1780:

> *From this place to Voluntown the road is very bad, one is continually going uphill and downhill, and always with rough roads. It was six o'clock & night had closed in, when I reached Dorrance's Tavern, which is only twenty-five miles from Providence.*

The Marquis de Chastellux remained three days in Voluntown, albeit in the not unpleasant company of one Miss Peace, waiting for his cart to appear. When it did, he wrote indignantly,

> *It is proper to observe that my servants, proud of possessing ample means of transporting my effects, had loaded it with many useless articles; that I myself, Being apprised that wine was not always to be met with in the inns, had thought proper to furnish myself with canteens which held twelve bottles, and having taken further precaution to ask for two or three loaves of white bread from the commissary at Providence, he had packed up twenty, which alone weighed upward of eighty ponds, so that my poor cart was laden to the point of sinking.*

Thomas Nichols, with the other four men of the regiment "on Command" to drive the wagons over the same rough terrain, would have endured an exhausting portage, given the marquis's assessment of the baggage and supplies packed for the journey. The wagon train's "greatest misfortune," as the marquis recorded, "arose from striking on the rocks, which had broken one wheel and greatly damaged the other."[71]

After exchanging the marquis's wagon for a smaller one, the entourage continued to Plainfield, Connecticut, and then to Canterbury, a village that pleased the marquis with its elegant homes. Leaving the pleasant streets of the village, however, "you reach the woods and a chain of hills, crossed by rugged and difficult roads six or seven miles further along, the country begins to open up again and you descend agreeably to Windham."

Still waiting for orders in Rhode Island, a detachment of the First Rhode Island Regiment was sent to guard stores in Providence in December, while the rest were recalled to their base encampment in East Greenwich. The regiment received a wagonload of its new white uniforms in late December, and Colonel Greene received orders to march and rendezvous with troops in New Haven on January 2, 1781.

Nichols's letter is dated January 18, 1781, though the medical attendant who took the dictation indicates that it was actually written on December 31, 1780. From Nichols's letter, we are given to understand that he had little in the way of clothing. This would seem to indicate that he and the others left Rhode Island without the benefit of the new clothing distributed to the other troops that December. The letter also seems to indicate that Nichols spent considerable time either trying to recover from what must have been a relapse of an ongoing condition or sickened by another debilitating illness.[72]

After driving three wagons with the other soldiers, Nichols was overtaken by the "old fits" that had plagued him months before. When he informed his commander, he was stripped of his wagoner duties and ordered to guard the wagons alone. Nichols refused; left the wagons, followed by two others; and walked back to camp to complain. Colonel Greene ordered the men back to their wagons, but as Nichols explained in his letter, he made it only as far as South Windham, and the suffering he had experienced since then made him feel as though he were no longer fit for duty. This might easily explain the sickbed offered to him by a well-respected militia leader, whose son also served in the Continental line.

Thomas Nichols spent weeks in the home of local militia leader Dan Murdock of Windham County. It was there that he was examined by a doctor and tended to by a surgeon's mate, who transcribed the letter dictated by the Black soldier to his former owners.

> *Windham January 18th, 1781*
>
> *Onered Master & Mistress I take this opportunity to inform you of my citiation att this time & desire your ade....After I drove 3 waggons as far as Windham I hade waggoner tookaway my badge of driving & ordered me to gard ye waggons which I refused & turned back to colonel green att Covintree & ye wagoner sent back two men after me Ye Colonal did not blame me but told ye men and me to go on again & that I should take my waggon again but being over worried with this tramp I got but 3 miles further than where I left ye waggons in So. Windham att ye house of one Dan Murdock where I have been confined with my old fits But have good care taken of me But I have a desire to Return to you Not having any money Nor Clows fit to wair & all strangers to me makes it something difficult for me I have had a Doctor and a Surgans mate to me which advize me to go to* [the] *corps of invalids at Boston where I may be under half pay During Life Remaining in this poor State of Body But I ante able to go thether Neither do I incline to with out advice from you But I have a desire that Master or Mistress would go to Colonel Green & see if you cant git me Discharged from ye War it being very Disagreabell to my mind as well as Destructive to my helth I suppose I could ride on a horse or att least in a Slay if you could obtain a Discharge for me So that I may Return to my Master and his family again baring* [?] *the will of god & your pleasure So No more att this time But I Remain your humble & dutiful Thomas.*
>
> *"N" His mark*

> *December 31, 1780, These lines I recv'd from ye Surgeon's mate whereas Thomas Nickols a soldier belonging to ye first Regiment in Rhode Island State hath been for some time attended with fits in this place & still likely to Remain unfit for military life.*[73]

These incidents would explain what occurred during de Chastellux's and other officers' long wait for their wagons. The French had clearly left the wagoners to their own devices. Was not this breakdown of discipline when the roads were so tough to be expected? In the end, Colonel Greene's order sending the men back to their wagons was obeyed, but the delay caused by Nichols's illness meant he was left behind as the entourage moved on, and he was apparently bedridden for six weeks, from the time of his illness to the time the letter was written on his behalf.

Nichols was not returned to the family who had enslaved him, as he had expressed his hopes he would be. Instead, he was transferred to the Corp of Invalids in February 1781. More than a year later, he was the subject of a letter from Major General Benjamin Lincoln to General George Washington:

> *I do myself the honor to inclose your Excellency a Certificate from Doctor Warren of Boston relative to the inability of a Soldier there as also an Extract of a Letter from Mr Green on the Subject—I saw the Man when I was in Boston and supposed him quite unfit for the Service but did not think myself authorized to Discharge him.*[74]

In the years after the war, the mystery of Thomas Nichols deepens. While the federal census of 1790 included two Indigenous servants and one free Black man, who may have been Nichols, in Benjamin Nichols's household, the census also found a "Thos (neg) Nichols" in Stratford, Fairfield County, Connecticut. This Thomas Nichols resided in a household of four people of color, presumably his wife and children. As Nichols does not appear in the 1785 count of invalid soldiers residing in Rhode Island, it is possible that the treatment and the respect he received in Connecticut during his recovery had convinced him to return to Fairfield County.[75] It may well be that he was introduced to the woman he would later marry during this time.

Whatever the circumstances, its contents notwithstanding, the letter is a unique account of a Black soldier's experience as dictated by the soldier himself. Nichols's plea to his former master to let him return to a life of servitude may seem remarkable to us as modern readers. But there is no doubt that his words reflected the thoughts and fears of a host of others enlisting for freedom in exchange for their service during the war, some of whom found the toil and danger too heavy a price to pay. To his credit, Nichols stood with his regiment at the Battle of Rhode Island and suffered the trauma that would continue to afflict him later, but he never deserted, as others might have done.

The circumstances surrounding the writing of Nichols's letter also give us a glimpse into how the war affected communities. The Murdock family was hardly alone in sheltering and caring for a sick or wounded soldier. Communities often paid families to do as much, as records throughout New England's historical societies show. Such circumstances also appear in diaries published after the war. The Marquis de Chastellux himself came upon a similar situation "six miles beyond Windham, at a solitary little tavern, kept by Mrs. Hill." Asking for beds, the marquis and his junior officer were informed that there was only one "spare" bed in the house, the other being already taken by "a sick traveler in the house whom she did not want to disturb."[76] The traveler was a sick soldier of the Continental army who had been given a furlough to return home for the benefit of his health "but had not a farthing either in paper or 'hard money.' Mrs. Hill notwithstanding, had given him a good bed as he was too ill to continue his journey, she had kept him and taken care of him for four days." The marquis paid his bill in "hard money" and gave some to the soldier to help him on his way, an act that deeply touched Mrs. Hill, who, like many throughout the war, gave of her own charity for a soldier far from home.

CHAPTER 3

GENERAL HOSPITALS, CONFISCATED HOUSES AND CAMP MEDICINE, 1775–1778

To correct long-standing inconsistencies in medical treatment, the Continental Congress agreed in July 1775 to provide twenty thousand men to render medical services, with hospitals under supervision of a Medical Department, and named Dr. Benjamin Church of Massachusetts as the first director and chief physician of the Continental army's Department of Medicine.

When Church assumed the post, the Continental army had but thirty "regional" hospitals, some of which were houses or buildings in deplorable condition. Many were run by inexperienced surgeons who had no practical experience in managing such a facility.[77] Some, however, had gained experience practicing in the field during the French and Indian War, and these men went on to be leaders with some influence during the war.

> *Experience with the British exposed some of the apprentice-trained colonial physicians to a higher level of practice than they had known before and familiarized them with the lower level operations of an army medical department. During the Revolution, even such men as Benjamin Rush, who had no previous military experience, expressed a wish to see the American Army Medical Department modeled more closely upon its British counterpart.*[78]

Overseen by a committee of three civilian practitioners, the British model included a physician general, a surgeon general and an inspector general, who oversaw lesser inspector generals assigned to the welfare of the army. As known by Church and others, "The principal, or general, hospital for such an army might have 400 beds and a staff of six medical officers (including a physician and two assistants, a surgeon and one assistant, and an apothecary) and fifty other workers."

The British also stressed getting wounded soldiers off the field as quickly as possible and created small, enclosed wheelbarrow-like wagons that could be transported by one man. Inside the hospital, good sanitation and ventilation were of prime importance, as was keeping the building from becoming overcrowded. During wartime, each regiment had its own surgeon and a pair of assistants. Each regiment also had its own hospital, whether a tent or a house near the encampment.

Many American physicians believed a smaller, more manageable space was a healthier environment for recovering from illness than a large congregation of the ill in one great hall or building. This belief was also widespread among the populace, who often took those who were "unfit for duty" into their own homes until they recovered as well as those who

Model of a British "flying ambulance." *Wikipedia Commons.*

were sick among the captured enemy soldiers. In May 1776, for instance, Rhode Island authorized payments to Rachel Cranston, "for boarding one Hamilton, a prisoner, who was sick at her house," and to Ruth Peckham, for boarding a wounded prisoner in Providence.[79] As historian Jeanne Abrams notes, "Public-minded Revolutionary-era women often tended to sick soldiers and…also took jobs as nurses and administered medications, attended to the hygiene of hospitalized men, and cleaned up after sick patients for meager pay."

Dr. Benjamin Church's term was short, however, and after months of conflict with colleagues, he was accused of treason when a suspicious letter written by Church was found that appeared to provide critical information to the British. Church was tried, found guilty and sentenced to prison in the West Indies. During his time as director, Church had sought to increase the use of general hospitals, large-capacity buildings where multiple patients could be treated, rather than smaller "regional" hospitals.

From its inception, the Medical Department faced daunting challenges to its mission of providing uniformly competent care to the fledgling Continental army—an army whose health was constantly at risk from poor camp conditions and inadequate food and clothing.[80]

The medicines needed to supply the colonies' hospitals had always been imported and had been in somewhat short supply even before the war began. These shortages drew early notice from Congress, which, by September 1775, had created a Medical Committee, whose purpose was to "devise ways and means for supplying the Continental Army with Medicines."[81] The committee's authority was gradually extended during the war until it oversaw the hiring and firing of hospital personnel, policies for inoculation and other measures. It was also responsible for resolving internal disputes within the Medical Department.

Those disputes were no small matter. The legislation that created the Medical Department did not extend to the regimental system, which was set up by each colony for the care of its regiments. Church's attempt to consolidate hospitals and lower the cost of providing men and supplies to these regimental hospitals continued to be largely ignored beyond Massachusetts.

Regimental surgeons often complained to the Medical Department that supplies and medicine were being denied to them by the general hospitals. Brigadier General John Sullivan complained, wondering to what purpose was the army "Dragging our sick…in Waggon Loads to Cambridge?" There, they had their wounds dressed at the general hospital while his regimental surgeons stood idle in camp. According to Sullivan, half the men ordered to go to the general hospitals refused to leave the camp, as "they would rather Die where they were and under the care of those Physicians they were acquainted with."[82] Washington, however, approved of the general hospitals and believed there was no need for camp hospitals in cases where "a General Hospital so near and well appointed" lay in the vicinity.

In October 1775, the Continental Congress appointed Dr. John Morgan from Philadelphia to be the new director general of the Medical Department, despite Washington's personal wish that Dr. John Shippen Jr. be given the post.[83] Morgan did not have the best reputation among his medical colleagues: he was better known for his sometimes conceited and vengeful behavior than his medical skills, though John Adams thought him of "very good" moral character at the time of his appointment.

Nonetheless, when Morgan assumed the post, he faced the persistent problems that had arisen from the disputes between the hospitals that were providing care to the troops. The general hospitals were now overcrowded, and the officers' inexperience in providing care for large numbers of men had already begun to take its toll. In addition, supplies were in disarray. While there might be five hundred mattresses on hand in army storerooms, for instance, those same storerooms were devoid of blankets. Most crucially, medical supplies were limited. At the time of Morgan's first inventory, the general hospital in Philadelphia had but twenty bandages, and while it was well stocked with more than one hundred items, those medicines most in demand were in limited supply.

The demand for supplies soon widened the rift between the two hospital systems. In an effort to force the regimental surgeons' hand, Morgan maintained that he had no orders from Congress to supply regimental hospitals. While regimental surgeons had long demanded supplies from the general hospitals, there was no oversight, and Morgan was determined to change that. He asked Congress to clarify the rules under which regimental surgeons served, "that may be devised for the Hospital, and the good of the service." However, while Morgan demanded accountability on the part of the regimental hospitals, he did not discount their purpose and their necessity during times of severe outbreaks of hostility during the war.

The results of Morgan's campaign became a resolution enacted by Congress on July 17, 1776, that clearly defined the general hospitals' role in supplying regimental hospitals with medicine and instruments but stated that any patient requiring more treatment than the camp hospital could provide should be sent to the nearest general hospital. The act also enabled representatives from the general hospitals to inspect regimental hospitals' supply chests and for supplies to be returned to the general hospital in the event that a regiment was depleted or disbanded. It also increased the staffing of hospitals, allowing one surgeon and five mates for every five thousand men and the hiring of "as many storekeepers, stewards, nurses, and hospitable employees as deemed necessary, to be appointed by individual hospital directors."[84]

An example of the way the system was intended to work can be viewed in the response of the Colony of Rhode Island to the act of Congress. In the summer of 1776, the Rhode Island General Assembly appointed a committee, which included Surgeon John Bartlett, "to procure upon the best terms they can, a suitable house, to be used as an hospital, for the colony troops stationed upon Rhode Island; and that the sick be immediately removed from the present hospital, and the house be cleaned."[85] By the close of the year, the assembly had appointed Jonathan Arnold as "Director and Proprietor of Hospitals, in this State; Isaac Senter, Hospital Surgeon; Stephen Wigneron and Joseph Joslin, Regimental Surgeons."[86] A general hospital was established in Providence, and other houses were occupied in service as "sick houses" throughout the state. As the war progressed, Rhode Island remained one of the few states that maintained active hospitals until the close of the conflict.

When the British evacuated Boston on March 17, 1776, one of the first tasks of the soldiers who had undertaken the long siege through the previous fall and winter was to find whatever stores of drugs and supplies the enemy had left behind. What supplies they found were immediately suspect, however, as Dr. James Warren testified:

> *When he entered the workhouse which the British had used as a hospital, he found the medicines in great disorder with small amounts of yellow and white arsenic mixed in with them. After learning that another physician had already removed twelve to fourteen pounds of this poison from among the drugs.*[87]

Warren recommended that the confiscated drugs be destroyed. Washington agreed and approved the confiscation of the well-known apothecaries of two Tory doctors in town. One of those whose pharmacopoeia was raided was Dr. Silvester Gardiner, who was born on the estate founded by his family on Boston Neck in North Kingstown, Rhode Island, in 1707. He was a sickly child growing up, and with long confinements in bed came a love of reading and learning. When his older sister married the Reverend James McSparran, Gardiner moved with them into their home so that he might get a proper education. As his interest in medicine grew, his family's wealth allowed him to study in London and Paris for a period of eight years.

By 1734, Gardiner had returned to New England and settled in Boston. Not long after beginning his practice, he was chosen to join the vestry at King's Chapel. He was a strong advocate for increasing oversight of medical practitioners in the city and began to publish his convictions in letters to Boston newspapers. He also authored articles for the benefit of the public, including an article on the measles published in 1736. Gardiner established his pharmacy on the corner of Washington and Winter Streets, at the "Sign of the Unicorn and Mortar," and later built a palatial home among the other fine houses on Winter Street.[88] He founded the Medical Society of Boston and gave lectures on anatomy. Gardiner also performed surgery at least once before an audience within his society, removing a large stone from six-year-old Joseph Baker, who had suffered from growth of calculi, or kidney stones, since birth. As noted in one account of the operation, "This calculus was oval and seven inches in circumference. For three days urine drained through the incision; following this, it returned to the natural channels. By three weeks, the urinary flow was natural."[89]

By the time the Revolutionary War began, Dr. Gardiner had broken his long-standing friendship with John Hancock. Now faced with his stores being raided and his name reviled, he fled to Halifax, Nova Scotia, with some two thousand pounds sterling.

By June 1776, the Medical Department had confiscated enough medicines, bedding, furniture and supplies to adequately stock the five regiments defending Boston. In anticipation of an attack to retake the city, a barracks was constructed on Prospect Hill that could house one hundred wounded.[90]

When American forces were ordered to shore up the defense of Manhattan, they left behind three hundred patients, men who were too ill to travel with the army, to be funneled into the new hospital system. When Director General Morgan was ordered on February 3 to report to New York and oversee the organization of a general hospital there, he left Isaac Foster in charge. The surgeon managed the task admirably, establishing a "Principal Hospital" in the confiscated mansion of Henry Vassall, the son of a wealthy Jamaican planter. Vassall built an elegant house in Cambridge on an estate that included a courtyard and a large carriage house and stables. By moving the patients into such a tranquil, rural-like setting, Foster kept the death rate low and recovery rate high, lowering the patient count to

Above: Display of colonial medicines. *Courtesy of Dan Newman.*

Left: Nineteenth-century portrait of Vassar House, Cambridge, Massachusetts. *Cambridge Historical Society.*

eighty men by April 22. "Within six weeks of receiving orders to move the department's main operations from Boston, he discharged the last man and settled all his accounts for the Boston hospitals."[91]

Foster was sent to Philadelphia, but New England was never far from his mind. His success in Boston led him to pitch himself to John Adams and thus the Continental Congress for a post overseeing a proposed new military hospital in New England, as he wrote on June 14, 1776:

> *It is not improbable the attempts of the abandoned British administration to Subjugate the United American Colonies may require such a part of the Continental Army for the defense of the New England Colonies, as to render the Establishment of a Military Hospital highly expedient, if*

> *not absolutely necessary there. If that should be the case, I beg leave to offer myself a candidate for, and solicit your interest towards my obtaining the directorship.*[92]

Not a humble man, Foster lauded the present governing body of Congress and then summarized his services as a surgeon from "the Day after [the] Battle of Lexington" to the Battle of Bunker Hill, where, he wrote, "[I] exerted myself in dressing and takeing Care of the Wounded, while my native place and most of My property were in flames before my face." In case Adams should not be swayed solely by his autobiography, Foster wrote:

> *Permit me to add that should a younger Man than I am, or one who has never been in the service be sent to New England as Director of the Hospital there, it would not only greatly lessen my reputation among my countrymen there, to most of whom I am personally known, but very unhappy in my own mind.*[93]

Morgan, of course, was chosen for the post Foster favored, but the physician continued to serve as the deputy general for the Eastern Department from 1777 to 1780, when he retired from the army.

At this critical time, General Horatio Gates, commander of the northern army, instigated several measures to improve the sanitary conditions of encampments, ordering an end to cooking over an open fire, confining the toilets to trenches covered daily with lime and evacuating any smallpox patients to Fort George.

The hospital at Fort George held over two thousand patients in July 1776, but by October, the patient load had been reduced to four hundred.[94] In June 1776, Dr. Jonathan Potts was appointed physician and surgeon to the northern army at Fort George. On his arrival, he found approximately one thousand patients suffering from smallpox, dysentery and fevers in a hospital staffed by only four surgeons and four surgeon's mates. Dr. James McHenry was assigned to assist Potts and immediately given the task of heading to Philadelphia to procure needed medicines.

The chief surgeon at Fort George during that time was Samuel Stringer, a physician from Albany who had accompanied General Philip Schuyler and his troops into Canada, relying on his own medicine chest to treat them. Once sent to the fort, he administered care as best he could during a most desperate time as the hospital saw an increasing population of smallpox patients.

On July 7, 1776, Stringer ordered newly appointed hospital director Dr. Jonathan Potts to "have the sheds along the lake shore fitted up with cribs or berths for their reception, and hurry those that are to be built where the old fort stood."[95] That month saw the completion of "two houses, capable of holding about three hundred and fifty"; additional hospitals and buildings were still under construction. The Reverend Ebenezer David wrote from Fort George that same month that he found

> *near 2000 sick between 20 & 30 dying in twenty four hours....Col. Read, now Briggadeer laying very low....But when I came to where the large sheads called Hospitals were erected, I stood still & beheld with Admiration & sympathetic anguish what neither Tongue nor Pen could describe....Here I tarried two days visited & prayed with the sick.*[96]

Rejoining his own regiment, David wrote from Ticonderoga on August 22:

> *Found my* [Colonel Bond's] *Regiment in a most sorrowful condition. The remaining Field officers both Sick with the fever and Ague. Oh how the Men were changed....The Regiment did not look the same...thin in flesh, badly dressed, spirits sunk &etc....I must inform you that the jaundice set in with the Col. Bond's first complaint....He soon proved very Bilious & putrid....Yesterday Morning he was a very sick Man....Last night at ten he fell asleep....Was buried to day in the front of the Regiment with the honors of war.*[97]

When Potts arrived with his appointment, Stringer had no intention of relinquishing his authority. By July, when McHenry still had not returned from procuring medicines, Stringer set out to collect his own supplies, and when the men's paths crossed, he fired McHenry—unbeknownst to Potts. By late summer, Potts had accepted a role subordinate to Stringer, perhaps simply to be on better working terms with the senior surgeon as he struggled to meet the needs of the increasing number of patients. Medicine continued to be in short supply, as Stringer had yet to return to the fort hospital. As detailed in Mary C. Gillett's history of the Army Medical Department,

> *Returns of late September suggest that in the northern army at this time, as many as 50 percent of all the enlisted men assigned to the camp may have been sick. Two to four times the number sick away from camp remained under the care of regimental surgeons in their tents, or quite possibly, within regimental hospitals.*[98]

Throughout the summer, Stringer had attempted to reduce the hospital population by dismissing some men from the army altogether and sending others to a newly established hospital in Albany. Despite the difficulties endured, records show that the general hospital held over two thousand patients in July 1776, but by October, the patient load had been reduced to four hundred.[99] Potts was eventually appointed to reopen the previously closed facility at Fort George for patients with contagious diseases, while the new general hospital tended to patients with a variety of other ailments.

The fall of 1776 was a crucial test for the Medical Department, as it faced the challenge of procuring supplies, especially medicines, for the regimental hospitals. Colonel Samuel Wigglesworth, who served as surgeon in Colonel Waldren's regiment of the New Hampshire militia, worriedly wrote to the committee of safety back home:

> *Near half this regiment is entirely incapable of any service, some dying almost every day. Col Wyman's regiment is the same unhappy situation. There are no medicines of any avail in the Continental Chest; such as there are, are in their native state, unprepared, no emetics nor cathartics, no mercurial or antimonial remedies, no opiate, no elixir, tincture or any capital remedy.*
>
> *It would make a heart of stone melt to hear the moans and see the distress of the sick and dying. I can scarce pass a tent but I hear men solemnly declaring that they will never enlist in another campaign without being assured of a better supply of medicine.*[100]

Wigglesworth's regiment was one of those twelve thousand militia enlisted in companies from the northern colonies that included men from neighboring Massachusetts, Connecticut, New Jersey, Pennsylvania and New York who had occupied the forts on either side of the narrows of Lake Champlain, at Mount Independence and Fort Ticonderoga, since the summer.

In November, a committee sent by the Continental Congress to investigate the hospitals of the Northern Department recommended that the hospital at Fort George be closed and that a general hospital for the northern army be constructed on Vermont's Mount Independence, across the narrow channel of Lake Champlain from Fort Ticonderoga. Morgan wrote that the hospital as he envisioned it

> *ought to be floored above, so as to make two stories each, and to hove* [have] *a stack of chimneys carried up the middle—it is further required*

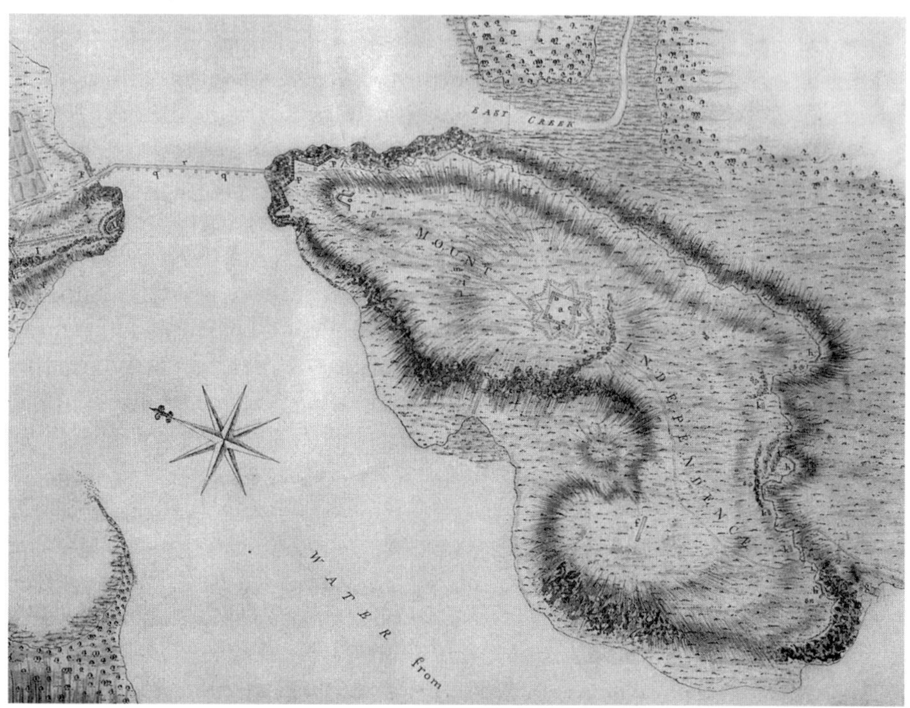

Map of Mount Independence by Charles Wintersmith. *Wikipedia Commons.*

> *that bed bunks be made, and straw be always in readiness for the sick, and a carpenter or two to be employed solely in the business of the General Hospital in making coffins, tables, and utensils of various kinds.*[101]

In early January 1777, the Continental Congress abruptly dismissed Morgan and Stringer from their posts, and by April, new appointments had been made in the Medical Department: William Shippen Jr. was given the director general's position, now supported by an assistant director, a physician general, a surgeon general, an apothecary general, six senior surgeons, seven mates, a commissary general, his assistant, two clerks and one steward.[102]

In March 1777, the construction of the general hospital at Mount Independence began. By June, the hospital was essentially finished, with a capacity for six hundred patients. Dr. Jonathan Potts was appointed the hospital's director. Surgeon James Thacher described the site in his journal:

> *Mount Independence directly opposite to Ticonderoga, is strongly fortified and well supplied with artillery. On the summit of the mount, which is*

Reenactors' encampment at Mount Independence. *Wikipedia Commons.*

> *table land, is erected a strong fort, in the center of which is a convenient square of barracks, a part of which are occupied for our hospital.*[103]

Conditions at Ticonderoga, however, were far worse than they appeared. General Gates wrote several missives to Washington about the wretched housing, complaining that the barracks constructed the previous fall were flimsy and had already fallen into ruin. Worse yet, they were too far removed from the defensive works to keep the troops close to their post.[104]

Within a few months, however, the mountain lay under siege. By August, the British had occupied the hospital and were using it for their wounded. When they left in November, they burned the hospital and destroyed the outbuildings: "So it would not come back into American hands, and the entire mountaintop was allowed to return to forest."

Dr. David R. Starbuck writes that during an archaeological dig conducted in 1990, researchers uncovered shingle nails, fragments of melted wine bottles, medicine cups, a single surgeon's blade, an ointment jar and a garbage pit that confirmed livestock had been brought to the hospital "on the hoof." Strikingly, Starbuck notes:

> *When we examined historical records and excavated many of the smaller cabins of the soldiers, it also became clear that the soldiers must have taken*

> *their medicines back with them to their cabins whenever possible, rather than risk the very real danger of being exposed to contagion in the hospital. We discovered fragments of medicine bottles in a great many of the soldier's hut sites, suggesting that the General Hospital may have principally served as a giant dispensary.*[105]

By the early summer of 1777, conditions at the three hospitals had greatly improved. As Gillett notes, "Supplies were adequate, and patients were, for the most part, housed in buildings specifically designed for their care.... Fresh vegetables were available from local gardens, and beef and sheep were delivered on the hoof to hospital commissaries."[106]

In preparation for the defense of New York City in 1776, an estimated forty regiments, or some twenty thousand men, descended on Manhattan. The majority of these men were from New England and had first marched as militia from their homes to the siege of Boston. Their transition into units of the Continental army made them part of the first Grand Army of the Republic. The Continental army established the principal hospital for the city at Kings College but also secured the city hospital in Manhattan, just recently restored after a severe fire, and established other hospital units at the city barracks and even in private homes.[107]

The taking of Trenton and Princeton allowed the Medical Department to establish hospitals in the Old Barracks at Trenton; it created a general hospital from the 1758 barracks of that town and other units in Princeton, Brunswick, Amboy, Mendham and Morristown.

Another general hospital was established during the summer of 1777 in the vicinity of Bennington, Vermont, to serve the militia units gathering there. The "hospital" was initially scattered among a series of houses in the countryside, where regimental surgeons tended to patients.[108] When the British effort to take the Bennington encampment was rebuffed, Dr. Francis Hagan reported to Potts that the army had confiscated a meetinghouse for the wounded prisoners and a pair of German physicians been placed in charge of their care.

Arriving in Albany, New York, on August 30, 1777, Surgeon James Thacher recorded his impressions of the young city and the hospital to which he had been assigned:

> *The city of Albany is situated on the west bank of the Hudson, or North River, 160 miles north from New York; and the river admits of sloop navigation between these two cities. It consists of about three hundred houses,*

> *chiefly in the gothic style, the gable ends to the street....The hospital was erected during the last French war, it is situated on an eminence overlooking the city. It is two stories high, having a wing at each end and a piazza in front above and below. It contains forty wards, capable of accommodating five hundred patients, besides the room appropriated to the use of surgeons and other officers, stores, &c.*[109]

Just a month later, the capacity and the preparedness of the hospital surgeons were tested as they received the wounded from battles at Paoli and Saratoga. The carefully mapped-out chain of hospitals and supply lines was undone on September 21, 1777, by the unexpected loss by Brigadier General Anthony Wayne at Paoli that led to the British occupation of Philadelphia a mere five days later. The evacuation from Philadelphia was one of the greatest challenges yet faced by the Medical Department, involving as it did the forced evacuation of all existing hospitals that lay within striking distance. Initially, one hundred wounded were sent from Paoli, followed by the evacuees from Philadelphia; the most seriously ill or wounded patients were transported in open wagons. Days later, on October 4, the defeat at Germantown sent another five hundred wounded men to the hospitals, all of whom arrived in the days and weeks that followed the battle. Though there was concern for the safety of the hospital at Princeton, it remained operational.

From Albany, Thacher recorded:

> *The wounded officers and soldiers of our army, and those of the enemy have fallen into our hands, are crowding into our hospital, and require our constant attention. The last night I watched with the celebrated General Arnold, whose leg was badly fractured by a musket ball while in the engagement with the enemy on the 7th instant. He is very peevish and impatient under his misfortunes, and required all my attention during the night, but I devoted an hour in writing a letter to a friend in Boston detailing the particulars of the late battle.*[110]

The hospital continued to care for the wounded after the surrender of Burgoyne, when the general himself was taken in custody to Albany. Such were the overcrowded conditions, however, that patients spilled from the building into local homes and a church in town. Thacher again described a vivid scene: the military hospital in the wake of a costly campaign.

> *October 24,*
>
> *This hospital is now crowded with officers and soldiers from the field of battle; those belonging to the British and Hessian troops, are accommodated in the same hospital with our own men and receive equal care and attention. The foreigners are under the care and management of their own surgeons. I have been present at some of their capital operations, and remarked, that the English surgeons perform with skill and dexterity, but the Germans, with a few exceptions, do no credit to their profession....Not less than one thousand wounded and sick are now in this city; the Dutch church, and several private houses, are occupied as hospitals. We have about thirty surgeons and mates; and all are constantly occupied.*[111]

By late November, some three thousand men were crowded into hospitals, churches, meetinghouses, schoolhouses and citizen's homes. A list of the number of patients occupying hospitals in the region that encompassed the "Middle Department" on November 24, 1777, shows that the hospital at Easton, Pennsylvania, had 400 patients, 283 of whom were sick, 40 wounded and 107 convalescing. The hospital at Bethlehem, Pennsylvania, held the largest number of wounded in its wards: 142.[112] In total, the list accounts for thirteen hospitals established throughout the states of New Jersey, Pennsylvania and Maryland. The list does not include the existing regimental and "flying hospitals," those tents in encampments for sick soldiers and the regimental surgeon that existed during this time.

At Valley Forge, at the onset of the winter of 1777, brigade "hospital huts" were constructed close to encampments that measured fifteen feet wide, twenty-five feet long and at least nine feet high. They were crudely built of log, and the resulting gaps were covered with wooden shingle but not caulked with mud to allow for ventilation. A chimney was constructed at one end of each hut, and there was at least one window on each. This environment, it was hoped, would allow troops to recover quickly and rejoin their units. However, a noted lack of discipline among the surgeons and mates at Valley Forge undermined Washington's plans, and ultimately, as the hospital huts were overcrowded and consistently low on supplies, the more seriously ill were transported to Albany.

That winter, another hospital was constructed at a site called Yellow Springs. A main building, situated on land owned by Dr. Samuel Kennedy, was erected and named Washington Hall. It was "three stories and an attic high, 106 × 36 feet in dimension, the first floor held a kitchen, dining room,

Soldiers' hut at Valley Forge. *Wikipedia Commons.*

and service rooms, while the second floor contained two large wards, and the third held many small rooms" for the surgeons and staff. Washington visited the facility in April 1778 and approved of its design and plan of care for the troops, but even in such a well-planned facility, overcrowding became an issue. A few nearby barns were enlisted to house patients, along with a convalescence unit constructed two miles from the main hospital.[113]

The hospital in Schenectady, New York, had also seen an increase in patients since the summer of 1777. Dr. Dirk Van Ingen hired two men and a pair of women to help out at the hospital, but still the patient load continued to increase until, by December 1777, the doctor and his staff were treating 312 patients crammed into two rooms and whatever available space could be allotted them from the barracks.

After a reshuffling of Medical Department personnel and facilities in March 1778, the Eastern Department oversaw hospitals in Danbury, Hartford and New London, Connecticut; Providence and Newport, Rhode Island; Boston, Massachusetts; and Fishkill and Peekskill, New York.

Physician General Philip Turner made the four-hundred-mile circuit to inspect each hospital that spring. Turner was a humble physician from Norwich, Connecticut. His service throughout the war would eventually bring him to the role of surgeon general of the army's Eastern Department in 1777, a post he held until the conclusion of the war.

The British evacuation of Philadelphia in June 1778 that led to the Battle of Monmouth and the withdrawal to New York City put the new chain of hospitals to the test. Wounded men from the Battle of Monmouth were originally housed in nearby buildings: the church, for instance, and the courthouse were utilized for the wounded and sick, many of whom had fallen prostrate from the heat in battle, who lay on straw layered upon the floor. Many died in the heat, and Washington ordered that the sick and wounded be sent to barracks at Brunswick, New Jersey, while he led the troops north to new headquarters at White Plains, New York. In fact, some of these soldiers, as well as those who fell ill after the evacuation, were sent to hospitals in Trenton, Princeton and Springfield, New Jersey, whose small hospital struggled to care for a patient population that had swelled to two hundred, before some men could be transferred to Morristown.

In Rhode Island, hospitals for the troops were established in Bristol, Coventry, Providence, South Kingstown, Tiverton and Warwick. The location of the early hospital in Bristol remains undocumented. Local historians believe that the town courthouse was used. A return from January 1778 shows but four patients in the hospital and another five "Sick in Quarters."

In the coming months, in addition to the number of sick troops carted there from the Bristol Ferry, the hospital at Bristol received a good number of men who had initially been taken prisoner during the British raids on Bristol and the adjacent town of Warren in May 1778. The men had been held on "prison ships" in Newport harbor, a fleet that included the HMS *Endeavor*, discovered in 2022. While the reputation of these ships did not match that of the "death ships" in New York, many prisoners found them "too cruel to endure." Early historian Benjamin Cowell wrote, "At one time in particular, there were one hundred and fifty-seven prisoners brought up from Newport to Bristol, all made sick by brutal treatment during their captivity; twenty-seven of whom were brought from thence to Providence."[114]

The hospital in Coventry, Rhode Island, was likely one of the "smallpox houses" put to use by the town in the area of Pottersville, close to its northern border with the town of Scituate. Several houses were reportedly used by the town for this purpose during the epidemics of the eighteenth century and after the Revolutionary War. Records are incomplete, but it appears that in Pottersville, the house of John Greene was utilized. Greene may also have offered the use of his farm for an encampment when needed.

Other private houses were used to shelter troops from nearby encampments. During the widespread epidemic of 1776, General Nathanael Greene's wife, Caty, opened their large home by the family forge in Coventry to nurse several soldiers who were suffering from smallpox. Several died while hospitalized in the house and were buried on the grounds of the homestead.

University Hall, Brown University. *Photo by author.*

A return from August 25, 1777, shows that twenty-four men of the First and Second Rhode Island Regiments were transferred from the Coventry Hospital to the Providence Hospital, suffering from a variety of ailments. Among them were four patients suffering from venereal diseases; four with "inflammation of the eye," an ailment commonly known today as pink eye; two men with whooping cough; two with ulcers, or bedsores; one with fever; one with rheumatism; and another with dysentery. The young fifer James Mitchell was diagnosed with scrofula, Asel Bennet, John Ranford and Samuel Cushing were convalescing. Four of the men on the list had diagnoses that are now indecipherable due to fading of the script.[115]

The general hospital in Providence was on the grounds of present-day Brown University. Now President's Hall, it was an impressive edifice on the hill above the town, then called Rhode Island College. In December 1776, following the British occupation of Newport, the college was closed and almost immediately confiscated for use as a barracks for the troops that had streamed into Providence. By 1778, the hall had been converted into a hospital. A return of patients made in mid-August 1778 lists about one hundred soldiers in the general hospital at Providence alone; considerably more soon filled the regimental hospitals in the state. As historian Benjamin Cowell notes, "The battle on the 29th of August, on Rhode Island, kept all the Surgeons busy for some time." A list of the "Sick Sent from Warren to Providence Sept. 4, 1778" (see appendix E), which consists of forty-four men, is divided between "Whites" and "Blacks"; four men of color are listed, including "Cato Chase & Black wife."[116]

Those regimental hospitals left behind after the Battle of Rhode Island continued to lack needed supplies. Documents of requests for supplies and medicines as the regimental surgeons prepared their units for winter show that regiments from South Kingstown and Tiverton, Rhode Island, and Freetown, Massachusetts, lacked key elixirs and powders for their medicine chests. The regimental hospitals also found it difficult to procure other needed supplies, as shown by a list of "Articles wanting in the Brigade Hospital of Gen. Stark" dated November 28, 1778:

2 Iron Pots (to contain 4 gallons each)
10 Tin porrengers
12 spoons
2 buckets
Sugar
20 thick blankets
10 bed sacks
Coffee, chocolate, tea
2 gallons Rum & keg
8 gallons claret & keg
Oatmeal

Among the medicines requested by the brigade hospital were opium, camphor and "a host of carthatics."[117]

Reports issued by the Medical Department in the late summer of 1778 show that "the number of sick within General Washington's army was running at 1,200–1,400 men per week, but not all of the sick soldiers were retained in the hospitals within the camp." An estimation by Gillett determined this to be 17 to 20 percent of the soldiers enlisted in the Continental army.

CHAPTER 4

THE CONSEQUENCE OF CIVIL WAR

Loyalists, Dissenters and Deserters

From the beginning of the conflict with Great Britain, many inhabitants of the colonies were deeply divided in their loyalties, and at times, these divisions ran deep within a single colony. Rhode Island landowner Thomas Cranston, a descendant of Governor Samuel Cranston, wrote to Beriah Brown, the high sheriff of Kings County, on April 26, 1775:

> *We are in the utmost confusion and which part we shall take is at present uncertain. I see nothing but destruction coming upon us, look which way I will....There is no person here that knows how to act or which part to take—if we should take up with the part that the government hath adopted we shall be laid in ashes—and if we take up the King's side we shall have all the sons of liberty upon our backs.*[118]

It was a perilous year for the smallest colony. The government itself was in peril as a crisis erupted in the wake of the reelection of Loyalist Governor Joseph Wanton in May 1775. The Rhode Island General Assembly, which had largely been behind the drive for independence through various measures and actions taken since the burning of the HMS *Gaspee*, a British revenue schooner, in 1772, now demanded that the governor swear an oath of allegiance to the Continental Congress. Wanton refused to take back the oath he had made to the Crown a year earlier. The assembly ousted Wanton but remained in turmoil for nearly a year until a new election was held.

Old State House, Providence, Rhode Island. *Photo by author.*

The Continental Congress had decided on its definition of treason just under two weeks before the Declaration of Independence: "Persons, members of, or owing allegiance to any of the United colonies…who shall levy war against the said colonies…or be adherent to the king of Great Britain…giving to him or them aid and comfort, are guilty of treason against said colony."

Those suspected of being loyalists were closely watched, their every move scrutinized, especially in coastal communities. Among those suspected early on were wealthy landowners whose business connections through British merchants were imperiled by the outbreak of war.

In Kings County, Rhode Island, many of those wary of war were the landholders of those large estates whose farms contributed to the flood of goods leaving Rhode Island ports for the West Indies. These included bricks, timber, iron and other tools and building materials; barrels of salted fish and mutton for the enslaved laborers on sugar plantations; and hay for the horses that drove the sugar mills. It was a lucrative agricultural enterprise that brought great wealth to the region. Many of those prominent farmers known as the Narragansett Planters were owners of enslaved workers on their own plantations, and some owned or invested in ships that plied the triangle trade, shipping rum to the west coast of Africa in exchange for slaves sold in West Indian ports, where the holds that bore the enslaved on the voyage were cleaned and then filled with sugar for the ship's return to Newport.

But it was not only the wealthy landowners who benefited from these exchanges. Many smaller farmers, lumbermen, fishing crews from Wickford, masons, craftsmen and suppliers of all kinds contributed to those exports from New England in support of Great Britain's production of sugar and its wholesale enslavement of thousands of individuals to meet the demand. As one might expect, the tensions between England and the colonies of North America were of great concern to those who favored keeping such valuable economic ties to the mother country.

Such was the wealth in Kings County that other loyalists' leanings came purely from the fear of losing the consumer goods they had become dependent on: the fine China dishware, tea sets, silverware, glassware; the silk for shirts, dresses and cravats; the books, portfolios and prints—not to mention teas from China, fine port from France and numerous other wines, spirits and imported liquors.[119]

One such gentleman of leisure who lived in the region was George Rome. The Englishman had arrived in Newport in 1761 at a providential moment. As it turned out, a once-prominent Newport cordwainer named Henry Collins had seen his firm file for bankruptcy. Collins owned a fine home in Newport and a large portion of land with a mansion house in Narragansett on Boston Neck. The land there was originally called Namcook by the Indigenous Narragansett people and was part of their summering encampment. A six-hundred-acre parcel on the northernmost portion of Boston Neck had originally been purchased by Captain Edward Hutchinson, whose family held the land through three generations. Henry Collins purchased the farm from Hutchinson and built a mansion house for his summer retreat, but risky ventures in privateering caused his fortunes to falter. When George Rome arrived, he took the opportunity to buy the fine home in Newport as well as the "summer residence."[120]

Rome went on to purchase adjacent properties that had been part of the original deed until he had acquired nearly the entire six hundred acres of Hutchinson's purchase. He improved the mansion house that Collins had constructed and spent his summers there, entertaining guests from nearby Narragansett but also from Newport and as far away as Boston in what he called "my little country villa."[121] Such a lavish lifestyle, of course, relied on a large contingent of enslaved workers. We will learn a little more about some of them later.

As Rome had come so recently to Rhode Island, and perhaps because he so lavishly upheld a bachelor life of English gentility in Narragansett, many of those who favored separation from Great Britain in the fervor after the *Gaspee* incident suspected him of being less than eager to support independence. In 1772, a letter Rome penned to an associate in London—criticizing the governments of Rhode Island and Massachusetts and, in effect, calling for the revoking of colonial charters and new governments that would be more sympathetic to the Crown—came into the hands of Ambassador Ben Franklin. The contents were soon published in newspapers throughout the colonies.

In October 1775, Rome was brought before the Rhode Island General Assembly, which was meeting in South Kingston. He was jailed in Kingston and then Providence before fleeing the country on the British man-o'-war *Rose*, then anchored off Newport. Rome's property was confiscated, and the auction of valuables left over from what the state had taken for supplies was overseen by Major James Cooke.[122] The property was largely purchased by merchant and shipbuilder John Brown of Providence, who, by 1780, resold the property to Supreme Court Judge Ezekial Gardner. With these and other holdings, Gardner became one of the largest owners of enslaved individuals in the state.[123]

The enslaved individuals who had been on Rome's farm were part of the property and would eventually form the nucleus of a Black community in Wickford, Rhode Island. During the Revolutionary War, several of those who had been enslaved on the farm under Rome, Brown and Gardner served in local militia, Continental regiments and even the American navy.

So-called confiscation laws were passed in many states to seize the property of known loyalists. These laws effectively criminalized dissent to the American Revolution. New York's was among the earliest legislatures to pass such laws and sought aggressively to seize property even before the state had ratified its constitution. In March 1777, New York's provisional government established "Committees of Sequestration" in each county to confiscate and auction off seized property for the benefit of the state's coffers. In 1779, the state passed "an Act for the Forfeiture and Sale of Estates of Persons who have Adhered to the Enemies of this State and for Declaring the Sovereignty of the People of this State, in respect to all Property within the same." The act included a list of New Yorkers who remained loyal to Great Britain and contended that these "offenders" had forfeited the rights to their property, authorized the seizure and sale of their estates and banished them from the state.[124]

Dissenters lived throughout the colonies and came from all walks of life. Twenty-first-century historians believe that White adult male loyalists were 15 to 20 percent of that population during the time of the Revolutionary War. In addition to these men, as historian Robert Calhoon has noted,

> *Approximately half the colonists of European ancestry tried to avoid involvement in the struggle—some of them deliberate pacifists, others recent immigrants, and many more simple apolitical folk. The patriots received active support from perhaps 40 to 45 percent of the white populace, and at most no more than a bare majority.*[125]

Dissenters were sometimes proactive in their resistance to the draft. When a call to arms came for part of Rhode Island's state militia to serve fifteen days in April 1777, a group of fifty-two men from Kent County petitioned local commander John Waterman. The petition stated that the men refused to serve because they needed to tend their crops at this critical time of the year in order to support their families. They asked the commander to forgo issuing warrants that would fine the men for refusing to serve, as such fines could cause them "unnecessary stress and ruin."[126]

The townspeople of West Greenwich and Exeter, Rhode Island, also protested the draft by refusing to enlist. The general assembly, at its session the following month, decried residents' "atrocious and high handed" refusal to raise troops from the town. The assembly requested that Major General Joseph Spencer send troops to the rebellious community, and in response, Brigadier General James M. Varnum was dispatched with a detachment of the Rhode Island militia to round up the "disaffected inhabitants of said town, or any other towns within this state."[127] Varnum reported on May 24 that he had seized several Tories in the town and sent them to Providence for trial. Even as these men awaited trial, the *Newport Gazette*, published by a Tory sympathizer, crowed, "We hear the town of West Greenwich has, almost to a man, refused to guard the shore, or to pay any fines."

Records of the February 1778 session of the Rhode Island General Assembly reveal that at least some of the local population were loyalists and had chosen to abandon their farms and businesses. The assembly noted it had received notice that "Samuel Boone, William Boone, John Wightman, son of Valentine, Ephraim Smith, Ebenezer Slocum, Charles Slocum, and Thomas Cutter, have gone to the island of Rhode Island, and have joined the Enemy." High Sheriff of Kings County Beriah Brown was ordered to confiscate and make a full accounting of all their property.

Towns throughout New England often used the draft to "smoke out" loyalists in their communities. When an individual did not appear, the local militia was sent to arrest the man. This led to violent confrontations and, in one instance in Rhode Island, the death of a dissenter. Simeon Tucker of South Kingstown was a member of a Quaker family. His father and two brothers were listed as exempt, having taken the oath of nonviolent principles, as required by the state for those conscientious objectors of that time. Tucker was a successful farmer and well thought of in his community. He does not appear to have been a practicing Quaker. When he was drafted in late September 1777, he refused to appear or to find a substitute. When he failed to pay the fine levied for his noncompliance with the law, a warrant of distress was issued to seize property to cover the penalty. When militia showed up at Tucker's farm, the officer in charge ordered his men to seize one of the farmer's best cows. When Tucker interfered, the officer ordered his men to fire, ostensibly to frighten him into submission, but one ball struck Tucker in the forehead, killing him instantly.[128]

Other citizens were suspected to be loyalists because they declared themselves what we now call conscientious objectors, refusing to fight because of their religious convictions. Some religious dissenters, like the Mennonites, refused to hold political office in any colonial government and eschewed those responsibilities that went with being a citizen in early America. Yet by the time of the revolution, they were eager to participate in governance at all levels.

The largest group of said objectors was the Society of Friends, or Quakers, as they were more commonly called. The Friends had been following the "peace testimony" issued by their founder, George Fox, and the Committee of Suffering, as the leading council was called since as early as 1660, when it was declared by the body:

> *Wars and Fighting proceed from the Lusts of men…out of which Lusts the Lord hath redeemed us.…We…utterly deny…all outward Wars, and Strife, and Fighting's with outward Weapons, for any end, or under any pretense whatsoever.…The spirit of Christ which leads us into all Truth will never move us to fight and war against any man.…We cannot learn War anymore.*[129]

As historian Sarah Crabtree writes of the Friends' stance in the colonies, "Drawing on the languages of spiritual warfare, Friends promoted a unique cultural and political identity that allowed them to remain separate from, but engaged with the outside world."[130]

Large communities of Friends existed in Pennsylvania, Maryland, New Jersey, Rhode Island and other colonies, but even where worshipers were scarce, a network of Friends remained intact. In November 1775, the Assembly of Pennsylvania, still controlled by Quaker elders as it had been since the colony's founding, issued instructions to their delegates at the Continental Congress that although they shared the Patriots' frustration at the oppressive measures leveled by Parliament, "We strictly enjoyn that you in behalf of this Colony, dissent from & utterly reject, any propositions, schd such be made, that may cause, or lead to, a Seperation from our Mother Country, or a Change in the Form of this Government."

So warned at yearly meetings, Friends took steps to distance themselves from any attachment to the coming conflict. Many Quakers in America took the edict seriously, and meetings across the colonies punished or evicted members who had taken part, in any way, in helping either side. So strict were these measures that even wealthy Friends who could have profited from the war took pains to shed themselves of any suspicion. At the start of the conflict, for example, Quaker merchant William Rotch of Nantucket loaded

Saylesville Friends Meetinghouse, Lincoln, Rhode Island. *Photo by author.*

the bayonets he had acquired in trade and rowed them out to the harbor, where he dumped them overboard.

Prior to the Revolutionary War in North America, Rhode Island was the only colony in which Friends fully adhered to the Quaker Peace Testimony. For a time, Rhode Islanders steeped in liberty of conscience, or the right to worship as one saw fit without interference from the state government, tolerated the society's conscientious objection to participating in war and allowed some Quakers to join militias without taking up arms—but that was always an uneasy alliance. As historian Arthur J. Worrall notes,

> *Even there in that rogues State of toleration, such forbearance was short-lived among the populace. The Quaker Government's refusal to enter King Philip's War, and the subsequent abjection of Governor William Coddington allowing the troops of the United Colonies into Rhode Island the resultant rampage of murder, pillage of encampments and goods, and the kidnapping of innocent indigenous people to be sold into slavery; meant the end of Quaker political influence.*

At the onset of the American Revolution, the populace had become more conservative and militarized against threats to the colonies. This reflected a mindset that was now less than tolerant of dissenters. As historian Sarah Crabtree observes, "Voluntary military service became central in the modern conception of citizenship," and thus the image of the valiant "citizen soldier" guaranteed that "the supreme embodiment of proper citizenship became a man's sacrifice on the battlefield."[131]

In Massachusetts, those who exempted themselves from the draft paid a fee in lieu of service. Rhode Island enacted a law requiring any man who was drafted to either serve or provide a substitute in his place. If any person refused to follow the law, as attorney and historian Christian McBurney has noted, "The law further provided that…the state had the authority to impose a fine on him for each day he refused to serve, and if the man refused to pay the fines, to seize his property, sell it, and apply the proceeds to pay the overdue fines."

Friends presented a different concept of their responsibilities: "Quaker men (and women) insisted that they labored on behalf of their religious nation much in the same way that the citizen soldier did for his country." Such notions challenged the ideology of the Quaker Peace Testimony, and Friends' lack of willingness to serve often made them traitors in the eyes of patriots. Those Quakers who had been expelled from the Society of Friends for their support of the Revolution grew more vocal as the society's insistence on abstaining from any civic responsibilities during wartime extended to withholding food, blankets, clothing and shelter for troops of either side of the conflict.

Even in the face of persecution, the majority of Quakers held to their creed: "As God's chosen people and members of a church militant, [the] Quakers' role was to serve as models for other Christians....[They were] divinely called upon to hold up a standard, or testimony, to the nations, against every species of war, as antichristian."

Aside from the Quakers' very direct stance of refusing to enlist and take up arms against others, the peace testimony brought an even thornier issue to the forefront. As historian Arthur J. Worrall explains,

> *A much more difficult question than loyalty, especially in New England, turned on tax and currency. If Friends accepted and used money of the states or Confederation and paid taxes even indirectly to support the war, might they not be said to participate in wars and tumults and in the overthrow of lawful governments?*[132]

Some Quaker activists like Job Scott, a schoolteacher and minister in Providence, drafted policy that strictly adhered to the peace testimony and refused to pay war taxes of any kind. Others, like Moses Brown, advised forbearance, leaving the use of money or paying taxes to individual Friends' own consciences. Still, as Worrall notes, "The Revolutionary War was nudging Friends into a more rigid position."

Local governments also toughened their stance. In February 1777, the Rhode Island General Assembly added the requirement that the local clerk of the Friends' monthly meetings provide certification of membership for any member of that community who was drafted. The following month, fourteen Quakers who had not obtained the required certificate were fined and jailed. The prisoners petitioned the general assembly for their release and a waiver of the fines imposed based on their nonviolent consciences.[133] The assembly responded by expanding exemption from military service to include any individual who "took an oath adhering to the principles of non-violence and not bearing arms."[134]

Outside of New England, the Quakers in New York refused to pay taxes both during the war and after, when all citizens were enjoined to contribute to the easing of the country's debt from the long war. Massachusetts had enacted a measure whereby those who exempted themselves from the draft paid a fee in lieu of service. Rhode Island, which still held a wealth of Quaker merchants, had no such law and protested the efforts by Congress to extract more funding from the states.

Pennsylvania's Quakers also held firm to the peace testimony, refusing both to bear arms and to use the locally printed currency. On January 30, 1776, Quakers John Drinker, Samuel Fisher and Thomas Fisher were called before the Committee of Observation and Inspection for the City and Liberties of Philadelphia to answer for their refusal to accept Continental bills of credit. The committee was not, apparently, impressed by the three men's solidarity on this issue, and less than a week later, it issued its findings, which condemned all three as "enemies of their country" and prohibited them from all trade with the inhabitants of the colonies. Following this statement, the Pennsylvania Committee of Safety directed local authorities to "seize all of John Drinker's books and papers and deposit them in a locked and sealed chest or trunk in his ship and to lock up the windows and doors of his stores and warehouses and nail them shut."[135]

New Jersey Quakers also suffered persecution after the state assembly passed acts requiring citizens to take an oath of affirmation to the new state government. Thomas Redman and Mark Miller read aloud the epistle from Philadelphia's Yearly Meeting of Friends in December 1776 to the members of their own meetinghouse at the Haddonfield Monthly Meeting. They were arrested and jailed in Gloucester, New Jersey.

The local governments of Pennsylvania and New Jersey continued to pressure Friends into "taking the test," as members called it. Both states passed laws extending the oath requirement to all males, with, as we have seen, loss of liberties as punishment. In 1778, Pennsylvania adopted a statute that required all schoolteachers to take the oath—an occupation that many young Quaker males had undertaken. Some Friends could not help but bow to the pressure.

Quaker meetings in these states, however, responded by strictly enforcing the peace testimony, leading in New Jersey to the disownment of 288 members out of 429 cases brought before the meeting during the course of the war. Pennsylvania Friends disowned 948 members from a total of 1,287 cases brought before the meeting for discipline.[136]

Such measures by lawmakers inflamed persecution of Quakers by local patriots, especially in Pennsylvania, but there were outbreaks of violence against Quaker communities throughout the colonies. In Philadelphia, life was especially difficult. Meetinghouses were confiscated for use by local authorities to quarter soldiers or store ammunition. American soldiers from

Maryland confiscated the meetinghouse on Market Street for a time, allowing members to meet while holding the building.[137] When the city was occupied by the British in late 1777, officers of the British army and Hessians alike confiscated rooms in houses and barns to quarter their livestock, with little regard for the population.

Perhaps the most egregious offense against religious dissenters was the episode initiated by New Hampshire General John Sullivan, who, in August 1777, wrote to John Hancock concerning the discovery of a letter from the yearly meeting in Spanktown, New Jersey, that contained information about and outlined the movement of American troops. General Sullivan accused the Quakers of being loyalists and traitors. His letter, along with the discovered letter, was forwarded to the Continental Congress. Though this document and others provided by Sullivan later proved to be forgeries, the episode and its publicity turned many against the Quakers.

In Philadelphia, twenty-two prominent members of the Society of Friends were rounded up by order of a special committee of the Continental Congress that included John Adams, Richard Henry Lee and John Duer. Lee himself fervently believed that the Quakers held "a uniform fixed enmity to American measures."[138]

The Congress had decided on the measure of "banishment"—that is, exiling suspected loyalists at least thirty miles from any coastline, from which they might escape, or within easy access of postal routes, by which their communications might be carried to the enemy. On September 9, 1777, the Congress ordered those arrested in Philadelphia to be marched under escort of Pennsylvania militia to Staunton, Virginia, where they were held for over seven months. They would have likely been there longer but for the efforts of Elizabeth Drinker and a group of fellow wives, who spent those months petitioning the government; penning letters to leaders, including General Washington; and meeting when they could in person with those men of authority who could free their husbands and, perhaps more importantly, their fellow Friends from unjust imprisonment.

While many who supported the rebels may have regarded the Quakers as loyalists, the diary of John Duer's wife, Elizabeth Drinker, makes clear the Friends' disdain for war and the vainglory that accompanied such times, as described in her entry of May 18, 1778:

> *This day may be remembered by many, from the Scenes of Folly and Vanity, promoted by the Officers of the Army under pretense of showing respect to Gen. Howe, now about leaving them,—the parade of Coaches*

> *and other Carriages with many Horsemen. Thro' the Streets towards the No. Liberties, were great many numbers of the Officers & some women embark'd in three Galleys and a number of boats, and pass'd down the River, before the City, with Colours display'd, a large Band of Music, and the Ships in the Harbour decorated with Colours, saluted by the Cannon of some of them; it is said they landed in south wark, and proceeded from the waterside to Joseph Whartons late dwelling, which has been decorated and fitted for this occasion—in an expensive way, for this Company to Feast, Dance, and Revel in,—How I insensible do these people appear, while our Land is so greatly desolated, and Death and sore destruction has overtaken and upends ever so many.*[139]

Another issue that arose during the war was the confiscation of loyalists' estates as they fled or were arrested by local sheriffs, placed on trial and put under house arrest or deported. The property of these convicted loyalists was auctioned off, and the revenue received was placed in the coffers of the state's General Treasury, under the supervision of the Council of War or Committee of Safety.

As the first wave of loyalists fled the growing rebellion in the colonies, many of those estates left behind were purchased by neighboring Quakers or the fields of the estate rented out for their livestock. In the eyes of those who strictly adhered to the Quaker Peace Testimony, such actions were incriminating, as they were considered contributions to the war effort.

As historian Worrall writes, "Throughout the war Friends maintained their earlier testimony against participating in military affairs, though the price was substantial. Many young Friends enlisted in the army, and this was the major cause for disownments." One such prominent disowned Friend was General Nathanael Greene. Historian William C. Kashatus III believes that Greene "wrestled with a fundamental ideological dilemma: 'Was it possible to balance an allegiance to the state without deviating from the principles of the Society of Friends?'" But after Greene's decision to establish a local militia corps with others in 1774, he seems not to have looked back. Amid the arrests of Philadelphia and New Jersey Quakers, which some legal experts lamented as "the most wanton Tyranny ever exercised in any Country," Greene wrote home to his wife, Catharine, "The villainous Quakers are employed upon every quarter to serve the enemy. Some of them are confined and more deserve it."[140]

As harshly as he might view his former fellows for their refusal to fight, Greene could be equally harsh with those who enlisted and shirked their

Portrait of General Nathanael Greene. *Courtesy of the Nathanael Greene Homestead.*

responsibilities or used their status as soldiers to inflict harm on others or their property. One such series of incidents occurred in the summer of 1780, when Greene was in command of the southern army. He wrote to Washington in August 1780 of the crimes and his intended punishment:

> *Sir,*
>
> *There has been committed some of the most horrid acts of plunder by some of the Pennsylvania line that has disgracd the American Arms during the War. The instances of plunder and violence is equal to any thing committed by the Hessians. Two soldiers were taken that were out upon the business both of which fired upon the Inhabitants to prevent their coming to give intelligence. I think it would have a good effect to hang one of these fellows in the face of the troops without the form of a tryal. It is absolutely necessary to give a check to this licensious spirit which increases amazingly. The impudence of the Soldiers is intollerable: a party plundered a house yesterday in spight of a number of Officers; and even threatened the officers if they offerd to interpose.*

It is the opinion of most of the Officers that it is absolutely necessary for the good of the service that one of those fellows should be made an example of; and if your Excellency will give permision I will have one hung up this afternoon where the Army are to march by.[141]

Greene then addressed another ongoing issue among the troops, that of desertion.

There is also a deserter taken three quarters of the way over to New York belonging to the 7th Pennsylvania Regiment which the Officers not only of the Regiment but several others wish may be executed in the same way that I propose to execute the other in. Several deserters are gone off yesterday and last Evening.

As it was, the desertion of soldiers who had enlisted or been drafted for the War of Independence was a constant source of irritation for Continental officers, especially during the first two years of the conflict, when desertion rates from the American army were as high as 25 percent, one-quarter of those who had been mustered.[142] Morale among the enlisted men ebbed and flowed with the fortunes of the army. Having begun as a spirited rabble of patriots, their numbers and enthusiasm for the war had dwindled and even threatened to dissolve the army before the taking of Trenton and Princeton rejuvenated the American cause.

While lesser officers felt little empathy for the common soldier, their commander in chief was all too aware of the many encumbrances faced by these men, who were now charged with living in crowded and sickly encampments and facing almost constant shortages of food and clothing—not to mention the lack of pay that was often promulgated by the Congress's inability to raise funds, as well as the effects of homesickness and fear of combat. It was not until June 1777 that Washington could write, "By paying off the Troops and keeping them well supplied with Provisions & ca. desertions have become much less frequent." At best, it was a temporary reprieve.[143] As the war reached its third year, procurement of supplies dwindled during the winter of 1778 at Valley Forge. Washington wrote on February 7, 1778, to the commissary general, "The spirit of desertion among the Soldiery, never before reached the threatening height, as at the present time." Brigadier General James Mitchell Varnum echoed that concern nearly a week later in a letter to General Nathanael Greene, writing that desertions that year were "astonishingly great." The harsh winter of 1777–78 set off a wave of desertions from encampments, including Valley Forge, where conditions were so harsh that Washington waived the usual punishment of death and reduced the sentence to one hundred lashes.

But by late 1778, another issue was revealing the weakness of the Continental Congress. Fewer states were supporting their troops with pay and supplies and the Congress with funds, effectively stalemating the war and prolonging the suffering of troops abandoned in the field. As noted by historian Joseph J. Ellis,

> *The...stubborn reality was the small size of the Continental Army....In fact, the Continental Army remained too small to conduct any major offensive operations between 1778–1781. The refusal of the states to provide men and money for the Continental Army was...a long standing problem.*[144]

The problem worsened after the French alliance. By the fall of 1780, shortages of support and supplies were seemingly about to dismantle the whole of the American army. The strength of the American forces fluctuated between three thousand and ten thousand men, but these numbers were deceiving, as Washington noted: "There is a greater disproportion between the total number and men fit for duty...than any army in the world." Between those bedridden by illness or starvation, those too ill clothed or shoeless to march and the men who had deserted, Washington felt his army "was constantly sliding from under us as a pedestal of Ice would do...in a Summer's Day."[145]

The following spring, conditions brought on a crisis, and Washington sent the young John Laurens to France in the hope of raising yet more funds to save his army. He wrote after his emissary's departure of the desperate situation:

> *The troops are fast approaching nakedness, and...we have nothing to clothe them with....The hospitals are without medicine's, and our sick without nutriment except such as well men eat; that all our public works are at a stand....It may be declared in a word that we are at the end of our tether.*[146]

The punishment for desertion was a sentence of death, handed down in a court-martial overseen by thirteen officers who acted as judge and jury of these cases. After sentencing, the Continental officers reported the results of the trial for General Washington's approval. While some sentences were approved, Washington was hesitant to inflict such harsh punishment unless circumstances demanded such an execution.

When sentences were carried out, the prisoner was paraded before his regiment and either lashed, hanged or executed by firing squad. Often, deserters received a pardon or a lesser punishment. Sometimes, a reprieve came at the last possible moment. Historian Joseph Lee Boyle recounts a case of eleven men who were scheduled to be executed in May 1780. All but one of these men had been convicted of desertion. Their graves had been dug, and eight had been forced to climb ladders with the nooses already placed around their necks when the reprieve came from General Washington. The ten men who had deserted were pardoned. The eleventh man, James Coleman, had been convicted of forging more than one hundred discharge papers, including his own. He was hanged for his crimes.[147]

Boyle also cites a study that found that out of 225 cases of men sentenced to death for desertion, only 40 to 75 were executed. In fact, General Washington issued four mass pardons for men who had deserted the army, beginning on April 6, 1777. To Washington's consternation, however, he found that many deserters could return to their communities and be taken in and even hidden from the troops who were looking for them in the weeks after their desertion.

In December 1782, a sizeable detachment from the Rhode Island Regiment, including one subaltern officer, three sergeants and forty-three rank-and-file men, marched under command of Captain Ebenezer Macomber to the state of Vermont, ostensibly to search for deserters. The actual objective of the mission was the capture of Judge Luke Knowlton of Newfane and Colonel Samuel Wells of Brattleboro, two known loyalists who were suspected of passing letters deemed "inimical to American interests" between the British in Canada and officers in New York. The two loyalists had escaped to Canada by the time their pursuers arrived, but the detachment managed to capture fourteen men who had deserted. The following year, Washington again complained that the "Grants," the wooded hills area between New Hampshire and Vermont, were "populated by hundreds of Deserters from this Army."

CHAPTER 5

"NO MEAT, NO BREAD, NO SOLDIER"

The Campaign Against Hunger, 1775–1779

During the first year of the Revolution," British historian Louis Clinton Hatch writes, "the troops were reasonably well fed. The war began in eastern Massachusetts, a thickly settled agricultural district inhabited by zealous Whigs, who were eager to supply the Army."[148] The quality of the provisions, however, was said to be poor. The bread was "sour and unwholesome," the beef so poor that complaints spurred General Nathanael Greene to launch an inquiry, in which a panel of butchers found the "beef" sold to the army to be horseflesh.

The truth was that within twenty miles of Boston, those farms in surrounding communities were largely small, self-sustaining ones, ill-prepared to provide for the needs of thousands of soldiers. Historian Jackson Turner Main notes:

> *In Suffolk County, which included the city, a group of inland villages near Rhode Island, were actually more extreme examples of the type ... Although the region had been settled for decades, the distance from Boston and Providence, together with the rough terrain and lack of navigable streams made transportation costly.*[149]

While the troops around Boston during the American siege of the city and those taking part in the defense of the Hudson in New York might have been well supplied and eating hearty dinners washed down with hard cider, the army was, it seems, utterly unprepared to supply those troops on an extended campaign, as was evident in the disastrous march to Quebec during the fall and winter of 1775.

Washington was buoyed by the daring raid led by Ethan Allen and his independent Green Mountain Boys on Ticonderoga and Crown Point that spring.[150] Immediately after the victory, Allen traveled to Philadelphia to obtain reimbursement but also to have his unit established as part of the Continental army. Congress granted his request with an order that he raise "a body of troops, not to exceed five hundred men," who would be called the Green Mountain Boys and be allowed to elect their own officers. Arnold immediately went to lobby General Washington, and subsequently, plans to invade Canada developed over the summer, with a combined force of Allen's and Arnold's men and others under General Philip Schuyler.

On September 8, 1775, General Washington laid out the specifics of preparations for a northern campaign against the British-held fortification at Quebec. Sadly, this excursion was to be a harbinger of things to come for those providers of the Continental army from its beginnings in 1775, with which some difficulties would persist throughout the war.

> *The detachment going under the command of Col. Arnold, to be forewith taken off the roll of duty, and to march this evening to Cambridge Common, where tents and everything necessary, is provided for their reception. The Rifle Company at Roxbury, and those at Prospect-hill, to march early tomorrow Morning to join the above detatchment. Such Officers and men, as are taken from Gen. Greene's brigade, for the above detatchment, are to attend the Muster of their respective regiments tomorrow morning at seven O'Clock, upon Prospect-hill, when the Muster is finished, they are forthwith to rejoin the Detatchment at Cambridge.*[151]

Within days of Washington's orders, the men who would make up Arnold's Army—some ten companies of musket men and another three brigades of riflemen—were gathering along the bank of the Kennebec River, "between Rueben Colburn's shipyard and Fort Western."[152]

Arnold's plan was to disperse his army into four divisions, which would depart Fort Western on consecutive days. While this plan may have seemed reasonable, mixing musket regiments and riflemen together in the belief that they would coexist and cooperate was a serious misstep—a boot in the muck, you might say. The riflemen were not inclined to fall under the command of anyone or follow any but their own commanders' orders, and Arnold finally had to relent to a sole rifle division under command of the Virginian Daniel Morgan.

From these men, an expeditionary force was sent out, not only to blaze the trail for the army to follow but also to send back needed information beyond what had been mapped out as the army progressed along the route. Surgeon Isaac Senter of Newport, Rhode Island, accompanied the "Secret Expedition to Quebec" that fall and winter. Its troubles would soon be no secret; even dispatches home began to carry a note of uncertainty. The difficult lessons the army learned from this expedition doubtless lessened the hardships of later campaigns, but this, of course, was an unknown comfort to those whom the army so severely tested.

On September 15, Senter wrote with the burgeoning enthusiasm of a young man going to war:

> *Transports now in readiness, we were ordered to embark this morning by 9 o'clock. Our fleet consists of 11 sail of shipping, sloops, and schooners containing upon an average 100 troops as we carry 1,100 men, officers included.*[153]

What followed was a week of rough passage, which periodically caused them to be taken by swells that "occasioned most of the troops to disgorge

Scene of soldiers using bateaux. *Wikipedia Commons.*

themselves of their luxuries so plentifully laid in ere we departed." Despite the questionable weather, they were piloted into the mouth of the Kennebec River: "The wind and rain continued exceeding hard, and with much difficulty we entered the river."

Continuing upstream, they passed through a narrow section of rough water called Hell Gate and on to Gardner's Town, where the bateaux that would transport the men and their provisions waited. The whole of these, however, were "not quite finished," and the ones that were had been constructed of "green pine boards, which made them rather heavy."

For those unfamiliar with their design, Thomas A. Desjardin, in his book on the expedition, *Through a Howling Wilderness*, provides a description of the bateaux (the French word for the northernmost settlers' preferred style of "boat"):

> *The size and shape of the bateau, varied in the colonies, but each was higher and pointy at the ends with a flat bottom for navigating shallow water. In Maine, these were generally smaller than in southern colonies, standing just three feet tall at the bow and stretching twenty-two feet from prow to stern. While they were rugged and durable, they weighed hundreds of pounds each, which made them a poor choice of vessel for an expedition that would be carrying them often. On land, as few as four men could carry them on their shoulders, but not without great exertion.*[154]

Members of the riflemen brigade were sent to survey the route ahead, and on September 25, Senter recorded that the army had about one hundred bateaux ready for departure: "To each of them a select number of bateaux men were ordered—in general about 5 per boat. In these all the provisions were put, tents and camp equipage, &c. All excepting what was necessary for that party that went by land."

Those who departed by river would soon find it an arduous journey. Because the boats were heavily laden with provisions, as they proceeded through shallow rapids, the men were obliged to leave them and guide the bateaux through waist-deep water. On October 5, the surgeon recorded, "By this time many of our bateaux were nothing but wrecks, some stove to pieces, &c. The carpenters were employed in repairing them while the rest of the Army was busy carrying over the provisions." Of those, however, barrels of dried cod lying untied in the boats had come open and spilled their contents at the feet of the troops and among the freshwater bilge. In addition, "the bread casks not being water-proof admitted the water in plenty, swelled the bread, bursts the casks as well and soured the whole bread. The same fate attended a number of fine casks of peas."

Surgeon Senter recorded the sobering future that now faced the expedition: "We were now curtailed of a very valuable and large part of our provisions, ere we had entered the wilderness."[155] The men still held a few barrels of salt beef among the remaining provisions, but even those, "being killed in the heat of summer, took much damage after salting....Our fate is now down to Salt Pork and flour." Worse still, some of the men began to fall ill with dysentery.

The men hired a pair of Seneca guides and proceeded upriver against a swift current to the Seven Mile stream. From there, they continued to "a very high waterfall named Caratuncah." The next stage of their passage would be the "Great Carrying Place," a stretch of twelve miles from the Kennebec to the Dead River interspersed with three ponds they would traverse along the route. Within but a few days, Senter recorded, "The Army was now much fatigued, being obliged to carry all the bateaux, barrels of provisions, warlike stores, &c. over on their backs through a most terrible piece of woods conceivable—sometimes in the mud knee deep, then over ledgy hills &c."

These items were all transported piecemeal: first the bateaux, turned upside down so the heavy gunwales rested on the shoulders of the men; next the barrels of provisions, hung with rope between two poles and carried by four men per barrel; and lastly the stores of powder and other "war provisions."[156] The expedition managed to transport all this roughly three and one-quarter miles to the first body of water, a stagnant pond, "quite yellow in color"—yet water with which "we were obliged not only to do all our cooking, but use it as our constant drink. Nor would a little of it suffice, as we were obliged eat our meat most exceedingly salt[ed]....This with our constant fatigue called for large quantities of drink."[157]

As might be expected, the number of cases of dysentery among the troops began to worsen, and by the time they'd marched and carried the bateaux to the second pond along the route, the sick were so many that the army was forced to hastily construct a blockhouse amid the swamp, christened Arnold Hospital, which was "no sooner finished than filled."

A council of war was called, with respect to the state of provisions, where the commanders of the separate companies in attendance voted on whether to resume the expedition or return home: "The question being put whether all to return, or only part, the majority were for part only returning."[158] As rifleman George Morison inscribed in his journal, "Increasing fatigue began at length to make a deep impression on some of us. Several sank under the weight of it. Their strength was exhausted: grew sick, and our provisions were vanishing away. It was deemed proper to send them back."

As evening fell on Thursday, October 26, some of the remaining men at the encampment likely wished that they had left with those returning. A disgusted Senter recorded the following day, "Our Bill of Fare for last night and this morning consisted of the jawbone of a swine destitute of any covering, that we boiled in a quantity of water, that with a little thickening constituted a sumptuous eating."

On Saturday, October 28, they received word that relief in the form of provisions awaited them at their designated meeting place with Arnold and the remainder of the army ahead. With this news, the officers decided that they should resume the march immediately. They pooled the provisions on hand, affording each man five pints of flour and an equal share of pork, which would need to sustain them for the journey remaining of "about a hundred miles."

The next day, Surgeon Senter discovered with disbelief that "some of the men devoured the whole of their flour last evening, determined (as they expressed it) to have a full meal, letting the morrow look out for itself." On November 1, he wrote a long, heartsick entry describing the horrid conditions that had overtaken the expedition:

> *Our greatest luxuries now consisted in a little water, stiffened with flour, in imitation of shoemakers paste....We had now arrived as we thought to almost the zenith of distress. Several had been entirely destitute of either meat or bread for many days. These chiefly consisted of those who had devoured their provision immediately, and a number who were in the boats. The voracious disposition many of us had now arrived at, rendered almost anything admissible....In company was a poor dog,* [who had] *hitherto lived through all the tribulations, became a prey for the sustenance of the assassinators. This poor animal was instantly devoured, without leaving any vestige of the sacrifice. Nor did the shaving soap, pomatum, and even the lip salve, leather of their shoes, cartridge boxes &c., share any better fate.*

The following day, the men lightened their load considerably, and after marching eight miles, they witnessed "a vision of horned cattle, four-footed beasts, &c., rode and drove by." A celebration soon ensued: "Echoes of gladness resounded from front to rear with a te deum" as the men realized they had reached an encampment that included eighteen Canadians, one American, three horned cattle and two horses. A heifer was soon dispatched and divided evenly among the men for cooking. While the men were engaged in these activities, a pair of birch canoes arrived carrying two more Canadians and provisions, including mutton, cornmeal and tobacco. It was decided at once to send back the mutton for the relief of those sick in the hospital.

The men learned with relief that they were but twenty miles from Arnold's settlement. The officers hired a Seneca guide, and the men proceeded downriver to a house that offered goods and, more importantly, a good meal. Provisions still proved difficult to find, but for one bottle of suspect New England rum for which Senter paid "one hard dollar." He wrote:

> *We were making enquiry at every likely stage, for this purpose* [we] *visited an old peasant's house, where was a merry old woman at her loom, and two or three fine young girls. They were exceedingly rejoiced with the company, bought some eggs, pork, sugar, sweetmeats &c., where we made ourselves very happy.*

In the weeks that followed, after reaching Arnold's encampment, the men were engaged with the siege of the city of Quebec. They no longer had to worry about provisions, but Arnold and other strategists among the fledgling Continental army knew they had miscalculated the length and severity of the march—let alone underprovided for the troops enlisted in engage in such a campaign. Many of those who survived the march to Quebec were taken prisoner as their assault on the citadel failed when they breached the gates but then became trapped within the city walls.[159] Arnold had been injured early in the attack and removed to a flying hospital nearby, where he sat propped up on a cot with his wounded leg dressed and a pair of pistols in hand. He and the others in the hospital would escape capture, but over four hundred American soldiers were taken prisoner. As for the American army, its method of placing stores at specific locations in advance of the arrival of troops came of the painful lesson in near starvation that Arnold's men endured.

In the spring of 1777, Congress began to address the problem of supplying the army by appointing Christopher Ludwig of Philadelphia to the post of "Superintendent of Bakers and Director of Baking for the Main Army." He was directed to furnish 100 pounds of bread per 135 pounds of flour supplied to him. The baker managed to deliver the required weight in bread from its equal weight in flour. Hatch reports in his history, "There was no more bad bread after he took office."[160]

Painting of the Invasion of Quebec. *Wikipedia Commons.*

For a time, supplies of meat and bread improved, but Washington notified Congress in a letter on July 19, 1777, "During the greater part of the last campaign and during all the present, the soldiers had scarcely tasted vegetables…[and] they were very inadequately supplied with beer, cider, and rum." Congress authorized the Board of War, a standing committee that oversaw the war effort, to increase supplies of bread and spirits and also ordered a hogshead of rum to be delivered to the gallant troops who had won victory at Brandywine.

Shortly thereafter, however, in October 1777, the quartermaster of the army, who had removed himself from the field due to illness in June, resigned from his post. The organization of shipping supplies soon began to rapidly decline. Rather than fix the problem of organization, Congress began to pressure Washington to confiscate goods and provisions from the communities that surrounded the army encampment. Congress reasoned—without, apparently, much faith in the army—that these lands and thus goods would fall into enemy hands. Local farmers resisted these efforts, refusing to thresh the wheat from their fields, and millers refused to grind corn and flour for the army. Washington sympathized with their plight and resisted taking such action beyond what he felt necessary, knowing what hardship it would cause the populace. Congress continued to press, giving specific orders that farmers within a seventy-mile radius of the camp be required to thresh their wheat or have it confiscated as straw and be paid accordingly.

On December 10, Congress passed a resolution declaring its "great concern" that while insufficient supplies were sent at great expense from afar, the army was not taking advantage of the "large quantities of provisions and cattle in the country nearby." What Congress did not know from afar was that the country surrounding the encampment was already exhausted, and local farmers, aware that Congress believed their lands might fall into enemy hands, may well have been holding out to sell their wheat in the weeks ahead to the British for a better price.

Other farmers actively sought to sell to the British for an ensured price rather than a certificate from the Americans that held no guarantee of payment. As historian Joseph J. Ellis notes, "The local farmers knew all the backroads, and trapped as they were between two armies waging a foraging war, selling to the British was less a political statement than the only way to sustain their families."[161] When a band of militia murdered two wagon drivers, some farmers sent their wives or daughters to drive the wagons to the British encampments, knowing that they would likely not be harmed.

The last month of 1777 was especially rough on the soldiers. The Thanksgiving celebration, for many, was servings of the same beef and flour they were given daily. Major Dearborne wrote about what the day brought: "The third day we have been without flour or bread." The major recorded that while he and his fellow soldiers were thankful to be alive, unlike so many of their friends, "We had for Thanksgiving breakfast some exceedingly poor beef which has been boiled and now warmed in an old short-handled frying pan."

Even as the army marched into Valley Forge for winter quarters on December 19, 1777, officers were pondering how to stretch the provisions. General Greene suggested a mixture of wheat and sugar, a kind of cereal for the troops. General Pickering recommended that every soup served as a meal be thickened with bread.

The suffering of that long winter of 1777–78 has been well documented: the lack of clothing, shoes, blankets and straw that brought such injury and discomfort. But adding to these physical miseries were the constant pangs of hunger. Supplies of any kind had not reached the troops since Brandywine. One surgeon recorded in his diary that they had nothing but "fire-cake and water" to live on. When it was learned that some officers had left camp to be housed and dined in private homes, morale plummeted from the fragile precipice of honor on which it had perched and insubordination, outright desertion and rebellion grew in the encampment.

In late December, Brigadier General James Mitchell Varnum, commander of the two Rhode Island regiments and a pair of Connecticut Continental regiments, wrote to General George Washington of the ominous problem that was beginning to gnaw away at the morale and general discipline of the gathered American forces. "According to the saying of Solomon," Varnum wrote, "hunger will break through a stone

Portrait of Brigadier General James Mitchell Varnum by John Nelson Arnold (1870). *Courtesy of the Brown University Portrait Collection.*

wall." The general was writing because for the past three days the men under his command had been without bread and for the past two "intirely without Meat." What beef had been procured was too vile to feed the soldiers, and the situation had come to a critical juncture: "The Men must be supplied, or they cannot be commanded."

Varnum noted that he himself was distressed to be giving the commander in chief this unhappy news, but the general was never a subordinate who minced his words or refrained from giving his opinion: "If you expect the Exertions of virtuous Principles, while your troops are deprived of the essential Neccessaries of Life, your final Disappointment will be great, in Proportion to that Patience, w'ch now astonishes every Man of human Feeling."

Other officers, those commanders comfortably wintering in the confiscated quarters of nearby houses, would likely not have written such a provocative letter. Indeed, many hardly set foot outside to review their troops until the arrival of Baron Von Steuben, who insisted on the commanders' presence during drills and reviews of the Continental regiments. It may have been Varnum's proximity to his troops at Valley Forge: he was but one hundred yards beyond the old star redoubt raised above the northern road, quartered in a small stone house that belonged to John Stevens. No doubt he saw his troops on a daily basis and received their complaints—"too urging to pass unnoticed," as he wrote to Washington—but just as likely, Varnum wrote with such passion to his commander-in-chief because many of the men who joined the siege of Boston as Varnum's Brigade had suffered through such harsh conditions before, when nearly one hundred of them volunteered for the ill-fated expedition to Quebec.

In one outburst, shouts of "no meat, no bread, no soldier" and the accompanying "callings and hootings like those of crows and owls" resounded throughout the camp. In early 1778, a near mass desertion was averted when some provisions were found at the last minute and Washington calmed the situation by addressing the men personally, praising their fortitude and sacrifice and urging them to be patient and rise above these "little accidents" of misfortune. He would not blame the army before the troops, but in a private letter to Congress, he wrote scathingly that his men, "with unparalleled patience…have gone through a severe and inclement winter, unprovided with any of those conveniences and comforts, which are usually the soldiers lot after the duties of the field are over."[162]

Crucial to the morale of the troops and the general health of the camp were the women who accompanied the men to Valley Forge. Several of the officers' wives accompanied their husbands to camp, but these, as noted earlier, were comfortably encamped in local houses, along with both free and enslaved domestic staff who had accompanied them. Among those accompanying Martha Washington were laundress Margaret Thomas, a free woman hired by the Washington household, and Isaac and Hannah Till, an enslaved couple who cooked for the Washingtons during the 1777–78 winter encampment.[163] Polly Cooper, a woman of the Oneida Nation, came with her sachem's expedition to the encampment bearing provisions, among them white corn. Polly showed soldiers how to prepare the corn as hominy and to grind it into flour for what were known as fire-cakes. This Indigenous woman also advised and assisted with medical care in the camp, as noted by Martha Washington.

Within the camp itself, a number of enlistees' wives and servants were also present, in addition to the population of unattached women who served as camp cleaners, cooks, laundresses, seamstresses, nurses and those "women of comfort," as they were known, who also followed along with the others. The majority of these arrived with the wagon trains that followed in the wake of the marching regiments, and they brought with them tents, gear and other possessions. Washington grudgingly tolerated their presence as necessary but enforced a strict discipline of discreetness and was not against drumming women who violated military regulations out of camp. Most carried out their duties at camp with little fanfare or favor, bearing the ills of camp life the same as the soldiers. It's estimated that between 250 and 400 women were present during the encampments at Valley Forge.

Among the officers' wives were Lucy Fletcher Knox, who at twenty-two joined her rebel husband at Valley Forge after her loyalist family disowned her following their marriage and fled Boston. Sarah Livingston Alexander, the fifty-six-year-old wife of Lord Stirling, enthusiastically joined other officers' wives in organizing a camp production of the popular play *Cato*.[164] While these efforts and Martha Washington's dance-filled parties helped keep the officers' morale high, it's likely few gave much thought to the common soldiers shivering in the makeshift huts with little to sustain them. When she arrived in January 1778, Catharine Littlefield Greene, wife of General

Nathanael Greene, took upon herself the task of visiting the troops and comforting those who were disabled and confined to quarters. She endeared herself to the soldiers as a "handsome, elegant, and accomplished woman" while translating Von Steuben's French curses as they drilled, singing with soldiers gathered around the campfire and listening to their stories of loved ones back home. She gave, as an aide to Von Steuben wrote, "a bright side to our distress," and to the soldiers encamped, she became "the lovable sister among the band of brothers."[165]

With the coming of spring, supply routes were reopened, and Congress ordered a commission formed to find a new quartermaster for the army. The commission settled on offering the post to General Nathanael Greene, the Rhode Island commander who had literally saved the army at Valley Forge in the closing weeks of winter when he led a contingent of troops through weeks of zealous foraging and enforcing the orders for impressments. Greene was fair but firm in enforcing these orders. Like Washington, he understood the hardship these impressments inflicted on the populace and made certain that those farmers whose horses, cattle and sheep were taken were issued government receipts for payment. He had nothing but contempt, however, for those who led their cattle and horses into the woods to hide them from the army. He wrote to Washington on February 17, 1778,

> *Sir, I sent to camp yesterday near fifty head of cattle. I wish it had been it in my power to have sent more, but the inhabitants have taken the alarm and concealed their stock in such a manner that it is very difficult finding any.*[166]

This was just as Congress had suspected, and its members were well aware that the general could "harden his heart," as he expressed it, against any protest a farmer might make for an exemption from the impressment order. No doubt Greene's actions went a long way toward convincing the commission that the general had the capabilities needed for the post.

Greene and his men foraged for another two weeks before Greene returned and wrote from camp that during the direst period of that winter, when thousands appeared ready to desert,

> *Relief arrived from the little collections I had made and some others and prevented the Army from disbanding. We are still in danger of starveing; the Commissary department is in a most wretched condition; the Quarter Masters, in a worse. Hundreds and Hundreds of our horses have actually starved to death.*

Now offered the opportunity to remake the department, Greene at first hesitated. He relished the role of field commander and had more than proven his worth to Washington, both as a leader of men in the field and as a strategist amid the flurry of unrolled maps and opinions that the commander in chief had to weather in every council of war.

The commission itself had concluded that the current state of confusion in the Quartermaster Department as well as the "depreciation of our Money, and the exhausted state of our resources," made the task of reforming the department and methods of supply at the same time close to impossible. Even so, Washington himself, along with a representative of Congress, pressed Greene personally to take on the challenge.

The general finally relented, taking the post and starting out at once with "not a moments time to be lost." He set in motion a plan to store more than one million bushels of grain for the army's horses in the coming campaigns, writing to Colonel Clement Biddle, quartermaster of the Pennsylvania militia, to "give all sorts of grain the preference to wheat....Oats first, Corn next, Rye next, and so on." He was determined ensure that the men had enough flour for bread and to never again bear witness to the inexcusable deaths of so many needed animals in the army's care.

No greater problem faced General Greene as the new quartermaster than the seasonal challenges of transporting goods for the army. The British blockades of ports along the coastline between Newport and New York had forced the Americans to transport goods by land routes, would-be roads that were often barely passable, rutted as they were with washouts from the long winter. A shortage of vehicles also plagued the army's efforts, as the commissary seemed in constant need of finding "transport carts, wagons, sleighs, sledges, oxen, horses, harness, packsaddles, wagoners, carters, and forage."[167] Forage was of the greatest importance, as it fueled the oxen and draft horses that hauled the wheat and grain for the remainder of the army's livestock. If a supply transport was delayed or the march became an arduous one, the forage might well be severely depleted by the time it arrived in camp with the rest of the goods.

While the blockade at sea made those transport routes nearly impassable, Greene did take advantage of the myriad streams and rivers that flowed through the surrounding countryside, notably constructing a warehouse at Reading, Pennsylvania, on the bank of the Schuylkill River, from where he could transport goods by boat downriver to Valley Forge.

On April 14, 1778, he wrote to Colonel Charles Pettit from the Red Lion, a tavern in Lionville, Pennsylvania, where he had arrived after an apparently unpleasant ride, reporting to the colonel, "The road from Camp to this place is exceedingly bad and as it is the great communication between Camp to Lancaster and between Camp and the Yellow Springs where our principle hospitals are, it is our interest to set about mending it as soon as possible." The quartermaster general ordered Pettit to "apply to his Excellency for fifty men to work upon this road and fifty upon the other."[168]

By April 29, Greene had received welcome news from Colonel John Davis:

> *I have sent by James Rowney, Wagon Master ten teams fully Equipd with 100 bags 240 bushels of Chopt Grain for Forage to be Delivered to Col. Biddle. I have sent 60 Single Horses by Robert Riddle for the Artillery. In two Days I shall Send ten Wagons and teames more.*

As the livestock began arriving, Greene took note of a distinctive feature and issued a complimentary letter to the colonel:

> *You did perfectly right in branding the horses, make it a constant rule for the future to brand all you purchase upon the Four quarters* [forequarters]. *I have no doubt that states have lost some hundreds of horses, for want of proper attention be*[ing] *paid to branding the cattle* [i.e., livestock] *that have been purchased from time to time.*

Challenges still faced the quartermaster general: while roads were being repaired and supplies moving more smoothly than before, some goods were still delayed or not conveyed in a timely manner. He learned in a report from Colonel James Abeel in Reading, Pennsylvania:

> *I am extremely Sorry to tell you that I find a very great abuse in the Wagon Mast'r Gen'ls Department at every place I have been. In the First Place some of the Waggon Masters do not drive there Waggons above Nine and Ten miles a day whereas they can with ease drive 20 miles. Besides if they come in of an Afternoon early instead of Cutting Straw drawing their Fodder and Provisions so as to be ready to set off early Next morning they take the greatest part of the day to load and draw Provisions so that they go only 3 or 4 miles at farthest that day.*
>
> *They make it a rule to Stop at every Tavern on the Road and Loiter there time away.*

Abeel suggested a plan of action that proved successful while he was quartermaster at "Suckasunny Plains," where he "made this agreement with the Waggon Masters that they shou'd Travel at least 20 miles a Day steadily on and that whatever they were short I deducted from their Wages. This made them do their duty and very few Horses were hurt by being drove too hard." This apparently had been a common occurrence: having rested at three or four taverns on the road, the wagon masters then "drove as if the Devil was Driving them" to make up for lost time.

As the rumors of a British evacuation from Philadelphia swirled in the early months of 1778, Washington sent a message of some urgency to Greene on May 17, while he was on his way back to Valley Forge after a visit to the quartermaster in Fishkill, New York.[169] The general wrote,

> *Every piece of intelligence from Philadelphia makes me think it more and more probable that the Enemy are preparing to evacuate it.…In any case it is absolutely necessary that we should be ready for an instant movement of the army. I have therefore to request you will strain every nerve to prepare without delay the necessary provisions.*[170]

Greene sent a flurry of missives to put the plan for stores into action. He wrote late in the month to Moore Furman,

> *It would be best to send some good trusty persons to see that your orders are faithfully complied with—a disappointment will be attended with the worst of consequences.…You will compleat your purchases as heretofore instructed as fast as possible, for I am really afraid all our exertions will fall far short of supplying the wants of the army.*[171]

When the British did leave, it was the consensus of the council of war that the departing troops "remain unmolested," much to the consternation of Greene and two other generals who wished to engage—or at least harass and delay their departure. The American army, then, essentially escorted from a respectable distance the British army on its long, slow march through the early summer heat and humidity of New Jersey.

Washington's plan and Greene's method of laying stores at strategic points along the fixed route proved successful. When men arrived at an appointed campsite, they found tents and supplies waiting to be unpacked.

The quartermaster general's next challenge was to supply the army gathering under General John Sullivan for an attack on the British-occupied island commonly called Rhode Island, which was an island off the mainland of the state comprising the towns of Newport and Portsmouth, now known as Aquidneck Island. The British had occupied the island in December 1776, thereby creating a stranglehold on all shipping between New England and New York. An aborted attempt by the Americans to invade the island in the summer of 1777 brought a new strategist on the scene in the form of General Sullivan, and when the French signed a treaty with the United States in the spring of 1778, Sullivan could formulate a plan for a real invasion. By midsummer, the French had sent a fleet of battleships to support the assault.

Greene wrote from the American camp at White Plains, New York, to his deputy in Rhode Island Ephraim Bowen,

> *The forces collected for this purpose will be considerable. Great exertions therefore, will be necessary in our department....A great number of teams and Boats will be wanted upon the occasion. Pray do not let the expedition suffer for want of anything in our line.*[172]

Greene rode the 170 miles from White Plains to his home in Coventry, Rhode Island, over the course of three days, arriving on July 30 just as darkness fell. He spent just a day with his pregnant wife and two young children before heading to Providence to take command of roughly half the troops that were gathering for the march to Tiverton.

Since Washington's directive, troops had been gathering from all over New England to descend on the encampments in place for the assault on Rhode Island. As in the campaign at Monmouth, Greene was asked to temporarily relinquish his role as quartermaster general and assume that of major general on the field. He marched the men under his command from Providence to Tiverton on August 4, followed a day later by the Marquis de Lafayette with his troops. Together, they commanded more than ten thousand men, including the newly formed First Rhode Island Regiment, largely composed of formerly enslaved men who enlisted to earn their freedom, as well as free Indigenous and Black men and a handful of European-born indentured servants. The unit had been formed in February 1778 after much debate—and even more curiosity, once they were drilling and marching through the streets of East Greenwich in preparation for this, their first battle.

The British watched the growing encampment with trepidation. The French fleet had been bombarding the British fortifications since arriving in Rhode Island waters, and the nearly seven thousand British and Hessian

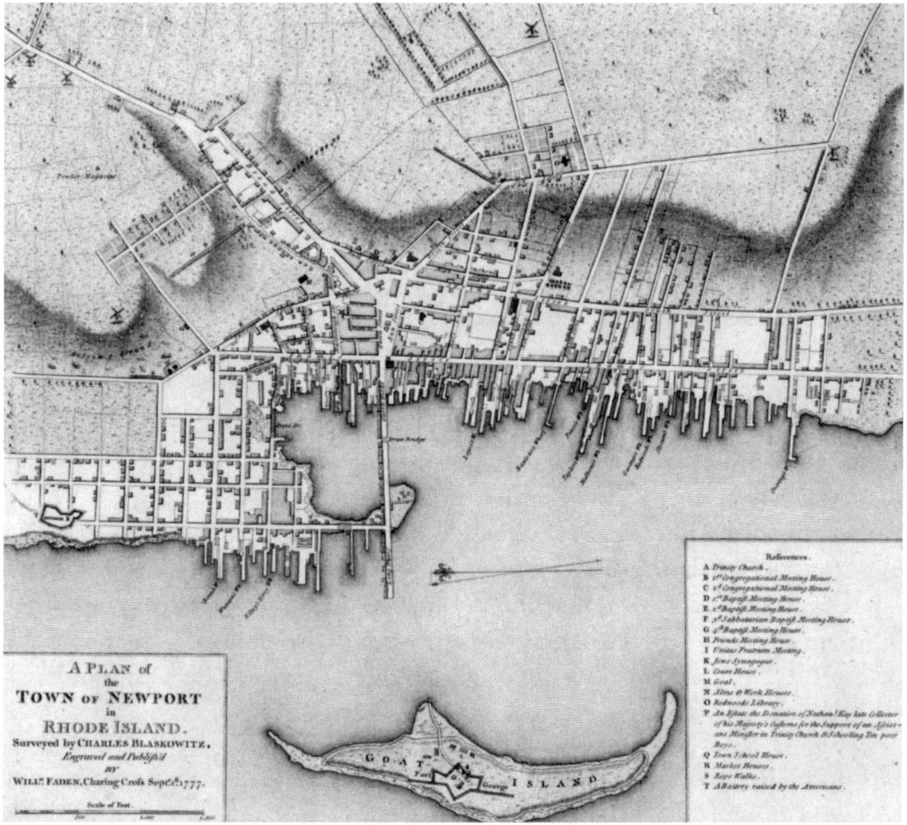

Map of Newport circa 1777 by Charles Blaskowitz. *Wikipedia Commons.*

troops held within their garrison waited anxiously for the British fleet under command of Lord Howe to arrive from New York.

Among those troops gathered was the New Hampshire State Regiment raised for the defense of Rhode Island in May 1778. They were placed under command of Colonel Christopher Greene, and on the eve of their march from Providence, Captain Sylvanus Reed of the regiment recorded that Colonel Greene offered

> *his most cordial thanks for the Officers, Volunteers & Soldiers who with so much alacrity repaired to this place to give their assistance in Exrepating the brutish Tirants from this Country. The zeal & Spirit which they discovuared are to Him the Most Pleseing Pro*[spect] *of Victory.*[173]

On August 5, the British burned four large frigates that lay in the harbor. One, named the *Lark*, set off a spectacular explosion, having some seventy-six barrels of gunpowder in its magazine. On August 8, some twenty houses in the city were razed to clear firing lines for their cannon. A large sailing ship that had been run aground near Goat Island to prevent a French seizure was also torched.

Around the same time, the French deposited four thousand marines on Jamestown, an island close to the western edge of Newport. When it was discovered that the British had abandoned posts on the hills of the north side of the island, General Sullivan dispatched around two thousand of the men to cross the East Passage and secure the forts.

The Americans now had over ten thousand troops gathered at Tiverton. General Sullivan, Major General Greene and Major General Lafayette's plan was to utilize these combined forces in a three-pronged attack. The Americans would cross the Sakonnet River to land on the eastern side of Aquidneck Island. The French marines would attack from the west, crossing from Jamestown, and the French fleet would keep up a continuous bombardment of the remaining British garrison. This plan was somewhat diverted on August 9, when the fleet of twenty ships under command of Lord Admiral Howe arrived to engage the French fleet.

As during the attempt the previous summer, foul weather was to play an important role during this planned invasion. On the night of August 11, a strong wind shook the tents in the field. At daybreak, a heavy gale, some believe with hurricane-force winds, ripped through the soldiers' encampments drenching ammunition, flattening tents and forcing soldiers to seek shelter where they could, huddling against stone walls to keep out of the wind. The storm lashed the troops and supplies for two days. Some men died of exposure in the fields; the horses reportedly suffered even more.

The storm abated and the skies cleared on the morning of August 14. The following day, Greene led a contingency of 1,500 troops, horses and heavy guns along the West Main Road toward Newport. Lafayette mimicked Greene's march down East Main Road. Among the soldiers with Greene were the First Rhode Island or "Black Regiment," as well as New Hampshire volunteers. They encamped about two miles from the British lines and dug in for a siege of the city.[174]

For several days, British and American artillery exchanged fire, with little damage to either side. Once again, an assault was delayed when the French retreated from the harbor to have their ships repaired in Boston. Their sails and rigging in tatters from the gale, they finally retired from the scene after suffering heavy damage from the British cannonading of the stricken vessels. Worse still, the French marines began to desert after witnessing the departure of their fleet. American militia also began to leave in considerable numbers: their allotted time for service had expired, and many wished to return home and harvest their crops. Greene counted a loss of some two thousand men after the French departure. By August 28, he had written to Washington, "Our strength is now reduced from 9,000 to between 4 and 5,000"—a predicament he found "vexatious and truly mortifying."

The planned assault was abandoned, and the exercise became one of evacuating the troops from Aquidneck Island. The troops under Greene and Lafayette began their withdrawal to the abandoned fortifications near Quaker Hill and Butts Hill in Portsmouth. As Greene biographer Gerald M. Carbone writes,

> *On both sides of the island the British drove American troops back toward their entrenched position in Portsmouth….Hessians attacked Greene's command, the American right flank where the Black or First Rhode Island Regiment was posted. This was a key posting, for if the British could overrun the flank they could press in on the sides and rear of the American line, cutting off their retreat.*

The Hessian troops charged twice and were fought off in fierce hand-to-hand combat. Frustrated, the British sent a frigate into position where it could barrage the site with cannon fire. Greene quickly ordered two cannons from the artillery to be placed into position and fire back. This effort, along with cannon fire from an American redoubt on Bristol Point, drove the frigate from the scene.

A third push by the Hessians succeeded in driving the regiment back, but Greene ordered the Second Rhode Island Regiment under command of Colonel Israel Angell into the battle. Alongside another Continental regiment, supported by light troops and Massachusetts militia, "We soon put the Enemy to route," Greene reported, adding, "I had the pleasure of seeing them run in worse disorder than they did at the Battle of Monmouth."[175]

Once again, however, the Americans had failed to expel the British from Aquidneck Island, and loyalist raids and the British embargo on trade to and from southern New England meant months more of scarce provisions and hardship.

General John Sullivan wished for Greene to remain in Rhode Island as some 3,500 troops were still encamped in Tiverton and wrote to Washington requesting that "the Sharer of my Confidences, the assistant of my Councils and partner in supporting the Burthens of War" remain a while longer.[176] Greene, however, felt an urgency to return to his duties as quartermaster general. "However agreeable it is to be near my family, and among Friends," he wrote to Washington, "I cannot wish it to take place, as it would be very unfriendly to the business of my department."[177]

That year, 1778, had also been disastrous for the wheat crop along the length of the Eastern Seaboard. As a result, the price of wheat rose exponentially as fall continued into winter. The prices of goods like flour, corn and grain, which had once been cheap and a certainty, were now so high as to be prohibitive. After a good number of horses were procured that spring for the artillery, Washington felt compelled to write,

> *The scarcity of flour will not allow any number of horses being brought into camp, but it is essential that horses and wagons should be collected at different places in the vicinity of camp, where they can be furnished with forage and drawn expeditiously into the army.*
>
> *Ps: As we may have to go to the No. River, magazines of forage should be provided.*

At the onset of the Revolutionary War, the market for the three varieties of flour produced in the colonies became very limited. Superfine flour, of the best quality, was exported, while "middling" and "common" flour ended up in homes and in the army encampments. The Atlantic trade, while it continued, became a risky business. Transporting flour overland also had its challenges, including spoilage. In January 1776, a vendor reported that several New England vessels were loaded with flour to be exported, one with "upwards of 4000 barrels on board." Other ships were carrying supplies "by permission of Congress."

The price of flour then was as high as fifteen shillings per pound. A few months later, when the Congress closed all trade with Great Britain, Ireland and the West Indies, the price per pound fell to twelve shillings. Such was the surplus of flour that complaints of poor and spoiled flour being sold to the troops pestered the Quartermaster's Department all summer. By August, prices had begun soaring. In September, the price of wheat increased by 33 percent from the month before.

The continuing decline in the value of Continental currency also contributed to the crisis. The price of wheat would continue to rise, with some fluctuation, over the course of the war. Wheat sold consistently at 12 shillings a bushel from November 1777 through June 1778, when another rise began, which continued until the price reached a peak in May 1779 at an astonishing 150 shillings a bushel.[178]

The president of Congress wrote in December 1778 of the crisis facing the army:

> *The Middle and Eastern states cannot supply more wheat this year than the inhabitants and the army will consume. New York, New Jersey, and Pennsylvania have been so much embarrassed and injured by military operations, as to afford at present but a small portion of their usual supplies.... The wheat in Maryland and Virginia, and I may add North Carolina, has been so destroyed or spoiled by a fly that infests these countries that but little flour and that in general of a bad quality can be procured here.*[179]

Supplies of food and forage, then, continued to be a major concern. Fodder had grown so scarce that urgent word went out from Colonel John Davis to purchase "all rye, oats, spelts, barley and corn you can in your neighborhood on as low terms as possible but the grain we must have, let the price be what it will."[180] When horses for the light infantry at Lancaster could no longer be cared for due to the lack of forage, rather than have them sacrificed, Greene approved a plan to evacuate them. They would eventually arrive to better pastures in Springfield, Massachusetts.

By November, Congress had called on the governors of each state to supply an informal survey of the "articles of consumption" that lay within their boundaries, particularly "flour, wheat, rye, barley, oats, corn and rice, beef, pork, working oxen and horses, cyder and vinegar." Replying in January 1779, Governor William Greene of Rhode Island wrote to Congress to explain that the inhabitants of his state did not have bread enough for their own needs and that the British occupied, with Aquidneck Island, "near one third of the best plow land in this state." The large island off the mainland contained the towns of Newport, Middletown and Portsmouth and had traditionally been prized farming and grazing pastures. Other acreage that would normally be plowed was now occupied by "large bodies of militia we have been obliged to keep on duty the whole time," and due to the large numbers of men thus occupied, Greene wrote, "We have not been able to improve the lands that we have remaining in our possession."[181]

Even though the army was better supplied as a whole, late in the year, complaints arrived from officers charged with obtaining goods. From

Pennsylvania, Greene heard: "All kinds of merchandise have risen in value here within these few days. The speculators have laid in for a winter sale; and should we want any foreign articles before the month of March, we expect to pay dearly for them.[182]

Most of Greene's time as quartermaster during the year 1779 was consumed with supplying Sullivan's campaign in the Susquehanna against the Seneca, a tribe that had remained loyal to the British since the French and Indian War. Feeding the troops and transporting goods through what was then still largely wilderness proved daunting tasks. On March 13, 1779, he wrote to Deputy Wadsworth, "We are upon the Wheel of Fortune and must take our chance of the round of things. Provisions are costly and scarce."

Greene wrote constantly to members of Congress asking for the support needed to procure horses, forage, pack saddles and tools to support expeditions. Receiving little in response, he grew wary of ambitious plans, such as Arnold's had been, made without proper thought to how needed supplies would be transported or placed strategically. He penned a long letter to Washington from March 17 to 20, detailing his uneasiness about General Schuyler's plan for an expedition in the Mohawk River Valley:

> *I am persuaded it will be attended with more risqué and expense and be less certain of success than if the Expedition is carried on by way of the Susquehanna.... The route appears to me long and tedious and so divided between land and Water carriage that it will require double preparations to enable the Army to move with ease and security.*[183]

The army at this time also faced a serious shortage of drivers and wagoners, largely due to the poor pay and provisions provided them. In March, Greene had received a petition signed by his deputy wagon master general and various conductors, masons and carpenters, declaring that they

> *have Endeavored to give satisfaction in their several Offices, and have satisfaction to find their Endeavors approbated.... But under the present Distressing Situation of Affairs... every species of clothing and Provisions are so scarce, and at so exorbitant a Price, that we find our pay inadequate, even to purchase necessary Cloathing, and by being allowed by Congress but one ration per Day our Families must in the Present Situation... Absolutely Suffer for the Necessaries of Life.*[184]

General Greene often heard other grumblings from subordinates and addressed their concerns to Congress in a letter to President John Jay on March 25, 1779:

> *I am sorry to find the...Resolution of Congress respecting the Waggoners is put upon a footing which I fear will defeat its intention. The Wages of the Waggoners is fixed at* [ten pounds] *per Month. I am persuaded that not a single man can be enlisted for this pay....In my letter...to His Excellency General Washington, I recommended giving the same Wages to those who enlisted dureing the War, as others might be hired for upon Annual service.*[185]

Economist and historian Anne Bezanson writes, "The critical problem of procuring waggoneers may be cited as one of the most serious bottlenecks of the war." She cites those wagoners paid in New Jersey on a contract basis, "which varied according to the supplementary allowances permitted in the way of supplies, forage, clothing, repairs and other expenses." Neighboring Pennsylvania attempted to set a rate of four pounds per day in September 1778 but was forced to increase it the following year by ten shillings, and by October 1779, as commissary prices continued to rise, the rate had to be reconsidered yet again: "A committee on behalf of the state, disregarding both the private rate and the New Jersey contract agreements, arrived at twelve pounds per day, which it hoped would be fully satisfactory and produce the desired number of teams."

At the same time, Greene's salary and those of his two deputy quartermasters had reached 2,400 pounds sterling, a sum that stirred controversy and not a little jealousy among the poorly paid members of Congress. That the salaries were paid with the constantly depreciating currency that Congress continued to issue mattered not a whit. Greene felt compelled to write in his defense,

> *There is not a man in the army that has been a greater slave to public business than I....I have been in every action that has taken place with the Grand Army since the commencement of the war, except those upon Long Island and at the White Plains; and although I have never derived any great military merit, yet no one has been more expos'd or more intent upon doing his duty.*

Part of the problem, clearly, was that Greene's deputies were often lax in filing returns to the quartermaster general's office. To Archibald Steele, Greene wrote in a scolding manner,

> *I must now once and for all give you warning that I expect to have abstracts of your Monthly disbursements of all Monies paid in your district in my Department....All these returns I must insist to be sent me monthly, made at the end of each Month, and sent forward as soon as possible. Whoever neglects in future will be dismissed* [from] *the Department as the Board of War and Committee of Congress will not excuse me upon any other terms.*[186]

Greene offered to resign, much to Washington's alarm. By June, the Congress had issued a proclamation of full support for the quartermaster.

Good news at last came from Colonel Ephraim Bowen at the close of October, after the British evacuation of Rhode Island: "The Enemy have left about Fourteen-hundred Tons of Excellent Hay," Bowen wrote, "Sixty [or] Seventy Tons of Straw, [and] upwards of three hundred Cords of Wood." It was the only good cheer Rhode Islanders would get that winter.

CHAPTER 6

AMERICAN PRISONERS OF WAR

The Sugar Houses, the Prison Camps and the Dreaded Ships

In August 1775, an exchange of letters between the British General William Gage and the American Commander George Washington served as the civil foothold on which both sides hoped to stand as the conflict began. Writing in the aftermath of reports of mistreatment of American prisoners in Canada, Washington desired that Gage fully know the consequences of any continuation of such practices:

> *My duty now makes it necessary to appraise you that, for the future, I shall regulate my conduct towards those gentlemen who are or may be in our possession, exactly by the rule you shall observe towards those of ours now in your custody. If severity and hardships mark the line of your conduct, painful as it may be to me, your prisoners will feel its effects. But if kindness and humanity are shown to ours, I shall with pleasure consider those in our hands only as unfortunate, and they shall* [receive] *from me that treatment to which the unfortunate are ever entitled.*

Gage, in his written reply, bristled at the thought that Britons, who were in his estimation "pre-eminent in mercy," should treat captives otherwise. He wrote that he had heard of "some of the King's faithful subjects laboring like negro slaves to gain their daily sustenance, or reduced to wretchedness and famine," but nonetheless declared to Washington, "Your prisoners…have hitherto, ben [*sic*] treated with care and kindness, and more comfortably lodged than the King's troops."[187]

In truth, Parliament saw those taking part in the rebellion in America as traitors in a civil war and therefore prisoners of the Crown. With the entrance of France and, later, Spain into an extended war of the Americas, historian William R. Lindsey explains, "The British government was dealing simultaneously with two categories of prisoners: those who were in the armed forces and merchant marines of powers which it recognized, and those who were American 'rebels.'"[188]

Britain's refusal to recognize Americans as prisoners of war meant that they were often held at the mercy of lower-ranking officers, jailers and even loyalists where Americans were captured or held. With little accountability, these men of authority could choose to treat prisoners with humanity or, as was more often the case, to wage vengeance indiscriminately, regardless of whatever intentions might have been penned on paper by their leaders.

Holding American prisoners, however, also proved to be a dilemma for the British government, as explained by Olive Anderson in her early work on the subject: "Captured Americans created exceptionally awkward problems, since neither wholesale release nor wholesale trial for treason or piracy was practical."[189] The British government needed to formally suspend habeas corpus in order to legally imprison rebels for a significant time, and as Anderson points out,

> *It was not until 3 March 1777 that the government provided both a solution and a deterrent in "North's Act," which suspended Habeas Corpus regarding persons charged with high treason in the American Colonies or on the high seas, or with piracy.*[190]

At this early stage of the war, the fate of prisoners hung on the temperament and conscience of those appointed to oversee their care. While the colonists had a handful of sympathizers in Parliament, those in charge of the makeshift jails held little regard for those imprisoned.

A grim reminder of this dilemma came on September 14, 1775, when Americans were informed of the deaths of twenty of the thirty-one American prisoners captured at Bunker Hill. While some soldiers undoubtedly died of wounds suffered in the battle, the suspicion of mistreatment and horrid conditions was prevalent among the officers, causing General Montgomery to write a threatening note to British officers that if such mistreatment continued, he would "execute with rigor the just and necessary law of retaliation upon the Garrison of Chambly."[191]

It was, in fact, a great risk to be taken prisoner, even more so when no policy of prisoner exchange had been agreed upon. Hessian recruits balked at enlisting for Great Britain and, through an emissary in the person of Sir Joseph Yorke, informed the Cabinet that "they did not want to fight without assurances of an exchange policy, or if they thought they might be subject to retaliatory action stemming from British mistreatment of prisoners."[192]

The Continental Congress took a step toward resolving the issue on December 2, 1775, when it passed a bill of exchange that would allow for an exchange of citizen for citizen, officer for officer of equal rank and soldier for soldier. For a time, it seems, this civil arrangement was the unspoken rule of law.

An early example of Britain's long-term treatment of prisoners came with the surrender of General Benedict Arnold's forces at the siege of Quebec in the closing hours of 1775. Private Jeremiah Greenman, who enlisted as a young man in Providence, was among the Rhode Islanders taken prisoner and marched "into a French Jessewit collage after taking away our arms. Hear we were very much crowded/no room for us to stur and very cold."[193] On New Year's Day, the prisoners were placed in a nearby convent and given a gill of rum "for a New years gift & sum bisquit." While the rooms they were kept in were cold, Greenman wrote, "We were allowed by the genl: 1 pound of bread and a half pound of meat, 6 ounces of butter a weak, a half a pound of boyled wrice in a day." They were also given casks of porter ale.

There remained little room among the prisoners, but that seemed to be their chief complaint, and by late January, Greenman could record that although he and his fellows were prisoners, "We live very happy & contented tho we are in such a dismal hole hoping the first dark night that our people will be in & redeem us." In the deep of winter, as death and despair affected some of the prisoners, others, like Greenman, showed a strong resilience. They sold their belongings, "so we have once in a wile Sum Caffe." "We live very Cold and Disag[reeable]," Greenman wrote, "but imply our Selvs in all of plays [games] that we can think of."

Through the coming months of isolation, smatterings of news, real or rumored, reached their ears through various sources. The prisoners gathered wood; plotted escape; underwent rigorous searches of their packs and rooms for arms and ammunition, when the British suspected locals of arming the rebels; and then worried that they were being poisoned by the biscuits given them to eat.[194] A note of despair crept into Greenman's journal entries: "Hear we live very discontented and quite out of hope of ever being reliv'd but keep up our hearts all we can." To keep up their spirits (or hearts, as Greenman put it), they melted down buttons to craft "a puter fife that we made out of all the buttons that we could get off our Cloths wich made us sum mery. So we passed away the long teatedus [tedious] time."[195]

In June, the prisoners voted to sign a "parole" agreement to "return to our friends & family again will promise not to take up arms against his majesty but remain peaceful & Quiet in our respective places of abode." Despite these promises, and talk of transports, their release was delayed time and again: "We begin to think that we are not to be sent home. We are put off from one day to another and next week but we keep our hearts up all we can."

In August, the prisoners were allowed to sign a parole agreement and transported to the *John & Christopher*. Suddenly being out in the open was "a very great chang of life after being in prison 7 month in a stone jayl." Thus began a slow journey to New York and liberty, as well as a reunion with the Second Rhode Island Regiment, then stationed at Fort Constitution. Nearly one hundred men of the militias that would eventually make up this regiment had volunteered for the Canadian Expedition in 1775, and most of them had been taken prisoner. In all, Greenman and the others had spent nine months in confinement.

By contrast, during this period, the time British prisoners spent in confinement was considerably less. Despite the Continental Congress's attempt to delegate rules for the confinement and treatment of prisoners of war, the states were largely left to their own devices. This was advantageous to those coastal communities that held prisoners and were eager to exchange them for their own imprisoned townsmen. But General Gage's early complaint to Washington was also based in truth. Some New England towns used prisoners to bolster crews for road work and other hard labor but also, in effect, rented them out to townspeople for specific labor needs.

Whatever efforts were made to establish civil exchanges of prisoners of war were disrupted by the invasion and then fall of New York City on September 15, 1776, and the capture, exactly two months and a day later, of Fort Washington, placed some 2,700 American prisoners into British hands. Another 1,000 were taken in the Battle of Brooklyn, and after a sweep through neighborhoods to collect suspected spies, overt political foes and other private citizens, the number swelled to 5,000 prisoners, who would have to be clothed, fed and given some form of shelter in the coming months of fall and winter.

After capturing Manhattan, the British occupied every house of worship in the city that was not affiliated with the Church of England to use as prisons. This included the Quaker meetinghouse on Queen

Old Quaker Meeting House, Flushing, New York. *Wikipedia Commons.*

Street. A large house on Broadway that had served as the meeting place for the city's chapter of the Sons of Liberty was immediately confiscated. Hampden House—as the chapter named its headquarters, for the English libertarian—became better known by locals as Liberty House. The British, seizing on the symbolism, promptly emptied the house and prepared it to hold American prisoners.

On the opposite side of Broadway, the newly constructed Bridewell House, whose intended use was as a new facility for the city's transient and poor, was also taken; eventually, it would house some eight hundred incarcerated soldiers. The Provost on the Common, which had served since 1759 as the municipal jail, was also taken for use as a prison. The jail, an imposing three-and-a-half-story structure with an impressive portico and Italian-style cupola, housed high-ranking officers through the course of the British hold on Manhattan, as well as a number of civilians charged with abetting the rebellion.[196]

The most infamous of the British prisons in New York were the massive "sugar houses," so named as they served as warehouses connected to the flourishing triangle trade in the years leading up to the war. Livingston's sugar house, tucked behind the Old Dutch Church on what was at the time Crown Street, was grimly described by historian Grant Thorburn in 1845:

> *A dark stone building...with small, deep windows exhibiting a dungeon-like aspect....It was five stories high; and each story was divided into two dreary apartments, with ceilings so low, and the light from the windows so dim, that a stranger would readily take the place for a jail.*[197]

New York sugar houses. *Wikipedia Commons.*

A second sugar house named Van Courtlandt's lay on the northeast corner of Trinity Churchyard. It functioned as a prison until it closed in 1777.

While commanders on the field had confiscated what they considered to be adequate shelter for prisoners, General Howe immediately understood the expense and inconvenience the British army was facing and soon began negotiating with Washington for a large prisoner exchange. Washington was eager to exchange prisoners as well and wrote numerous letters in the weeks that followed the capture of the prisoners to

> *governors, committee members and councilmen of the surrounding states* [asking] *to have all the Continental Prisoners of War (belonging to the Land Service) in the different Towns in your State, collected and brought together to some convenient place, from whence they may be removed hither, when a Cartel is fully settled.*[198]

The calls to collect prisoners, however, initially rang hollow. The governments of Connecticut, Massachusetts and Rhode Island, having, as indicated earlier, been left without a firm agreement from the Continental Congress, had already been initiating negotiations and exchanges of prisoners for some time.

Looking at Rhode Island records, we find a document titled "A List of the Names, Time of Commitment, and Discharge of the Prisoners of War Committed to Providence Gaol Since the Commencement of the Present

War to 5th Day of September AD 1777" (see appendix A), which shows that the jail incarcerated seventy-four prisoners of war over the course of 1776, many of whom were crew members of British registered vessels taken by privateers. Prisoners were kept an average of 2.2 months, the longest held being John Smith and James Wilson, "committed November 16th and discharged March 3rd" and the shortest held one Captain Stanhope of the ship *Glascow* and his midshipman Matthew Scanlon, who were taken prisoner on December 2 and released four days later. The ship, as we will see, was on its way to New York to transport American prisoners home.

Representatives of Rhode Island had written to Washington before receiving any indication of an exchange, having seen a notice in the newspaper that Deputy Governor William Bradford wrote to the general on September 26, 1776,

> *Sir:—Having seen in the public papers that Your Excellency and the British admiral have agreed upon an exchange of prisoners in the naval department, I beg leave to apply to you in behalf of a mate of a vessel, and four seamen, all belonging to Warwick, in this state; some of whom are connected with very respectable families. They were all taken in the merchant service, and are prisoners on board one of the ships of war, now in the Sound.*
>
> *We have a mate of a merchant ship, and four seamen who were taken in a transport, with part of one of the Highland regiments, to give for them.*
>
> *I request Your Excellency's directions, as soon as they may be, whether we shall send the prisoners directly to you, or how I shall proceed to procure the exchange; which will much oblige many worthy people here.*[199]

Like other states, Rhode Island was mindful of the tremendous expense that could arise from keeping a multitude of prisoners, and the assembly proved to be quite lenient when petitioned for release by those captured at sea by the state's sanctioned privateers. In October 1776, the assembly reviewed one such petition:

> *Whereas, James Smith, James Stable and Henry Barnes preferred their petition to this Assembly, setting forth that with the deepest concern they find themselves, after having been captured and brought into this state, unhappily considered as enemies to the rights, liberties, and privileges of America, and detained as prisoners; that having neither in thought, word, or deed, injured the cause of liberty, or joined, adopted or approved of, the present measures,*

they humbly conceive and pray that the wonted justice, mercy, and humanity of this Assembly will be extended to them.

After consideration, the assembly voted that

the petitioners have liberty of purchasing a suitable vessel, not exceeding the burthen of one hundred and fifty tons, for transporting themselves to Great Britain…and that two of the captains and five mates, who have last arrived within this state, be detained, to exchange for that number of masters and mates belonging to the United States of America, who are now prisoners on board the British ship of war Syren, *commanded by Capt. Tobias Furneaux.*[200]

Connecticut's Governor John Trumbull balked at releasing some prisoners, as the state was utilizing some of the more skilled craftsmen among them to bolster fortifications along what would prove to be a vulnerable coastline. From what Trumbull wrote to Washington, he had no wish to let them go so quickly and indicated that some of them might be inclined to stay, rather than return to the drudgery and danger of army life. The governor empathized with "such of the Privates as are Mechanicks & some Others who have a strong inclination to Abide & remain in the Country…[who] must be forced & Obliged to return & be exchanged."[201]

As for the unskilled prisoners, the State of Connecticut sought to negotiate for exchange, and by November, it had informed neighboring Rhode Island of the opportunity, prompting the Rhode Island General Assembly to take action on its own:

Whereas, it appears, by express from due authority in New London, in the state of Connecticut, that a flag of truce is there arrived from Lord Howe, for a general exchange of prisoners, confined in the marine department.

And whereas, this Assembly is well informed, that a considerable number of subjects of the American states have been captured by the British navy, as well as those who sailed in American privateers, as in merchantmen; that all are promiscuously confined under decks in large numbers, in a very sickly condition, and under short allowance; therefore for the relief of such,—It is voted and resolved, that the brigantine which the masters and mates of the prizes lately captured and brought into this state, purchased agreeably to an act of this Assembly, together with each and every person who hath a permit to proceed in said brigantine, be detained, and not suffered to depart

> *until further orders from this Assembly, that it may be known, whether if they depart from this port for Great Britain, by permission of the Assembly, a like number will be exchanged for them.*[202]

The assembly also voted "that Thomas Church and Daniel Rodman, Esqs. Be, and they are hereby, appointed to a committee to proceed forthwith to New London, to negotiate with any person or persons, authorized by Lord Howe, an exchange of prisoners."

Faced with the enormous expense of caring for the privateer's prisoners, the assembly clearly wanted to take advantage of any opportunity for an exchange:

> *Resolved, that the said committee take an authentic list of their names and stations, and confer with the person or persons authorized by Lord Howe, as aforesaid, whether if said persons be permitted to proceed from this state, as aforesaid, they will be considered as so many prisoners delivered up to Lord Howe; that upon the conditions of exchange being agreed upon, His Honor the Governor be requested to order all the prisoners in this state, that are not under said parole, to be collected together, and sent under proper guard, to the place agreed on, for the exchange, aforesaid; observing first to exchange the prisoners belonging to this state; and then for prisoners belonging to the United States in general.*

While Rhode Island looked to cut expenses by exchanging prisoners as quickly as possible and cutting its losses, Connecticut's Governor Trumbull pointedly asked Washington to request of Congress some reimbursement of "the Charge & expence Attending the keeping [of] the prisoners."[203] Washington, of course, could only request that money be sent and was powerless to sway Congress in anything but military affairs, and so, as the months passed and winter approached, the general's hopes for a wholesale exchange waned.

So, too, did the hopes for release held by the American prisoners in New York. At Harlem, a long line of prisoners was herded into a handful of farm buildings, where they waited for two days before being given any bread or water. One Connecticut soldier recalled that when they were given food, it was "as if to so many hogs. A quantity of biscuits in crumbs, mostly moldy, and some of them crawling with maggots, which they were obliged to scramble for." The following day, the prisoners "had a little pork given to each, which they were obliged to eat raw."[204] The prisoners were then formed up for the ten- to twelve-mile trek to Manhattan. When they arrived in Manhattan, the officers were divided from the enlisted men and taken to the Baptist church. The remainder of the prisoners were marched to Liberty House, where captives from the Canadian campaign and Brooklyn's lost battle were already imprisoned.

While the officers were prisoners, they were treated as gentlemen, as was the European custom during wartime. This meant that they could choose to share quarters with other imprisoned officers in one of the mansion houses that had survived the bombardment of the city and were allowed to wander about the city "on their honor" that they would return to their house of imprisonment by curfew. They were allowed to keep their personal belongings, and they carefully cultivated friendships among the guards and nearby merchants who could obtain goods for them in exchange for fair compensation.

As they were free to walk about the city, some of the officers tried to visit the churches and other prisons and report on the condition of the enlisted men. What they found shocked them. Captain Alexander Graydon wrote mournfully of "those abodes of human misery and despair…[where] thousands of my unhappy countrymen were perishing under the hand of a proud, unfeeling authority."[205] Having been captured at Fort Washington, Captain Graydon recorded his own experiences as a prisoner, when:

> *We were marched to an old stable where we found about forty or fifty prisoners already collected, principally officers.…We remained on the outside of the building; and, for nearly an hour, sustained a series of the most intolerable abuse*[s].[206]

The prisoners were soon moved to a large, newly constructed barn at the estate of Colonel Morris, which the American army had used as its headquarters prior to the battle. There, they were incarcerated with a large number of other prisoners. Graydon wrote, "There were from a hundred and fifty to two hundred, comprising a motley crew, to be sure. Men and officers of all description, regulars and militia, troops Continental and State, some in hunting shirts, the mortal aversion of a redcoat."

When the prisoners from Fort Washington arrived in the prisons of lower Manhattan, they were overcome by the true extent of what faced them. The American officers taken prisoner debated what to do. They considered writing to General Howe, but some voiced concerns about repercussions against them and reasoned that surely Howe must already be aware of the conditions in British prisons. Ethan Allen, an officer from Vermont who had been returned to New York after a year in prison in Great Britain, grew determined to write such a missive after visiting the churches and sugar houses and composed several rough drafts until the officers agreed to a version of the letter that would be sent, bearing their signatures, to the British commander.

As this handwringing continued, conditions only worsened for the prisoners. As described by historian Edwin R. Burroughs in his work *Forgotten Patriots*, "The bodies were piling up so rapidly…that burial details fell further and further behind. Twenty to thirty Americans died every day. A Connecticut soldier wrote sadly, 'They lie in heaps unburied.'"

On December 24, 1776, General Howe ordered the release of American prisoners in New York—with great fanfare for this "humane act of kindness," though it was certainly done to relieve the pressure caused by the maintenance and man hours required to run the prisons. Undoubtedly, the cruelest act committed against the captured Americans took place on the day of their release, when Provost Marshal William Cunningham ordered the bread given to the prisoners before they were released to be poisoned, reckoning that the majority would perish before they reached home. Cunningham had been abused by a mob made up of members of the Sons of Liberty and he had taken his vengeance throughout his years as provost marshal—especially with this final act, a war crime among others for which he was never brought to justice.

On the morning of December 24, 1776, 225 prisoners were collected on the Albany pier and placed aboard the *Glascow*, the same ship that had been detained in Providence earlier in the month. It had been hired by the British to transport the prisoners from New York to Milford, Connecticut. More than two dozen men died during the weeklong journey. Literally left on the beach, the emaciated men straggled into town and told their names and stories to the shocked villagers they encountered. The citizens did all they could for the released prisoners. They took some one hundred of the sickest men into their homes to nurse them. Despite their efforts, the prisoners were in such poor condition that almost half of them died in the coming weeks.

Others died on the journey home, and some brought disease and death with them. Oliver Babcock returned to his Connecticut family, and one of his first acts on his return was to write a note of thanksgiving in his diary, desiring that from then on, he would "live to honor and praise God all the days of my life." He met with Governor Trumbull and his council on January

7, 1777, where he "related the sufferings of my poor fellow prisoners at New York." Less than two weeks later, he died from the smallpox he contracted while imprisoned. His passing was followed, shortly thereafter, by the deaths of two of his children, who had become sickened after his return.[207]

It is estimated that some 1,800 American prisoners were released that December. Another release occurred in February 1777, as indicated in the postscript of a letter to Washington from Rhode Island Governor Samuel Cooke: "Agreeable to your Excellency's recommendation, I have sent to Newport all the prisoners in the land service, that were in the care of this state, and enclose you one of Lord Percy's receipts for them."[208]

Historian Burroughs draws on the cumulative effect this tragedy had on New England communities:

> *Of the thirty-six men from Litchfield, Connecticut who helped defend Fort Washington, four were killed and thirty-two taken prisoner. Twenty died in the prisons of New York, another six on the way home. Only six returned to Litchfield. A company of one hundred men raised in Danbury, Connecticut was captured at Fort Washington and confined in one of the sugar houses. Two survived. Some towns may have lost everyone.*[209]

On January 4, 1777, Jonathan Trumbull recorded he had learned that "seventy-seven prisoners went into the Sugar House. N. Molly says 800 were in Bridewell. The doctor gave poison powders to the prisoners who soon died—some were sent to Honduras to cut logwood; women come to the prison gate to sell gingerbread."[210] Near the end of the month, Trumbull heard from a Mrs. White that "General Lee was under guard in a small mean house at the foot of King Street."

The governor also learned that on December 1, 1776, some three hundred men were taken from the churches and placed on a prison ship. This was the *Whitby*, a large transport vessel that would be the first ship to be anchored in the Wallabout, a backwater bay off the East River. The *Whitby* was moored just off Benson's Mill in late October. As with the prison ships that later joined it in the bay, its masts were stripped of sails and rigging and then removed. The hold was completely stripped until the ship was an empty hulk that could hold as many as three hundred prisoners at a time. It was joined by the *Grosvenor*, and the two vessels were said to have held some 750 men between them.

Great Britain's use of prison ships began with housing Scottish rebels in 1745. They were used again for prisoners captured during the Seven Years'

War. As the American rebellion disrupted the practice of shipping convicts to distant locations (including the colonies), Parliament passed the "Hulk Act" to enable the government to hold prisoners in hulks along the Thames as an answer to the overcrowding in the infamous London jails.[211] The practice spread to other riverside communities—and then became a solution to the problem of political prisoners in the rebellious colonies.

In the aftermath of the British occupation of Aquidneck Island (then commonly known as Rhode Island) in December 1776, prisoners taken on land and sea were transported to prison ships in Newport Harbor. As news of the horrific conditions aboard the prison ships reached Rhode Island newspapers, concern for the prisoners aboard the ships off Newport grew: "Great complaints had been made that the prisoners were not properly treated, that suitable provisions were not made for their accommodations, and moreover, they were half starved." These concerns led the Rhode Island Council of War to empower Colonel James Barton

> *to proceed to Newport with supplies and necessaries for the prisoners on board the ships, in the jail and hospitals of Newport; and that he inform himself particularly of their state, treatment, and wants, and procure and bring an exact list of them.*[212]

It is believed that as many as three prison ships and a hospital ship occupied Newport Harbor during much of the time of occupation. By December 1778, Captain Cook's once-famous ship the HMS *Endeavor*, which had been sold and renamed *Lord Sandwich*, had been taken back into service by the British navy as a transport vessel. It was then refitted for use as a prison ship in the harbor, and it was one of eight vessels scuttled by the departing British forces in October 1779.

Other British ships, often with an illustrious history of service, were stripped to hulks and outfitted to hold American prisoners. With the fall of Fort Moultie at Charleston, South Carolina, in May 1780, some 5,266 American prisoners were captured. They were initially held in wooden barracks, and many of the prisoners found ways to escape—so many that Cornwallis informed General Clinton at the end of June that "not less than 500 prisoners have made their escape since the Town was taken." Some historians estimate that upward of 1,000 men escaped within their first year of captivity.[213] A good number of the remaining prisoners were transferred to prison ships in Charleston Harbor between 1780 and 1781. An incomplete list of American prisoners during this period shows them divided between

The HMS *Jersey* prison ship. *Wikipedia Commons.*

the ships *Torbay*, which held seventy-six men, and the *Pack Horse*, holding thirty-nine prisoners.[214]

After the surviving prisoners had spent thirteen months in captivity, British General Cornwallis was prepared to send them to the West Indies. Only the reprieve of a last-minute exchange saved the men from that fate.[215]

The prison ships off New York gained the most notoriety when revelations were published by survivors and men who had somehow escaped from the ships, the most infamous being the *Jersey*, placed into service as early as 1779. Memoirs of those who survived and letters from men who did not are numerous. The horrors suffered aboard the *Jersey*, along with others, left an indelible memory on the soul of the country. In an oration given on the Fourth of July 1800, Jonathan Russel of Providence, Rhode Island, brought back the memory of the ship and the sacrifice the prisoners endured:

> *On board one of those prison ships above 11,000 of our brave countrymen are said to have perished. She was called the* Jersey. *Her wreck still remains, and at low ebb, presents to the world its accursed and blighted fragments. Twice in twenty-four hours the winds of heaven sigh through it and repeat the groans of our expiring countrymen.…Every rain that descends washes from the unconsecrated bank the bones of those intrepid sufferers. They lie, naked on the shore, accursing the neglect of their countrymen.*[216]

Survivor and poet Philip Freneau penned a composition on the prison ships with these grim concluding lines:

Each day at least six carcasses we bore
and scratched them graves along the sandy shore
By feeble hands the shallow graves were made,
No stone memorial o'er the corpses laid
In barren sands and far from home they lie
No friend to shed a tear when passing by.

Survivor Henry B. Dawson also wrote a firsthand account that recalled how even during his time of confinement in 1780,

> *The bodies of the dead lay exposed along the beach, drying and bleaching in the sun, and whitening the shores, till reached by the power of a succeeding storm, as the agitated waves receded, the bones receded with them into the deep....*
>
> *The whole shore, from Rennie's Point to Mr. Remson's dooryard, was a place of graves; as were also the slope of the hill near the house, the shore, from Mr. Remson's barn along the millpond to Rappelye's farm, and the sandy island between the flood gates and the mill-dam, while a few were buried on the east side of the Wallabout....*
>
> *The whole Wallabout was a sickly place during the war. The atmosphere seemed to be charged with foul air: from the prison ships; and with the effluvia of dead bodies washed out of their graves by the tide.*[217]

On June 15, 1779, *Rivington's Gazette* included the instructions that "Privateers arriving in New York Harbor are to put their prisoners on the *Good Hope* or *Prince of Wales* prison ships." The *Good Hope* had been a hospital ship of good reputation for a time. When converted to a prison ship, it was known to have some of the worst conditions aboard, and it would ultimately be set ablaze during an escape.

Other prison ships in the bay included the *Falmouth* and *Good Intent*, as well as the hulks of the sloops *Scorpion* and *Hunter*. The fire ship *Strombolo* would also be utilized, anchored in the North River and said to have held two hundred prisoners. In all, an estimated sixteen prison ships were anchored in Wallabout Bay during the war. Americans taken at sea by Royal Navy ships were generally brought to England, while privateers brought their prisoners to New York, as indicated in the newspaper notice mentioned earlier.

Prisoners' depositions taken after their release show that conditions in Great Britain were only slightly better than in the prisons that held Americans in North America. The deposition of Eliphalet Downer, a surgeon taken prisoner from the privateer *Yankee*, describes how a few days after their arrival on the river Thames the prisoners were

> *relieved from this situation in the middle of the night, hurried on board a tender, and sent down to Sheerness, where the deponent was put into the* Ardent, *and there falling sick of a violent fever in consequence of such treatment, and languishing in that situation for some time, he was removed, still sick, to the* Mars.[218]

Downer was eventually moved to a hospital ashore and recovered to make his escape.

Captain Seth Clark of Newburyport, Massachusetts, was taken prisoner on September 17, 1777. He was first taken to Jamaica and then placed aboard an armed British vessel and forced to serve as a common sailor on its voyage to England. From Port a Pie, the crew, with Clark in tow, took a schooner to Charleston, South Carolina. On the ship's arrival at Spithead, Clark was removed again to the *Monarch*, where he was ordered to perform duty as a "fore-mast-man"—that is, an ordinary seaman rather than an officer. When he protested that he was physically incapable of the task, he was severely flogged. He was then placed aboard the *Bar-fleur*, where he met several American prisoners who informed him of the recent transport of many prisoners to the East Indies and the coast of Africa. When his condition worsened, Clark was sent ashore to the hospital at Haslar, where he met a

> *Captain Chase of Providence, New England, who had told him he had been taken in a sloop of which he was half owner and master, on his passage from Providence to South Carolina, by an English transport, and turned over to a ship of war, where he was confined in irons thirteen weeks, insulted, beat, and abused by the petty officers and common sailors, and on being released from irons was ordered to do duty as a formast man until his arrival in England, when dangerously ill he was sent to said hospital.*[219]

Other prisoners taken at sea were transported to prisons in England, the most famous of these being the Old Mill Prison in Plymouth, where, early in the conflict, Charles Herbert found himself confined. Like Eliphalet Downer, he was held aboard a pair of vessels before being committed to the Old Mill, where he kept a journal for the entirety of his two years of confinement. Secreting his diary in a false bottom of the chest that held his belongings, Herbert recorded every detail of prison life. On arrival, he noted, "Our allowance here in prison is a pound of beef, a pound of greens, and a quart of beer, and a little pot liquor that the greens and beef were boiled in."

While it seems the prisoners lived with a constant gnawing hunger—one recalled another prisoner eating the insects while digging the allotted plot for a garden—they were allowed to grow a small vegetable patch in season, given a yard to exercise within and visited by empathetic villagers, who passed provisions and clothing through the gates. Some became industrious enough to craft a living by selling items to the visitors, as did Herbert himself, who sold handmade boxes.

Security from the British guards also seems to have been somewhat lax, as even though Herbert wrote that ten prisoners could be expected to be admitted each day, "they were constantly digging their way out." He recorded a plot during the summer of 1777 to escape by "digging a tunnel eighteen feet underground to get into a field on the other side of the wall." On August 3, 1777, Herbert wrote, "There are 173 prisoners in the wards. On the fifth thirty-two escaped, but three were brought back. These were confined in the Black Hole forty days on half allowance, and obliged to lay on the bare floor." On January 7, 1778, his entry reads, "289 prisoners here in Plymouth, in Portsmouth there are 140 prisoners. Today the prison was smoked with charcoal & brimstone."[220]

In America, a report from the Board of War on January 21, 1778, stated that there remained 900 privates and 300 officers in New York, the privates being "crowded all summer in sugar houses, and the officers boarded on Long Island, except about 30, who have been confined in the Provost Guard."

CHAPTER 7

BRITISH AND HESSIAN PRISONERS OF WAR IN AMERICA

As the Continental army began to gain prisoners of its own, the commander in chief and Congress debated about the treatment they would receive. After his surprise attack on Trenton, New Jersey, on the morning of December 26, 1776, some eight hundred Hessian and British prisoners surrendered into Washington's hands. He shepherded the prisoners across the Delaware, and by December 30, he had marched them to Philadelphia.

In his groundbreaking work *Captives of Liberty: Prisoners of War and the Politics of Vengeance in the American Revolution* (2020), historian T. Cole Jones exposes the anger and frustration that consumed many Americans—and, ultimately, Washington and Congress—at the treatment their sons and brothers had received from the British. "For many Americans," writes Cole, "justice required that these prisoners be punished for their crimes. But Washington had other plans"—at least in this instance.

A few months earlier, a prisoner had advised American officers that much of the Hessian troops in the employ of Great Britain had been recruited under threat of violence and that, if treated well by the Americans while imprisoned, they would "all lay down their arms" and have "no desire to return to their Regiments again."[221] Jones assesses the situation Washington was in and points out:

> *With neither commitment to Parliamentary Supremacy nor vested interest in the outcome of the conflict, the hessians were not only potential recruits for*

> *the Continental Army but also potent political weapons. Once exchanged, these prisoners, provided they were civilly treated and shown the benefits of American citizenship, might destabilize the British war machine by spreading dissatisfaction among their colleagues.*[222]

Congress offered "all such foreigners" who agreed to become citizens of the United States "the rights, privileges, and immunities of natives" and promised to "provide, for every such person fifty acres of unappropriated lands in some of these states to be held by him and his heirs in absolute property."[223]

Two Hessian soldiers who took advantage of this offer settled in Cumberland, Rhode Island. Adam Polsey and George Christian Thomas found each other in Providence after separate circumstances led to their separation from the German army. Posley seems to have simply deserted outright from Newport, while two stories exist concerning George Christian Thomas. Local tradition has it that Thomas was assigned to maintain the grounds of a large estate confiscated by a British officer on Prudence Island, and having stayed for some time and earned the officer's trust, he simply disappeared after being sent on an errand to the mainland. The Schwaim Historical Association's records of German soldiers who remained in North America after the war state that Thomas was captured in Newport in August 1778 and deserted while being held in Providence in April 1779.[224]

Adam Posley married Mary Jillson, daughter of Enos Jillson of Ashton. The family lived for several years in a red cottage by the millpond in Ashton. Their sons would eventually work in the nearby Lonsdale Mill. George Christian Thomas found work in a Providence tannery and then established his own business before marrying Lydia, the daughter of Timothy and Catharine Mason. The couple settled in Cumberland in 1800. They owned a home at the junction of Mendon and Albion Roads. Local tradition has it that the two families were the first to celebrate with candlelit Christmas trees in Cumberland, their Catholic religion allowing a festive celebration of the holiday of the kind that was discouraged by more conservative Protestants. In this largely Baptist town, their dwellings were identified as "the Hessian houses" in early histories.[225]

The Hessian prisoners from Saratoga were moved quickly out of Philadelphia, marching on January 8, 1777, to the barracks at Lancaster, Pennsylvania. Rather than the open, unprotected, dungeon-like floors of the sugar houses and churches, the state barracks at Lancaster held seventy-six rooms "of approximately 263 square feet, each with a fireplace and windows." The barracks were surrounded by a fifteen-foot-high palisade and thus provided a "secure and commodious place of confinement."[226] Provisions were plentiful, and authorities encouraged prisoners to hire themselves out to local farmers or tradesmen. As these employers were required to provide provisions at work and pay prisoners a wage of at least "fifteen stiver daily," this relieved the government's expenses for maintaining the Hessians.

The British prisoners, however, received no such coddling. While the Hessian prisoners were marched to Lancaster, the British prisoners were confined in the state prison in Philadelphia. There, they were not protected from the anger of the populace. Overcrowding and growing fears of an attempted jailbreak caused their removal to jails and barracks in the backcountry. A good many were sent to the barracks at Lancaster where the Hessians enjoyed so much comfort and freedom. The redcoat prisoners were confined to the barracks for any infringement, especially after inebriated prisoners lit a bonfire in the prison courtyard to celebrate the king's birthday on June 4. Subsequent efforts by American guards to quell the disturbance took an ugly turn when the prisoners grabbed the guards' firearms and threw them into the fire. This brought out "an entire regiment" with two cannon, which fired on the gathered Hessians, killing some and wounding others.

The riot at the Lancaster barracks alerted Congress to a need it had ignored for some time: to establish a government-supervised prison system. Washington had approved a commissary general to administer to the affairs of the enemy prisoners, New Jersey lawyer Elias Boudinot. However, as Congress had allowed each state to put in place its own "Board of War" to oversee the handling of its prisoners, the commissary general found it difficult to assert any authority. Nevertheless, Boudinot worked to advocate on the prisoners' behalf, even spending from his own pocket when Congress delayed funding.

Washington's hope to utilize the British prisoners as leverage in securing the release of the Americans still held in New York was effectively derailed for some months by the capture and imprisonment of General Lee. The general was extremely popular among members of the Continental Congress, many of whom had wanted him to be named commander in chief over Washington. By the end of January 1778, word had gotten to Connecticut Governor John Trumbull that "General Lee was under guard in a small mean house at the foot of King Street."[227] The revolutionary press seized on the general's popularity to stir anger among the populace over the miserable conditions in which Lee was supposedly being kept. Washington doubted the severity of what was published in the press—and he was right—but the reports swayed many Americans toward demanding vengeance for the British treatment of American prisoners.

Perhaps no event generated more such hostility than the capture of the British troops under command of General John "Gentleman Johnny" Burgoyne. While his surrender to General Horatio Gates after the battles at Saratoga in September 1777 was a great victory for the revolution, which was still in a precarious state, the terms of surrender drawn up by the American general drew the wrath of Congress. While Washington and even Gates's junior officers assumed that the six thousand prisoners taken after the surrender were prisoners of war who could be used to haggle for the release of Americans, the terms on which Gates agreed to the surrender of Burgoyne's army effectively made them a "Conventional" army, which would be allowed to be marched under guard to Boston, where they would be able to procure a ship bound for England. Washington and others understood that such an agreement meant those British soldiers who had signed the parole agreement not to take up arms again in America could simply replace other British soldiers who were on duty at home, and a contingent of fresh troops would then return for a British campaign in the spring.

Both British and German officers were astonished by the initial civility of the Americans. Gates and his subordinate, Major General Philip Schuyler, "delighted in showing their European adversaries every courtesy and comfort."[228]

News of the impending arrival of Burgoyne and his troops upended Boston. The city was still recovering from the long siege laid by Washington to free it from British occupation. While once again free, the citizens were burdened by high costs, nearly worthless currency distributed by Congress and a severe shortage of firewood as the winter approached. The yearslong siege had deforested the land for miles around the city, so much so that wood had to be procured from Maine at exorbitant cost. Residents wondered aloud and in letters to the newspapers how the city would obtain enough flour, beef and other provisions to supply some six thousand prisoners, let alone enough wood.

As the captives were the responsibility of the Continental army, the responsibility for their welfare, and of relieving the citizens' burden, fell to Major General William Heath, who at once complained to Washington of the "wide and difficult field" he now had to plow "to provide quarters, provisions. Fuel, &c. for five or six thousand men." As for the prisoners, their expectations of marching into the city to find a ship already procured and waiting to embark for Great Britain were dashed when they arrived. Instead, the prisoners were divided again: the Hessian soldiers were marched to quarters on Winter Hill, outside of Cambridge, and the British to less comfortable accommodations on Prospect Hill. The barracks that the prisoners there were forced to occupy were the makeshift and dilapidated shelters built for the American rebels during their siege of the city in 1775–76. Little used after the rebels' departure in September 1776, the barracks had last housed smallpox victims and were then abandoned. Now, they were virtually uninhabitable. The floors had no foundations, and the walls were shabbily held together "with boards through which the rain and snow penetrate from all sides."[229] Officers were housed in better barracks, though in close quarters. Burgoyne himself was installed in a tavern in Cambridge.

As winter approached, a kind of desperation began to grow among the prisoners. Some had already sickened and died during confinement, and the Continental Congress seemed exceedingly slow in sending supplies and provisions in spite of Heath's barrage of letters to the Congress and the efforts of the Massachusetts Council and Washington himself. Heath had informed his supervisor that the cost of provisions and fuel was running to about $20,000, and with few trained guards to hold them, "the prisoners were escaping in droves."

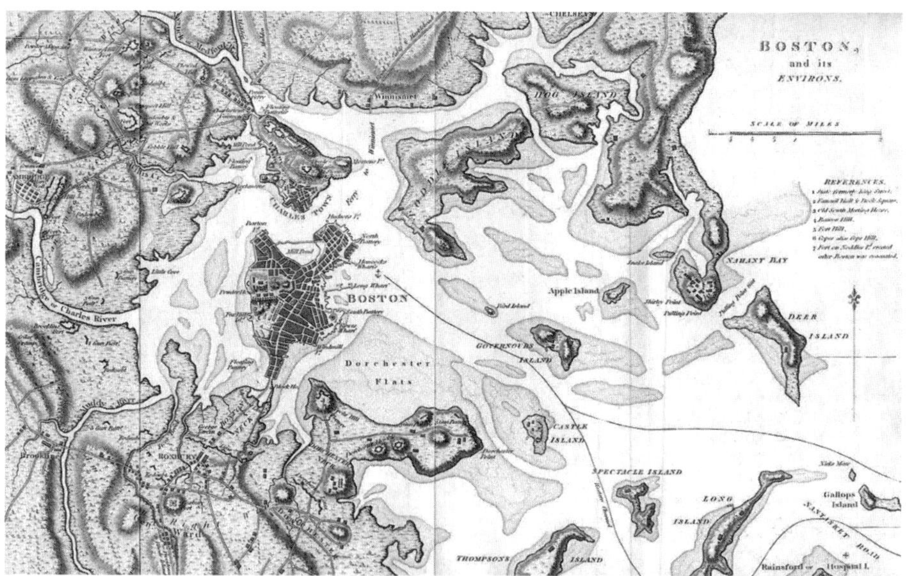

Detail of map of Boston showing Winter and Prospect Hills. *Author's collection.*

When Burgoyne openly complained to Congress about the treatment of his British soldiers, infuriated members responded by declaring an investigation into the treatment of American prisoners. The British general and his "Conventional Army" were delayed in departing from Boston, even as they learned that transport ships had reached Newport.

The emotional debate in Congress over what would be termed the Saratoga Agreement was described by Richard Henry Lee, president of the Continental Congress, in a letter to George Washington in November 1777.

> *It is unfortunately too true, that our enemies pay little regard to good faith, or any obligation of justice and humanity, which renders the convention of Saratoga a matter of great moment and it is also, as you justly observe, an affair of infinite delicacy.*[230]

According to the etiquette of eighteenth-century warfare, an agreement between high-ranking opposing officers was ironclad. Though the members of Congress were against Gates's generosity toward the British—this was perhaps the issue most rankling members who had sons of constituents in the New York prisons—the newly declared country could not turn its back on convention if it was to command the respect of the countries on which it would rely for loans of men, mariners and money in its pursuit of independence. Lee cautioned that "the undoubted advantage they will take, even of the appearance of infraction on our part, and the American character, which is concerned in preserving its faith inviolate, cover this affair with difficulties."[231] After considerable debate about what action would be taken, not to mention the wording of the resolution, Congress voted on January 8, 1778, to "suspend the embarkation of the troops" back to Great Britain until England conformed to civilized treatment of American prisoners.

As had the prisoners at Lancaster, the incarcerated British on Prospect Hill grew restless and then violent in their confrontations with guards. Colonel David Henley reported that winter that the prisoners were growing mutinous and showing increasing insolence toward their American guards. One guard had been struck senseless by a rock thrown by a British prisoner; others were threatened by mobs of prisoners who "arm'd themselves with clubs &c and taunted the guards to fire upon them."[232] Though the guards managed to quell the uprising on the first day, a greater mob grew on the second, culminating with Colonel Henley running a prisoner through with his sword. When Burgoyne heard of the riot and the killing, he filed a formal complaint with Heath. Following normal procedure, evidence was brought forward, and Henley would face trial.

In the aftermath of the uprising at Prospect Hill, Colonel Henley decided to house some prisoners in the very way that struck fear into American soldiers and repulsed the Congressional leaders struggling with the affairs of American prisoners. The Americans removed forty-four of the more rebellious British prisoners to a prison ship in Boston Harbor.

The same tactic the British used off the islands of Manhattan and Newport was, in fact, adapted by some coastal communities that were holding—and affecting their own exchanges of—prisoners. Rhode Island, with its active and often successful privateer fleet, had only community jails in which to hold prisoners of war. The jail in Providence at that time was a narrow three-story structure that could have held but a dozen prisoners at a time. Other prisoners were marched under guard to the jail in East Greenwich. By 1780, the city had installed a prison ship off Fox Point, where the Seekonk and Providence Rivers flowed into Narraganset Bay.

Connecticut also maintained a prison ship in New London Harbor, but Boston's use of a prison ship was in pure retaliation, and the constant shortages of food, fuel and medicines ensured that the treatment of the prisoners held in it was equal to the suffering the Americans continued to undergo in the prison ships in New York Harbor. Massachusetts authorities would consign over two hundred men to the ship, many already with "the countenance of famine." One officer taken prisoner and consigned to the ship at Boston recorded that in the hold of the ship, "every crevice is filled with vermin."[233]

Burgoyne learned of Congress's decision to delay his troops' and his own return to Great Britain. He also learned of the provision that any debt owed to Massachusetts for food and provisions would have to be paid before their release. Not surprisingly, authorities in Great Britain viewed this as an effort to extort money that could be used to bolster the American cause. Burgoyne and other officers were left to finance their own ticket to freedom.

In May 1778, Richard Henry Lee wrote to Arthur Lee, "Gen. Burgoyne has leave to return to England upon parole. But his army is detained untill the Court of London shall notify to Congress their Ratification of the Convention of Saratoga."[234]

That spring, over three hundred of the British prisoners died as an epidemic of smallpox spread through the barracks, and Bostonians clamored for Congress to provide relief and move the British to another location. Washington, along with Massachusetts authorities and General

Heath, continued to hope for a negotiated exchange of the prisoners for Americans held in New York. Washington had pressed for negotiations through the winter, but Congress refused to relent unless prisoners' expenses were paid.[235]

To relieve Boston, Congress initially authorized Heath to move several hundred prisoners some fifty-five miles inland to the town of Rutland. They were hardly welcomed there. Some reported that the prisoners there were "treated with great severity, very badly supplied with provisions." Townspeople refused to open their homes to British officers. By mid-September 1778, an aide of Heath had been enjoined to stop sending prisoners of rank to the community, as "I have not the least prospect of procuring Quarters for the officers. It was with great difficulty that the officers already here is quartered."[236]

As tensions in Boston reached an incendiary level, on November 9, 1778, what was left of the captives taken at Saratoga were marched to Virginia. Some 1,100 men had died or escaped during their imprisonment outside Boston. After an arduous march, they arrived during one of the worst winters in memory and with the Township of Charlottesville, in Albemarle County, ill-prepared for their arrival. The prisoners were led to land owned by Virginia's Congressional delegate John Harvie, who, nearly destitute, had wrangled funds from the government to build housing for the prisoners on his farm. He expected that he could run the "prison camp" as a plantation, with prisoners improving his land. When the British captives arrived, however, they found that the "barracks" where they were to be housed were simple, unfinished huts, with little running water available nearby.

Governor Patrick Henry was dismayed by the government's decision to burden the small hamlet with the prisoners and bickered with Thomas Jefferson, who favored the government money coming into Albemarle County and used his influence in Congress to keep the prisoners there. By 1780, they had become a heavy burden on the local economy. Waves of death and desertion plagued the Convention troops there as well, and within months, they were relocated to Pennsylvania. So long was their confinement that when emissaries arrived in New York to begin peace negotiations to end the eight-year conflict, most of Burgoyne's men were still imprisoned in the United States.

Other prisoners, however, had the opportunity to plead their case by petitioning the local Council of War in those coastal towns that held American prison ships. One such petition came from a man named Benjamin Clarke, who claimed that he, like many, was simply swept up—or, in his unfortunate case, shipwrecked—into the hands of one warring nation or another. Clarke petitioned the Board of War in Providence on February 3, 1780, writing of his circumstances as

> *Master of the Schooner Polly who was upset in a violent gale of wind on Thursday August 26, 1779.... Three men perished I remained with four of my men on the wreck until the 30th of the month when I was picked up by Capt. Jacobs of this town in a very poor condition.... He carried me into Boston from thence sent me to Providence and put me on the prison ship where I now remain a prisoner at present in a very poor condition for the want of clothes and bedding therefore I beg the honorable Board of Warr to take my unhappy situation into consideration and Grant me the Liberty to goe to New York. I shall with the greatest honor send a man in my Room which I am shure there is Numbers of Gentlemen suffering in the same condition that I do at present.... So once more I beg of the Honorable Board of Warr to take my unhappy situation into consideration and Grant me my request which shall forever be remembered by your humble and unfortunate petitioner...*
>
> *Benj. Clark*
> *Prisoner of Warr*[237]

During that same meeting, another petition was heard involving a casualty of traveling during a global war. The unfortunate prisoner was a Prussian doctor taken prisoner by a legendary Rhode Island privateer vessel. The doctor wrote at length to the board of his circumstances in a most officious manner:

> *The humble petition of Jacob Heisser, now a prisoner of war, a native of Prussia, and in the service of his Prussian majesty....*
>
> *Herewith... that your petitioner was Doctor on board of the ship George, one of the Jamaica fleet taken by the Providence Ranger and Queen of France, Continental frigates on the 20th of July 1779 and carried into Boston.*
>
> *That your petitioner have liberty from Capt. Simpson of the Ranger, to come to Providence, and take the opportunity which* [was] *offered at that time, to ship himself on board a Vessel bound to St. Eustice, and from thence to go to Holland on his way to Prussia/having a kind of furlough only for a few months from his King, and was desirous in that time to see the West Indies, therefore entered into the Line in which he was unfortunately taken prisoner.*[238]

Upon your petitioner's arrival here, the Vessel was gone down to Bedford, he was endeavoring to proceed there, but was stopped and confined on board the prison ship, then below Foxes Point for three months, notwithstanding there was an exchange of prisoners took place during that time with Newport, but the British having no doctor to exchange him, would not then be of the number.

Having been confined for up to four weeks, Hessier wrote,

Your petitioner's health through the inclemency of the weather and distress for clothing was such as to oblige him to go to the Hospital—and when he became reinstated, lent all the assistance to the facility which he was Master of, and that his Art afforded him for upwards of seven weeks....

Your petitioner in consideration of his long and tedious imprisonment and services, prays their honor of the Gentlemen of the Board of War, will consider the hardships of his case, and permit him to go to New York on Parole, and to send a person of Equal Rank from thence to exchange him, or in failure thereof to return to his former imprisonment.[239]

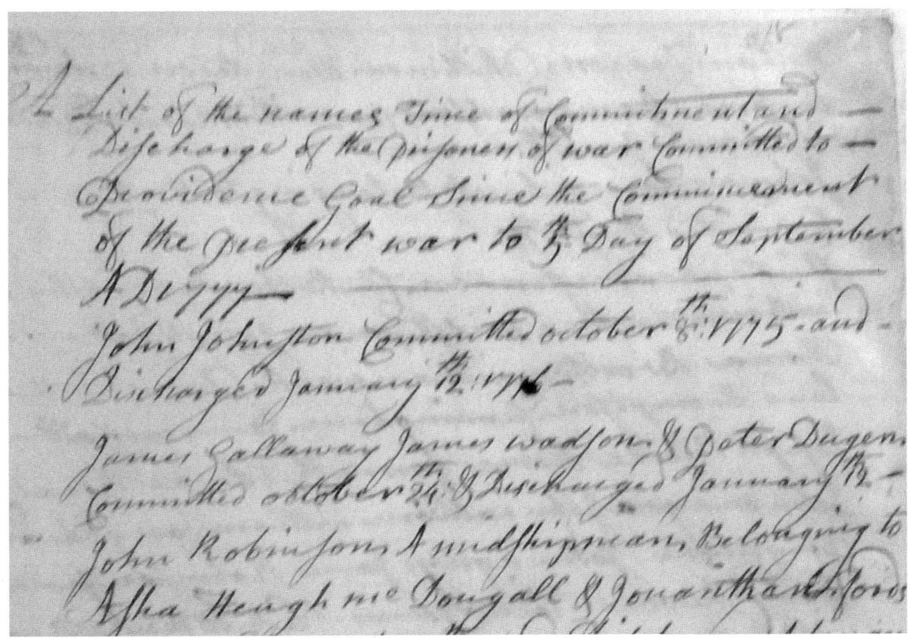

A List of the names Time of Commitment and —
Discharge of the Prisoners of war Committed to —
Providence Goal Since the Commencement
of the present war to 7th Day of September
AD 1777 —
John Johnston Committed october 8th 1775 and —
Discharged January 12th 1776 —
James Gallaway James wadson & Peter Dugen
Committed october 24th & Discharged January 12th —
John Robinson A midshipman, Belonging to
Asha Heugh mc Dougall & Jonathan Fords

"List of Prisoners of War...Committed to Providence Gaol." *Courtesy of the Rhode Island Historical Society.*

The following month, however, fifteen prisoners succeeded in escaping from the ship in Providence. The Council of War determined that "wheras Silas Gardner and others laid before the Council an Account of them charged against the State for their Time and Expense in apprehending Fifteen prisoners who escaped from the Prison Ship at Providence, and securing and delivering them to East Greenwich," the council would pay them 203 pounds, 2 shillings "for the use of himself and other Persons who assisted him in said Service.[240] As for the prisoners themselves, those who could be removed were quickly dispatched. An order from the council the following day resolved:

> *All the prisoners of war in this state, who lately made their escape from the Prison Ship at Providence, be immediately sent to Rutland, and that it be and hereby is recommended to the Deputy Commissioner of Prisoners in this State to send them forward accordingly, and that it be recommended to Colo. Greene to furnish a sufficient Guard for that purpose.*

The First Rhode Island Regiment marched from their encampment at John Greene's farm in Coventry to pick up the prisoners in the East Greenwich jail and march them, as ordered, to the prison camp in Rockland, Connecticut.[241]

On May 10, 1780, the Council of War ordered the removal of prisoners from Newport:

> *Resolved that the sloop Endeavor…be chartered and fitted as a Flag at the Expense of the State to transport a number of prisoners to New York and to bring back from there an equal number of the Subjects of this and the other United States who are now prisoners in New York.*
>
> *Resolved that it be and hereby recommended to Col. Greene or the Commandant of the Post at Newport for the Time being to deliver to Capt. Thomas Jackson all the naval Prisoners lately arrived at Newport who are fit to be removed; he being appointed by this council to carry them to the sloop Endeavor as a Flag of Truce to New York to be exchanged for an equal number of American Prisoners.*[242]

That summer, the Rhode Island General Assembly ordered the removal of the remaining prisoners of war, decreeing on July 21, 1780:

> *Whereas, it has been represented to this Assembly, that a number of British officers, who were captured by the fleet of His Most Christian Majesty, are now prisoners of war in the town of Newport; and whereas, their being at large in the said town, in the present situation of affairs, may be attended with inconvenience to the public—*
>
> *It is therefore voted and resolved, that it be recommended to Major General Heath to request Lt. General Rochambeau to cause the said officers to be sent to Cumberland, in the county of Providence, there to remain until exchanged, or until the further order of the said General Rochambeau.*[243]

Cumberland, though officially within the county of Providence, was far removed from anything the British and Hessian officers would have defined as civilization. There were but a few large houses along what is presently Mendon Road or in the area of the Elder Ballou Meeting House Road that may have housed the prisoners. As the state had confiscated a "wild tract of land" from one Richard Smith, a loyalist who fled to Britain, his estate may have been used. The town had contributed a significant number of men to the revolution, mostly composed of those who had enlisted in the Cumberland and Smithfield Ranger militia.

The Old Jail, East Greenwich, Rhode Island. *Courtesy of the East Greenwich Historical Society.*

Officers, as we've seen, were usually kept on "house arrest" in such communities—though around this same period, those in newly reoccupied Newport were not welcome in town and were likely confined to the "new jail" constructed in 1772 and still in existence today as the Jailhouse Inn. The Rhode Island Regiment, as well as the Kentish Guard and the Kingston Reds, were stationed on the island and likely were assigned in turn to guard the prisoners, but as the French occupied the town and repaired major buildings for their use, Rochambeau clearly wanted them gone from the island.

In 1781, the Council of War received another petition from the crew and passengers of a Bermuda-bound vessel:

> *Whereas David Clegg, Master, and William Smith, mate of the schooner Flying Fish; and Samuel Spencer and Josiah Hodges (for himself, his wife, and two children), passengers in said schooner preferred a petition, and represented unto this Assembly, that being bound from New York to the island of Bermuda, of which they are all inhabitants, they were taken and brought into this state, and here detained as prisoners of war, at a great expense; and that if they may be permitted to return to the said, island, they will engage upon their honors to send back, either from Bermuda or New York, a like number of prisoners of equal rank; and thereupon they prayed this Assembly to permit them, at their sole expense, to hire a small vessel, to be qualified as a flag of truce, to carry them to the said island.*[244]

The Council of War granted their petition on June 1, 1781, recording, "It is voted and resolved, that the prayer of the said petition be granted; they giving their paroles to the commissioner of prisoners in this state."[245]

Desiring to rid themselves of the costly responsibility of maintaining such prisoners, Rhode Island sought to discharge them as often as could be expedient to the state. The council decreed in early December 1781,

> *It is voted and resolved, that his Excellency, the Governor, and His Honor the Deputy Governor, be, and they are hereby, severally requested to order the two flags which have lately sailed from Providence, with prisoners from Boston to New York, in order to relieve the prisoners belonging to the Commonwealth of Massachusetts, into Taunton River to land them; and that His Excellency the Governor be requested to write immediately to the Governor of Massachusetts informing him that said flags will be sent there.*[246]

During the Southern Campaign, those prisoners who were taken at the fall of Charlestown were released from the prison ships in the exchange agreement of May 1781, and prisoners were taken on transport ships through the coming months. Those months, however, would bring skirmishes and battles that produced more prisoners on both sides.

A shared statement by American and British authorities issued on June 3, 1781, declared that "all the militia prisoners of the war, citizens of America taken by the British arms in the Southern Department...shall be immediately exchanged for all the prisoners of war, subjects of Great Britain taken by the American arms in said department." But the British refused to release all the militia in their prisons. They took exception to those prisoners who had been paroled earlier only to break that parole and be captured taking up arms against the king. Those Americans who were exchanged were made to disembark at Jamestown and Pennsylvania. Many, miles from home and short on cash, relied on strangers for food and a bed on their journey home.

At Yorktown, however, the victorious American and French forces had captured some 8,300 prisoners while losing 500 men captured by Cornwallis and his forces. After this battle, the negotiations became bogged down as the Crown refused to recognize Congress's demand that Britain acknowledge American independence and the rights of their prisoners under a sovereign state.

Washington was also hesitant to release the prisoners from Yorktown, fearing they would be exchanged for prisoners taken by the British navy from American privateers captured at sea. Some American and British officers attempted to work out an acceptable framework for an exchange but ultimately failed to reach an agreement.

One sticking point, to General Nathanael Greene in particular, was the British refusal to release certain militia during the earlier general exchange. While Greene had no wish to be burdened by prisoners, he remained skeptical of negotiations. Still, he continued to write to Major General Paston Gould, the temporary commander of British troops in South Carolina, and then to correspond with Gould's replacement, Major General Alexander Leslie, who wished on arrival to negotiate a prompt prisoner exchange. Greene insisted that all militia be released, while Leslie still took a hard line on British deserters who had taken up arms against their countrymen.

In the meantime, conditions for those American prisoners aboard the prison ships in Charlestown continued to worsen. The *Lord Howe* and the *Esk* were both said to be "sickly vessels," the latter so rotted that rain poured through its deck onto the prisoners below. Greene wrote to Leslie on April 12, 1782, about his concerns with "the deplorable state of our prisoners in your possession." He suggested, as a gesture of good faith, that officers from each army be allowed access to their respective prisoners and to inspect the living conditions in which the men were held.[247]

The general also applied pressure on Leslie for the release of American General Robert Stark, who had been taken prisoner. When Greene ordered that British officer Henry Barry be taken off parole and placed in confinement, Leslie relented, even though Stark, it seems, had acted with such reproach toward his British captors that the major general considered him "too obnoxious a person to be set at liberty."[248] Leslie countered, as the Americans consolidated control of South Carolina, that if no cartel was reached, he would take the American prisoners with him when the British evacuated the state.

Despite setbacks and rhetoric flung like cannon fire through missives from both sides, emissaries slowly moved negotiations forward for the exchange of prisoners in the Southern Department. The officers ultimately negotiated two exchanges in the fall of 1782, the first signed on October 23 at the Accabee Plantation on the Ashley River, a few miles outside of Charlestown, by Major Ichabod Burnet of Greene's staff and Major James Wemyss of Leslie's entourage. In spite of Leslie's threat, the British officer was so eager to make a deal that the American prisoners arrived in Charlestown before the ink was dry on the paper.

The cartel released "all the non-commissioned officers and privates" in the Southern Department and "all militia and citizens both American and British prisoners of war by either army." A separate agreement for the exchange of officers was reached on November 26, which freed all officers taken during the southern campaigns but for those taken captive at Yorktown and some 170 prisoners who had been taken at either Charleston or Camden.[249]

These prisoners were under control of the Continental Congress, and their plight received little attention that fall. Moreover, the Congress was not satisfied with Greene's agreed-upon prisoner exchange. Greene felt that, as commander of the southern army, he held the right to negotiate and follow through with such exchanges, as did others in the field and individual states. But members of Congress, it seems, now demanded complete oversight, borne from their frustrations in seeking negotiations between two sovereign nations and from the reluctance of other members to agree to pay compensation for the prisoners' cost of confinement on release.

On December 14, 1782, the British evacuated Charlestown, and by then, all prisoners from both armies in the Southern Department had been exchanged. Two weeks later, on December 30, American and British emissaries in Paris reached a preliminary peace treaty. Among its provisions was a call for "the immediate release of all prisoners of war."[250]

In February 1783, army financier Robert Morris recommended the release of all remaining prisoners as a cost-cutting measure, but the Congress still refused to release the prisoners taken at Yorktown. It would not be until July 1783 that agreements resulted in the release of all remaining British and American prisoners of war.

Chapter 8

"NO MEAT, NO BREAD, NO SOLDIER"

The Second Campaign Against Hunger, 1779–1783

The winter of 1779–80 came early, and General Nathanael Greene, as quartermaster general, had the responsibility of finding a suitable location for setting up winter quarters for some twelve thousand men. As the British had consolidated almost all their forces into New York, Washington wanted the encampment at a good distance and, fearing a winter assault, to be located on defensible ground. General Greene wrote that he scoured the countryside that autumn for a suitable location. He recommended a grove call Jockey's Hollow in Morristown, New Jersey. Washington approved the location on November 30, 1779, with the winter already gaining a foothold in the Northeast.

The troops marched from West Point to their winter quarters, arriving on December 2 amid a storm that pelted them with wind and hail. A heavier snowstorm arrived three days later, setting the precedent for an unrelenting winter of snow, ice and freezing weather. By the first week of January, snow lay four feet deep, with drifts as high as twelve feet. Teams of horses were unable to draw sleighs or sleds to camp, and provisions that Greene had stored in the countryside around the camp became impossible to retrieve. Greene wrote to his deputy quartermaster, "Our army is without meat or bread, and have been for two or three days. Poor Fellows! They exhibit a picture truly distressing, more than half naked, and above two thirds starved."

A few cattle arrived that week for some relief, but on January 7, some of the men took matters into their own hands, wading through the waist-deep snow to plunder Morristown's houses and farms. Washington sent a missive to a dozen county magistrates the following day, apologizing for men's actions but informing them of the army's dire situation. He appealed

Washington's marquee tent, pictured at the Smithsonian Institute, 1911. *Wikipedia Commons.*

to the "Virtuous inhabitants" of New Jersey to send cattle and grain to the encampment. Greene, at the same time, wrote to the local militia leader, asking him to bring teams of oxen to "break," or plow, the road between camp and Hackensack, New Jersey, where supplies lay in store. The letters prompted the citizens to action, and whether from patriotism or the opportunity to earn much-needed money, their contributions and efforts likely saved the army, once again, from disbanding during a brutal winter.

This time, however, relief did not come with the spring. Greene, now with the army at Morristown, wrote of the dire situation: "The Army is ready to disband this moment for the want of proper provisions. The soldiers are neither fed or paid; and are getting sour alarmingly fast." On May 25, a regiment of Connecticut troops raised a loud protest, beating drums and forming a line to march out of camp. Private Joseph Plumb Martin recorded in his journal that:

> *The men were now exhausted beyond endurance. They could not stand it any longer, they saw no alternative but to starve to death, or break up the army, give all up and go home. This was a hard matter for the soldiers to think upon, they were truly patriotic, they loved their country and had already offered everything short of death in its cause, and now, after such extreme hardships to give up all, was too much, but to starve to death was too much also.*[251]

When British and Hessian troops landed in New Jersey in June 1780 and marched into New York, Washington at once anticipated an attack on West Point and moved troops closer to the citadel on the Hudson. He left one thousand troops behind in Springfield, New Jersey, under command of Quartermaster General Greene. This was the third time during the war that Greene was assigned double duty as both the quartermaster general and a commander in the field.

The boom of alarm guns and the rapid riff of the drummers' call to arms warned of the enemy's approach in the early morning on June 23, 1780. Greene moved his troops to the hills above the town, and saw the "5,000 infantry, large body of calvary, and 15-20 Artillery" approaching in a swift and compact manner toward the town. He dispatched Colonel Israel Angell and his Second Rhode Island Regiment to move cannon to the bridge at the Rahway River to harass the oncoming troops and slow their movement toward the town.

Surgeon James Thacher relayed:

> *"Their whole force of five or six thousand were actually held in check by these brave soldiers for more than forty minutes, amidst the severest firing of cannon and musketry." The forces under Baron von Knyphausen would eventually overrun the Rhode Islanders and advance into Elizabethtown where they burned the church, and "twenty or thirty" houses.*[252]

In July 1780, the Congress overhauled the Quartermaster's Department, paring back the duties of the quartermaster general, as well as the number of deputies under his command. Those deputies who remained could expect to see a cut in pay. To say that Greene resigned in protest is to understate the mistrust and bitterness that existed between Congress and the quartermaster during this period. Greene's letter to Congress, and his subsequent demand of a Congressional committee that the act be repealed, nearly caused his removal from the army.

> *"My best endeavors have not been wanting to give success to the business in my care," Greene wrote in a seething tone, "and I leave the merit of my services to be determined hereafter by the future management of it under the direction of another hand.*
>
> *"My rank is high in the line of the army, and the sacrifices I have made on this account, together with the fatigue and anxiety I have undergone, far overbalance all the emoluments I have derived from the appointment.*

> *Nor would double the consideration induce me to tread the same path over again, unless I saw it necessary to preserve my country from utter ruin and a disgraced servitude."*

Only Washington's intervention prevented his removal from occurring, and Greene agreed to stay on until a replacement was found. The commander-in-chief immediately tasked him with supplying his next campaign. Greene spent his last months as quartermaster general collecting what boats, food and forage he could for the general's planned attack on the British stronghold of New York.

The department, however, was now short of deputies, and Greene found procuring any supplies increasingly difficult. By August, with time running short, Washington ordered Greene to take whatever hay, grain, cattle and horses were needed from the surrounding farms in New Jersey and New York. Unfortunately, some of the soldiers on these foraging missions took their orders as an excuse to harass and plunder the inhabitants, so angering Greene that he took the unprecedented step in his career of setting the ultimate harsh example. Fuming to Washington that he wished all to hang, he asked his blessing to "hang one as an example"; he would later reveal that he hanged one man from the Tenth Pennsylvania Regiment.

As these difficulties continued, Congress sought ways in which to supply the army. In February 1780, it "called on the several states for specific supplies of provisions and forage," an action that would eventually be enforced through quotas for beef and produce. By the final years of the conflict, each state was contributing much to the war effort beyond the fathers and sons sent as the Congress raised enlistment quotas.

In Rhode Island, a committee appointed by the general assembly "relative to the ways and means for procuring supplies for the Continental Army" reported in March 1780

> *that, after considering the great expense and risk of importing the necessary articles, and the uncertainty of their being procured seasonably for the service, the state of the treasury, and other matters, your committee are of opinion, it will be most for the interest of the state to procure the supplies in the following manner, to wit:*
>
> *That the farms not yet leased out, be rented for such quantities of beef as can be had for them, so far as those who hire will contract to pay in beef, and no disadvantage arise to the state by demanding the beef in preference to other articles of produce.... That salt shall be procured by purchase,*

Rhode Island farm, circa 1760. *Photo by author.*

> *either imported or manufactured; that the rum may be procured, either by purchasing molasses and having it distilled, or by purchasing Continental, French, or West India rum, which shall appear most for the interest of the state, that, for procuring the necessary quantity of hay, the farm lately belonging to Messrs. Joseph and William Wanton, on the island of Prudence, be leased on shares for cutting, making &c.*[253]

By November 1780, the committee had reported:

> *From the best information we have been able to obtain, we find that six hundred barrels of beef have already been purchased by the purchasing commissary; that one hundred barrels will be furnished by the towns of Westerly, Richmond, and Hopkington agreeably to a resolution of this Assembly; that one hundred barrels may be expected in payments of rents due for the state's farms; and that there will remain a deficiency of two hundred barrels of beef to complete this state's quota.*[254]

The Massachusetts General Court requisitioned some 2,400,445 pounds of beef from towns within the state, and the towns responded in varying ways depending on their situation. While the town of Amesbury, for instance, duly drove thirty-three oxen weighing approximately nine hundred pounds each to meet its quota, the town of Harwich, in Barnstable County, pled poverty and said that a drought had caused such shortages that only one-quarter of the town's population had meat of any kind. Elsewhere, the town of Wells purchased twenty thousand pounds of beef to contribute its quota, while Windham voted to send cash instead. Vermont, which had yet to be considered a sovereign state by the Continental Congress, chose to stock its own garrisons.[255]

Thomas Pickering, the former chairman of the Board of War, was chosen to replace Greene on September 30, 1780, and he set out at once to enforce the reforms Congress had mandated. Historian Louis Clinton Hatch opines:

> *Pickering was initially touted as "a more careful and frugal manager than Greene....But the new system did not improve the condition of the army; it is doubtful indeed, if any reform might have been of much service in this respect so long as the soldiers had to rely upon state supplies. By October 1780, the army was obliged to live on the country."*[256]

Washington wrote to John Sullivan, now an elected representative to the Congress from his native New Hampshire, that the army had gone ten months without receiving pay and that no one would afford any more credit to the encampment. He called on Congress for better organization and suggested shifting the vendors from large-scale suppliers to smaller businesses and individuals. "I am well convinced," Washington wrote, "that for want of system in the execution of business, and a proper timing of things, that our public expenditures are increasingly greater than they ou[gh]t to be."[257]

Improved systems or not, economist and historian Anne Bezanson's work clearly shows the increasing level of inflation for goods during the war, largely due to the continued depreciation of the currency. In a graph of the "annual percentage changes in prices of fifteen commodities" covering April 1779 to April 1880, the historian shows how prices continued to inflate as the war progressed:

> *The November 1778 to November 1779 comparison reflects the alarming depreciation of the close of 1779. Beef, common flour, pork, and pepper rose 1100 to more than 1900 per cent above the price of the same month the year before. Only one of the other commodities rose less than 341 per cent....In the percentage rise from April 1779–1780, some West India*

> *goods, notably molasses and rum, rose briskly, as did pork, but their behavior was only slightly more extreme than the mounting percentage climb of other domestic items like beef and tar.*[258]

During the same period, Bezanson shows, the "quantity of certain staples" that could be purchased continued to plummet throughout the war, especially supplies of flour and beef, until the Continental currency was abandoned.

By December, the army did not have enough credit to buy wood to make doors for the huts it had constructed. Food was also scarce. On December 10, surgeon James Thacher recorded that it was their third day without sufficient food. That same day, Washington ordered General Heath to discharge a portion of his troops as the army could not feed them.[259]

In January 1781, Pickering came up with a plan to sell some of the produce provided by the states in order to earn enough money to transport the remaining goods to encampments. The Board of War continued to be held in limbo by Congress as it waited for payments to settle old contracts before credit from merchants would be extended again.

The continued reliance on the states for provisions began to take its toll on the communities that were expected to provide a set quota of goods for each state. That same month, the Rhode Island General Assembly passed an act for "apportioning to the several towns in this state and for collecting fresh beef for supplying the Army of the United States." Each town was given a proportioned amount with which to pay its farmers for cattle on the hoof. The act levied strict penalties on the towns should they not follow through in the allotted time.

> *It is further voted and resolved, that in case any town shall neglect to pay the money assigned them, and within the time foresaid, such delinquent town shall forfeit and pay into the general treasury, for the use of this state, double the sum in which they shall be deficient, to be collected by adding the same to the next succeeding tax.*[260]

While this reliance on local towns and villages to provide for the militia may have been a boon to local merchants and a handful of suppliers, it remained a hardship to farmers and householders, many of whom opened their barns to store wares for the army and their homes to house officers or serve as hospitals for the sick, along with their churches, courthouses and schools.

In July 1781, the Rhode Island General Assembly requested that the town of Cumberland supply 1,823 pounds of beef for the army. Unable to fulfill the request, "the town sent over 36 pounds sterling in gold and silver as an alternative. Since paper currency now was worthless, gold and silver were collected from the people of the town to be melted and used for the needed money."[261]

In his new role as commander of the southern army that year, Rhode Islander General Nathanael Greene would come face the "great disorder" that permeated the chain of supplies through the southern states. The general "complained repeatedly that supplies meant for the Continental Army in the South were being intercepted, confiscated, and issued elsewhere by militia officers."[262] On May 2, 1781, Greene wrote in exasperation to Congress,

> *The distance is so great and the waggoners so unfaithful that great abuses prevail on the road, and besides it has been so much the custom for Stores to be stopped on the way by order of the different Governors and officers either commanding or residing in the different States through which the Stores pass that packages are often broken and issues made without being accounted for.*

Greene's words reflect, as well, the distressed situation of many communities in the South and the resulting bitterness toward the army's tactics in engaging stores and supplies from local inhabitants. Virginia Governor Thomas Jefferson cautioned Greene that the state's "free People think they have a right to an Explanation of the Circumstances which give rise to the Necessity under which they suffer."[263]

As he had to address the situation in Morristown, New Jersey, Greene issued orders to officers to "treat the Inhabitants with tenderness," to leave the best of their stock behind and to issue compensation certificates so they would not feel as though their farms had been plundered. As in Morristown, however, these orders were largely ignored by those desperately seeking supplies. That same spring, Greene received a letter from Jefferson complaining of transgressions by several officers, the most severe of which was the confiscation of a Thoroughbred valued at 750 pounds, which had then been traded "for a gelding…and Two Hogshead of tobacco to boot."

The saving grace of the southern army, as it turned out, was in the person of Colonel Edward Carrington, whom Greene had appointed deputy quartermaster for the Southern Department. A former officer in the Virginia Artillery, Carrington would prove his worth in the months and campaigns that followed.

In one instance, however, the untimely arrival of supplies caused an unpreparedness for battle. In April 1781, Greene marched his troops through thick woods and swamplands en route to a planned siege of Camden, South Carolina. Finding the fort there too large and well-fortified, he led the troops to the highest point nearby, a "sandy, pine-covered ridge running three-quarters of a mile from east to west about a mile and a half north of Camden" called Hobricks Hill. The troops arrived at the hill tired and hungry from their march. They had already been without provisions for two days. Greene reconnoitered the area surrounding the fort and sent a messenger to bring up the artillery. He had hopes of drawing the weaker troops of the British Commander Francis Lord Rawdon out to fight. His wish was granted sooner than the army was prepared to meet it.

On the morning of April 10, the troops awoke to find that Lieutenant Carrington had arrived with wagons full of supplies in the predawn hours, and the men were allowed to stack their guns and avail themselves of the newly arrived food. Unbeknownst to Greene and his army, Lord Rawdon had indeed decided to send a force out to strike the encampment. The rations relaxed the men: some set to washing their clothes in a rivulet that ran through camp, while others took off to bathe in the nearby Little Pine Creek. Others were cooking breakfast with the newly arrived victuals when the alarm signaling the assault was sounded.

Greene's army repulsed the attack for a time and then retreated into the swamp and thickets to fight another day. The unfortunate timing of the arrival of much-needed provisions was an indication of the difficult terrain the horses and supply wagons needed to traverse to try to keep up with an ever-mobile southern army, especially when a shortage of good horses continued to slow the progress of supplies.

Greene wrote again to Congress in exasperation:

> *I can see no place where an Army of considerable force can subsist for any length of time; and the horses are so destroyed in this Country that subsistence cannot be drawn from a distance. The Country is so laid waste and the means of transportation so unequal to the business of collecting supplies from a distance for an Army, that it is difficult for me to conceive how an Army is to be subsisted in this Country any longer unless its strength is such as to enable it to take post on the Congaree.*[264]

Throughout his campaign in the Carolinas that year, Greene would face innumerable difficulties in obtaining supplies, culminating in his famous

Portrait of Robert Morris.
Wikipedia Commons.

description of the southern army as one whose "wants are without number, and our difficulty without end." The disorder of supplying the campaign was compounded by enslaved men and women who left southern plantations in droves to seek refuge with the British army, often bringing good horses and packing them with supplies as they fled.

By the summer of 1781, Congress had again overhauled its administration of affairs, replacing the Treasury Board with a superintendent of finance endowed with great authority "to make such arrangements for feeding the Army as he should deem best." The man Congress came to choose to fill the office of financier was Governor Robert Morris of New York, who immediately determined, counter to Washington's interest, that feeding the army under contract from one large supplier was the best path forward. By December, he had signed an agreement with Mr. Comfort Sands and Co., "in which they promised to deliver at certain specified places, as many rations as should be called for." Any complaints about the quality or quantity of provisions were to be heard and settled by a three-person board, two of whom were appointed with congressional oversight.

Although it seemed a laudable plan on paper, its execution proved to be problematic. Washington wrote that provisions at West Point had become so scarce that "should the enemy besiege it, the fort could not hold out for three days." Historian Hatch observes that during these months,

> *The Army was frequently without food. It was said that when salt meat rose, Sands left the troops unsupplied, waiting for a fall in price. He also arranged that his droves of cattle should not arrive until they were needed, and so save the expense of maintaining them at camp. If there was any delay on the road, the Army might suffer, but the profits of the contractors were secure.*[265]

Morris initially continued to support Sands, but after letters from General Washington in May and June 1782 and Sand's own continued demands for payment for subpar provisions, the supplier was released from his contract. The superintendent of finances found other suppliers who were willing to wait three months for payment, the caveat being that the army now paid a considerably higher rate for goods than it had to Sands.

The winter of 1782–83 brought heavy snow, again blocking roads that were key passageways for supplies. Farmers could or would not bring sleds of provisions to camp. Washington placed the blame on Quartermaster General Pickering, penning an angry letter on Christmas Day 1782 concerning the lack of forage and its toll on the horses in camp. The general wrote that the horses had been without feed, "long or short," for some fourteen days and that General Gates had already lost "two fine horses." His own horse had been without forage for four days, and he had been obliged to buy feed from his own pocket to save it from starvation. Pickering, for his part, protested that he had foreseen such a difficulty and planned to lay up supplies in reserve but could not get the money from Congress to purchase them. The scarcity of provisions proved to be only temporary, and as in years before, once roads were cleared, supplies came steadily into camps once again.

During the final year of the Revolutionary War, the supply of provisions stabilized, due in large part to the Congress finally dispensing with the circulation of Continental currency and paying wages and accounts with acceptable specie. While there was finally plenty, there was also no shortage of the unscrupulous suppliers who had undercut and overcharged the army and its soldiers throughout the conflict. Henry Knox wrote disparagingly in February 1783, "The beef contractors go from bad to worse. There are now forty cattle killed, so infamously poor that the troops absolutely refuse it although their provisions were out last night."[266]

While the supply of provisions to the northern army had stabilized, the troops engaged in the southern campaign, of which the former quartermaster general was now commander, still relied on the state and the communities of the territory in which they were engaged. This reliance on the devastated southern states placed the brunt of the fallout from the American sieges on the quartermaster. At Yorktown, for instance, the stores had been devastated by the time of the American victory, and Virginia refused to furnish the quota that Congress demanded. In addition, "North Carolina failed to raise money to transport their supplies to camp, the quartermaster was also without money, so little assistance was given from that state."[267] South Carolina attempted to provide its share but also fell short. Georgia lay exhausted of any provisions and was unable to contribute any monetary assistance to the army. Virginia, though refusing the quota, did attempt to maintain its own troops, though in truth, the state had suffered greatly since 1781. One county that year refused to provide its quota on the grounds that the county had been taxed enough.

Historian Louis Clinton Hatch, in his early twentieth-century work *The Administration of the American Revolutionary Army* (1904), takes a severe look at what was undeniably a failure to provide for the soldiers engaged in the cause of liberty. He writes: "The story of the sufferings of the Revolutionary Army has usually been recorded as glorious proof of endurance and patriotism, and this it is, but it is also a proof of weakness and folly on the part of Congress and the Country." The British historian avers that even allowing for those

> *young, ill-organized people, who were inexperienced in great affairs...the fact remains that the Army starved, not because the country could not furnish food, but because the people were not willing to endure taxation, and because Congress themselves did not understand the importance of administrative centralization. Some of the hardships the Army endured were indeed unavoidable, but the greatest part of them were caused by incompetent or negligent Officers, bad management, and an excess of paper money.*[268]

Anne Bezanson poses a less political view, acknowledging the role of the depreciating currency and the Congress's stubbornness in continuing to circulate the nearly worthless paper but noting:

> *Though monetary factors were the dominant influence in the extravagant rise of prices, the part played by shortages cannot be overlooked....Apart*

> *from monetary inflation, shortage of goods and increased costs raised prices in specie terms 50 to 100 per cent. These shortages developed now in one sector of the economy, now in another....They were not persistent, except in the case of salt and specialized military equipment.*[269]

What cannot go unaccounted for as well are the losses from British raids on communities during the war. To give but a few examples: In April 1777, loyalist New York Governor William Tryon led a group of loyalists and a British force to raid Danbury, Connecticut, destroying some 1,800 barrels of beef and pork, 700 barrels of flour, 2,000 bushels of grain and other provisions collected for the rebel forces.[270] The following year, 1778, was especially successful, with British raids from coasting vessels affecting New Bedford and Fairhaven, Massachusetts. Rhode Island saw the loss of some 60–70 head of cattle and 900 sheep plucked from Prudence Island in Narragansett Bay. In September that year, a raid on Martha's Vineyard netted some 10,000 sheep (some from the already destitute Indigenous people of Gay Head), as well as 300 oxen.[271] In 1779, during growing season, the British returned and requisitioned from the islanders 900 hogs, 137 bushels of grain and 698 heads of cabbage, as well as leather, lumber and other provisions. A raid on the town of Royalton the following year burned dwellings and destroyed "16 new barns filled with hay, slaughtered about 125 cattle, and all the sheep & swine they could find."[272]

And on it went throughout the war, as both loyalist and rebel militia destroyed property and provisions in partisan plundering of those farmers whose sympathies lay with the American forces or those loyalists who had supported British troops during an occupation and were left vulnerable and defenseless in the wake of their departure.

Through all these challenges, both citizen and soldier gave great sacrifice. In one of Greene's letters at the close of the war, he expressed his gratitude for his army's

> *zeal and activity with which they attempted and persevered in every enterprise, and for the patience and dignity with which they bore their sufferings. Perhaps no army ever exhibited greater proofs of patriotism and public virtue. It has been my constant care to alleviate their distresses as much as possible, but my endeavors have been far short of my wishes, or their merit.*

Greene paid a greater price than the guilt he may have felt about falling short of his promise to provide for the troops. He fell heavily into debt after the war, having signed on as creditor to an unscrupulous supplier who absconded in the closing months of the war. South Carolina and Georgia had given General Greene two plantations in gratitude for his efforts in winning the war in the South, and thus, in hopes of alleviating his debts, the northern general who had advocated for and supported the raising of a regiment of enslaved men in his home state of Rhode Island now found himself a slave owner dependent on their labor. He died on his Georgia plantation and was buried with great ceremony outside of Savannah, just three years after the war.

CHAPTER 9

GENERAL HOSPITALS, CONFISCATED HOUSES AND CAMP MEDICINE, 1779–1783

After the British evacuation of Philadelphia on December 13, 1778, the Hospital Department reopened the wards at Bettering House. This facility continued to be used throughout the remainder of the war. The city's charity hospital housed the overflow of troops, and a limited number of cases was also admitted to the Philadelphia Hospital. As occurred throughout the conflict, the use of hospitals in their varied locations changed with the amount of activity in the region. For months, facilities might have but a few patients, and then the wards would fill again with wounded or sick soldiers from the campaigns.

The general hospital established in Baltimore in the summer of 1778 was closed by September. While use of the facilities at New Brunswick, Princeton and Trenton, New Jersey, continued though the year, patient populations remained exceedingly low until an outbreak of smallpox filled the beds at Princeton in 1779.[273]

By the fall of that year, three hospitals were in service in Pennsylvania, located at Fort Pitt, Sudbury and Fort Sullivan at Tioga. These housed the wounded and ill from that summer's campaign led by General John Sullivan against loyalists and their Indigenous allies of the region.

Again, hospital rolls show that most patients were admitted with a wide variety of ailments rather than suffering from the wounds of battle.[274]

Two new hospitals were opened that same year in New Jersey, at Basking Ridge and Pluckeman, which would share the burden of patients from Washington's encampment at Morristown. The hospital at Pluckeman

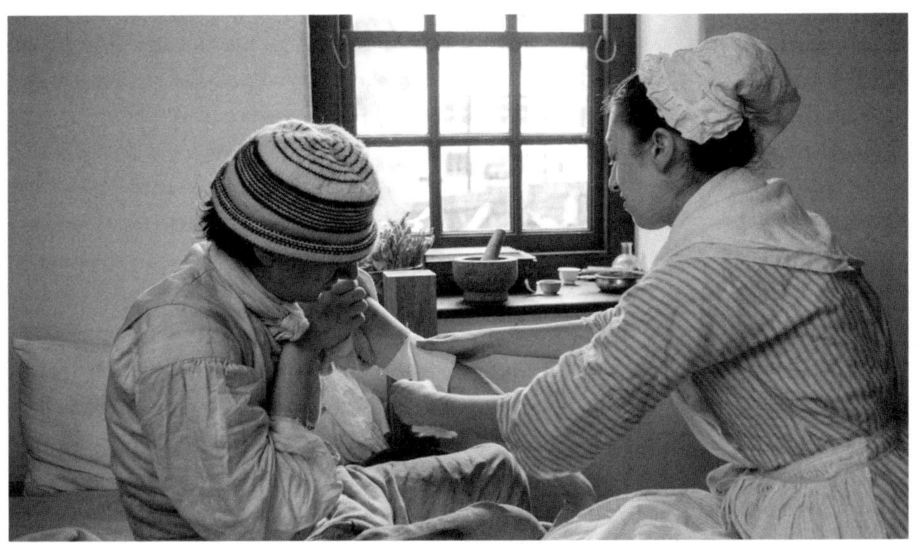

A hospital nurse tends to a patient. *Courtesy of the Trenton Barracks & Hospital Museum, Trenton, New Jersey.*

was opened in the summer of 1779 after renovations had been made to the "hospital huts" built the previous winter by Henry Knox and his artillerymen. By the fall, once those who had been patients in Morristown were transported, the new facility was housing some ninety-eight patients.

These "hospital huts" were usually of simple design, though one "experimental hospital" designed by Dr. James Tilton was an expansive log building. Another innovation of Tilton's was the building of smaller huts based on the Indigenous *wetu*, with a fire

> *built in the midst of the ward, without any chimney, and the smoke circulating round about, passed off through an opening about four inches wide in the ridge of the roof. The common surface of the earth served for the floor. The patients layed with their heads to the walls round about, and their feet were all turned to the fire. The wards were thus completely ventilated. The smoke contributed to combat infections, without giving the least offense to the patients, for it always rose above their heads before it spread abroad in the ward.*[275]

By the summer of 1780, another hospital had been opened within the encampment at Morristown. The huts built there, however, were soon in a state of disrepair, reputedly because of the "disorderly behavior of the patients." Nonetheless, they continued to be put to use. As late as the fall of 1780, patients were moved out of harm's way from Paramus, New Jersey, to the shabby huts at Morristown. The hospital huts there were finally closed in 1781.

Other hospitals in the region opened at Fishkill, New Windsor and at Robinson House, an elegant estate located on the east bank of the Hudson River. Surgeon James Thacher, reassigned from Albany, would pen a description on his arrival on June 11, 1778:

> *The house was erected by Colonel Beverly Robinson, a respectable gentleman from Scotland, for his summer residence, but being induced to adhere to the British interests, he has, with his excellent family, removed to New York, and thereby forfeited his large estate.... Robinson's house, with the out buildings, is found very convenient for a hospital; the farm and gardens are very extensive, affording excellent pasturing for horses and cows, and containing three or four large orchards abounding in fruit of various descriptions.*[276]

New England also opened various hospitals in the period between 1778 and 1783. Among the largest of these was the facility in Danbury, Connecticut, which admitted some 938 patients during the months of September and October 1778. Other hospitals at Bedford and Poundridge, approximately twenty miles northeast of White Plains, New York, were also opened. A facility was opened at Hartford that year but closed by March 1779. The following spring, 1780, the Continental Congress ordered director Shippen to establish a large facility in New London for the housing of British prisoners, who were to be returned to a healthy condition and exchanged for American prisoners. Historian Mary Gillett reports that this facility was little used and closed in the spring of 1781.

Rhode Island hospitals remained quite active during this period and seem to have been consistently well staffed. A return of the "Officers and Nurses in General Hospital at Providence" on April 23, 1779, shows D. Townsend as senior surgeon and Stephen Harding and Henry Stephens as junior surgeons. Joseph Bowen served as surgeon's mate, and a handful of other men filled roles in the commissary, as clerk, steward and ward master. Now listed as matron, Sarah Stainor oversaw six nurses, including Elizabeth Jenkes, Anna Barnes and Nancy Brown.

After the British evacuation of Newport in October 1779, the French troops under General Rochambeau took occupation of the ravaged city the following summer. They likely used the Congregational church, as the

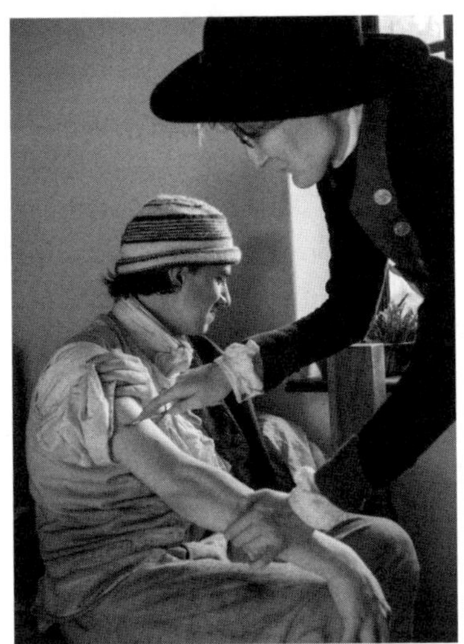

A surgeon examines a patient.
Courtesy of the Trenton Barracks & Hospital Museum, Trenton, New Jersey.

British had, for a hospital, but also ferried their sickest troops off the island, making use of an old house on Highland Road in Tiverton just above Sin and Flesh Brook.[277] This house may have been in use as early as June 1778, when a return penned by Surgeon Stephen Wigneron shows two men were in "Col. Topham's hospital," one with "symptoms of the small pox."

Another regimental hospital was located on the Vassal farm on Popasquash Point in Bristol, an estate confiscated by the state in 1779, after Vassal and his family fled with the British.[278] There, a "burial ground" was established for those men who had died as allies far from home. Those soldiers who most urgently needed care were sent to Providence.

Between 1780 and 1783, the general hospital in Providence mainly tended to French soldiers from Newport or encampments in Tiverton and Providence. The French encampment in Providence extended from Toll House Lane (now Williams Street in Pawtucket) past the Sayles Tavern (later the Pidge Tavern) south to Burlington Street. The encampment took over the hillside from there up to what is presently Hope Street and extended north from there to the present Blackstone Boulevard. This large encampment packed up in June 1781 and would eventually serve alongside Rhode Island troops at the Battle of Yorktown.

As detailed by Revolutionary War historian Norm Desmarais, some twenty-five French soldiers died at the Providence hospital during this period. A good number of these soldiers had survived an earlier smallpox epidemic, only to succumb to an outbreak of yellow fever that swept through the portside communities of Providence while they were stationed there. Most of the deaths occurred in the months of September and October 1780, the youngest being François Gouvey of Captain de Bien de Cheviny's company. He was an *enfant de troupe*, the son of an officer who would have been admitted with other peers when he was as young as six years of age. Such boy soldiers were paid a half wage as drummers until the age of sixteen, when they could enlist in the infantry. The boy was but thirteen when he died on November 5, 1780.

As the war shifted to the southern colonies, the Hospital Department made use of already existing hospitals as well as establishing new ones. The first hospital in the southern states was established in June 1776 by Dr. David Oliphant for the use of "state troops, militia, sailors and negroes in the public service." However, as there was yet little activity in the southern region, the hospital was not officially recognized or supported by the Hospital Department. Nonetheless, as the war headed south from New England, Dr. Oliphant was encouraged to work with Dr. Hugh Williamson and expand his organization to include Georgia and the Carolinas. These efforts were disrupted by the British taking Charleston on May 10, 1780. Oliphant was taken prisoner as an officer. Both he and Dr. Williamson spent time as prisoners, caring for their fellow Americans in British hospitals, Oliphant at Charlestown and Williamson at Camden, South Carolina.

In 1780, Dr. William Rickman was named director of the General Hospital for the Southern Army, but care remained largely in the hands of militia and regimental surgeons.[279] Rickman had developed a system of hospitals in Virginia before his appointment that had also remained independent of the Hospital Department. A facility outside of Williamsburg

Regimental surgeon's tent. *Photo by author.*

called the Vineyard Hospital reportedly served both the Virginia militia and Continental troops who had previously been dispersed among private homes. Separate "smallpox hospitals" had been established as early as 1777 at Dumfries, Colchester and Alexandria.[280]

Another hospital had been established in 1778 at Fredericksburg to service the troops under Major General Benjamin Lincoln during his time of command. A report from October 25, 1778, lists some 562 patients installed there. The following year, as Washington began transferring troops from Virginia and the Carolinas south, another hospital was established at Petersburg, Virginia, a facility that was plagued by severe shortages of supplies and staff. Rickman established a final hospital at the Chesterfield Court House in the spring of 1780, a facility that would continue actively treating patients into the spring of 1781.

It would not be until September 1780, when the Hospital Department was reorganized, that the southern hospitals already established were finally recognized and supported by the Congress—recognition that was imperative for the support of troops under the new southern commander, the Rhode Island native General Nathanael Greene.

At the time of Greene's appointment, the village of Hillsborough, North Carolina, was the hub of the southern army under General Horatio Gates, but all discipline seemed to have gone awry. As historian Hugh Rankin wrote, "There were frequent clashes between the military and civilians, especially among the militiamen."[281] Rankin noted, "The supply situation blackened the picture....The courthouse had been designated a warehouse, but there was little surplus to be stored therein, certainly it was not as full as the church that had been converted into a hospital."[282]

Sometime after his appointment in October 1780, General Greene visited the hospital at Charlotte, North Carolina, and reported the conditions there were "shocking to humanity." The following month, the Hospital Department appointed Dr. James Browne medical director for the state, perhaps as a favor to the general, whose men had been previously cared for by Dr. Browne at a hospital in Cheraw, South Carolina. The efforts to reorganize the southern hospitals suffered through a rocky start. A planned move of the general hospital from Charlotte to Salisbury, North Carolina, had to be abandoned and the patients in Charlotte evacuated when Greene was forced to retreat into Virginia.

Dr. David Oliphant was released from British captivity during the winter of 1781 but chose to remain in service of the American prisoners as director of the British hospital for the captives at Charlestown. By spring, he was free to return to the American cause, and he was appointed deputy director of the southern hospitals with a staff at his disposal, including a chief physician, a deputy purveyor and two hospital physicians. The director and his staff had much to do. The majority of hospital stores had been taken in raids by the British, and hundreds of men fell ill during the summer, even as General Greene moved the men to the high hills of Santee, South Carolina, for the fresh air and cooling breezes.[283]

Dr. William Reed was then directed to leave his post at Charlotte Hospital and join with Greene's encampment, where he would establish a "flying hospital" to support the soldiers. By the fall, "many hundreds were still sick, and supplies of bark [to make quinine]…were totally exhausted by mid-October."[284]

In the spring of 1781, as Cornwallis marched his army into Virginia, the main hospital for the southern army of the Continental line was removed to Williamsburg. After the Battle of Green Spring in July, ninety-nine wounded were installed in a nearby church. By August, most of these men had been moved to a general hospital established at a private home in Hanover. At the close of the month, the number of patients had swelled to the extent that medicine and other staples became in short supply, and multiple buildings were taken for use to house the sick and wounded. Convalescing soldiers were enlisted to care for the sicker patients and were pressed into greater service when the only appointed physician to the hospital expired in September, and these untrained orderlies became the only semblance of medical practice that remained.

The condition of the American camps during the same period was poorer than what the French managed in Newport or even Providence. What the Comte de Clermont-Crèvecoeur found on his arrival in the American camp in New York on July 8, 1781, was far different than what he expected from an army that had, improbably, fended off a British victory for six years:

> *I went to the American camp which contained approximately 4,000 men. In beholding this army I was struck, not by its smart appearance, but by its destitution: the men were without uniforms and covered in rags; most of them were barefoot. They were of all sizes, down to children who could not have been over fourteen. There were many negroes, mulattoes, etc.*[285]

By contrast, Surgeon James Thacher thought the troops, though less elegantly dressed than the French, had made a good impression during the review by Rochambeau on his arrival to confer with Washington. Thatcher

Surgeon's medicines at a regimental camp. *Photo by author.*

had the good fortune to be invited to dinner at the allied encampment, where, he recorded, "We were politely received under an elegant marquee, our entertainment consisted of soup, roast beef &c. served in the French style. The gentlemen appear desirous of cultivating an acquaintance with our officers, but being ignorant of each other's language, we can enjoy but little conversation." Thacher noted, "Their military dress and side arms are elegant, the troops are under the strictest discipline, and are amply provided with arms and accoutrements." Little wonder the French officer was astonished to witness the ragtag army of America parading with muskets and fowling pieces. It was this army that would, in the coming months, descend on the village of York.

The siege of Yorktown brought some 15,000 men into the region. At least three more hospitals were established at Williamsburg to provide care for 250 patients, including the Wren Building at the College of William and Mary, which was utilized by the French after being rejected by Rickman for use some months before. The Americans sheltered patients in the old palace-like hall, reputedly in poor condition, as well as a pair of churches in town. Flying hospitals were also established within the encampments of French and American units.[286] Malaria took the greatest toll among the Americans at Yorktown, far greater than those casualties of battle or the later outbreak of smallpox. Historian Gillett notes, "New England troops especially were suffering from the remittent and intermittent fevers considered endemic in that area."[287]

After the British surrender, some six hundred Americans remained too ill or incapacitated by injuries to be cared for in the camp hospitals. Four hundred were patients housed in the hospitals at Williamsburg; another two hundred were sheltered at facilities in Hanover. It was Washington's desire that as many of the sick as possible be housed in Williamsburg, with separate houses or facilities found for those suffering from smallpox. He hoped that the victory at Yorktown would add to the army's coffers and provide monies for improvements and supplies for the hospitals and that a swift signing of the Articles of Peace would enable him to move the army away from the unhealthy environment as soon as possible.

General Greene moved his men southeast toward Charlestown, but for the soldiers who had to be left behind at the hospital in the Santee hills. Another hospital in Charlotte, North Carolina, continued to be used into early 1782. Greene's men were soon joined by units under General Wayne and Major General Arthur St. Clair, but by the time of their arrival, having marched through stagnant swamps "full of little insects," many were afflicted with fever and had to be hospitalized in a private house in Ashley, North Carolina: "A very disagreeable place—all sick and some continually dying."[288]

Perhaps the site of suffering for the majority of the survivors of Yorktown was the general hospital in Philadelphia. One of the last of the northern regiments to leave Yorktown was the Rhode Island Regiment, a combined unit of what had been the First and Second Rhode Island Regiments prior to 1781. The First Regiment was the so-called Black Regiment composed partially of enslaved men who had enlisted to earn their freedom, and the Second Regiment had evolved largely from General James Mitchell Varnum's Continentals. Historian Daniel M. Popek chronicles the "slow and harrowing voyage" the men made to Head of Elk, Maryland. One of the first to die was Private Matthew Hart of Olney's Light Artillery Company, who died on November 1, 1781. By the close of the month, another nine members of the regiment had died.

On their arrival at Head of Elk, two of the Rhode Island delegates to the Continental Congress informed Rhode Island Governor William Greene that the regiment had arrived

> *after having experienced almost every kind of distress in a long passage by water from Yorktown. The regiment is very sickly, the small pox has got along the last recruits. In this case they are not alone, many from other regiments being down with it.*[289]

Within a few days, the remaining healthy men were marched to Philadelphia. Commander William Allen of the Second Company would relate to a friend in Providence that during the voyage, "great numbers of the soldiers were hourly taken sick in a manner so uncommon that the surgeons were unable to tell the disease, much less afford them relief."[290] He continued that since their arrival in Philadelphia, another thirteen men had died, "though they are tenderly taken care of, and everything provided for their comfort that a hospital can afford." The hospital reached a peak of 314 patients in November 1781.[291]

By the end of December, another forty-three men of the Rhode Island Regiment had died at the Philadelphia Hospital, and the sick of the regiment were scattered throughout the region: sixty-three men were at other hospitals in Wilmington, Delaware; thirty-seven men at Head of Elk, Maryland; thirty-six in Trenton, New Jersey; fifteen in New York; two in Williamsburg, Virginia; and one back home in Rhode Island. Such was the fate of virtually all the regiments that had fought at Yorktown and other sites throughout the war, vindicating once again the adage that where soldiers go, plague will follow.

A good number of the older facilities of the Hospital Department remained open after Yorktown, along with the Philadelphia hospital. The West Point facility was active throughout 1783, when a measles outbreak filled its wards. The hospital at West Point was strained by the admittance of some 1,149 patients in the month of February 1782. The majority of these, just over 1,000 men, were afflicted with smallpox. The medical report from March 1782 shows that among 345 patients remaining, some 100 were afflicted with smallpox and 42 with "bilious fevers." Hospitals east of the Hudson River housed some 367 sick soldiers.

During the same period, the hospital at Albany provided services for some fifty-four patients. Other facilities in operation during the year were located at New Boston, on the Hudson River and in New Windsor, New York.

In the spring of 1782, the long-used hospitals in Albany and Boston were finally closed. The hospital in Boston had for some years housed the "Corps of Invalids" from the northern army. By the time of its closure, they had been disbanded and returned to their own communities. A turning point had occurred, and the army now had to adapt, from supplying far-flung camp or flying hospitals to providing care at more centralized locations.

Historian Mary C. Gillett writes, "Although there was no major action after the victory at Yorktown and Congress had faced the closing of some of the major hospitals even before the end of 1781, the concerns of General Washington and...of the Hospital Department were not diminished." Indeed, the general himself would visit hospitals during this period on inspection, urging directors to keep stores amply supplied.

Gillett's analysis of medical treatment during the Revolutionary War, given the limited medical knowledge that existed, is summed up in her closing chapter on the revolution within her history:

> *Administrators may have learned much more about the management of a military hospital system in the course of the revolution and individual surgeons undoubtedly added to their skills while confronting injuries and disease of which they would never have encountered in such numbers, but no significant insights into the prevention, diagnosis, or treatment of disease appear to have resulted from the American Revolution.*[292]

Surgeon James Thacher would likely have disagreed. He and other surgeons who enlisted believed that they were at the forefront of a turning point in medicine. An important discovery proven during the war was the effectiveness of a new treatment for smallpox, as Thacher described in his journal on April 1781:

> *All the soldiers and the women and children who have not had smallpox, are now under inoculation. Of our regiment one hundred and eighty-seven were subjects of the disease. The old practice of previous preparation by a course of mercury and low-diet, has not been adopted on this occasion, a single dose of jalap (a tincture distilled from the pokeweed) and calamel, or of the extract of butternut...is in general administered, previous to the appearance of symptoms.*

Thacher felt that the discovery of the effectiveness of the butternut extract was "highly important, and it may be considered a valuable acquisition to our *meteria medica*." The Brown University–educated surgeon acknowledged that this was not a "newly discovered" treatment: "The country people have for some time been in the practice of using it." The plant had long been known for its fruit, also known as the white walnut, and its medicinal benefits

Illustration of a Continental regiment surgeon. *Courtesy of Alan Archambault, artist.*

seem to have been borne from the same homeopathic experiments that had long contributed to locally known cures. What was unique to the Army Medical Department's use of it was that "it operated without creating heat or irritation," as the young private Joseph Plumb Martin and others had experienced, and the extract was also found to be useful in treating dysentery and "bilious complaints."

The availability of the butternut tree, which was then widely dispersed throughout the East Coast, the mid-Atlantic states and as far south as northern Georgia, meant that officers would no longer need to collect supplies of the quinine constantly in need at the "flying hospitals." These camp hospitals were also an innovation borne of the Revolutionary War. They were, of course, the predecessors of the field units used so successfully in World War II and the MASH units that the U.S. Army has employed since the Korean War to keep life-saving medical treatment close to the front lines of battle.

Another result of the war experience was that after the conflict ended and those who had served as army surgeons returned home to their communities, nearly all began immediately to inoculate their new patients. Their experience, in effect, brought back to the community helped dispel long-held fears of inoculation, especially in rural communities—if they had not already found the benefits of the butternut tree.

By the latter part of century, a plethora of pamphlets, periodicals, almanacs and books that fully described and illustrated common surgical procedures had been published, including several well-regarded books on surgical procedures and practices that were published to assist army surgeons in the field. One of these was the Austrian surgeon Baron Gerhard van Sweeten's work *The Diseases Incident to Armies with the Method of Cure*, republished in 1776 along with extracts from British army medical manuals for the benefit of the Continental surgeons.

Another indispensable book proved to be William Northcote's groundbreaking discussion on wounds of veins, arteries, nerves and tendons. Northcote, who had penned *A Concise History of Anatomy, from the Earliest Ages of Antiquity*, was unparalleled in his teaching on the subject during his time as an academic. Among the practices he discovered was a method of healing ruptured tendons in the field. Northcote specified:

> *If tendons were wounded, they were to be splinted, but not sutured to avoid suppuration, which would tend to shorten them. If major nerves were completely severed, the limb would have to be amputated, because*

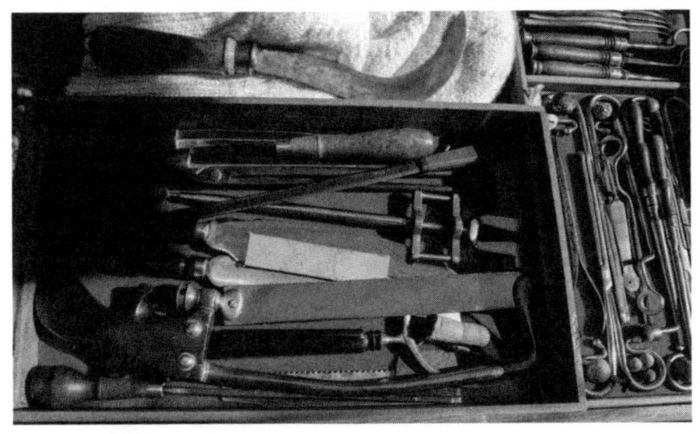

Regimental surgeon's tools. *Courtesy of Dan Newman.*

> *the arteries below the cut would not be able to function without their nerve supplies. However, nerves that were only partially severed could be expected to heal after Peruvian Balsam had been poured into the wound.*

Thacher also cited a work by the Philadelphia surgeon John Jones published in 1775 titled *Plain Remarks on Wounds and Fractures* that he considered indispensable in the field during the war. This medical text published by Dr. Jones is widely accepted as the first American textbook on the subject. Within its pages were many detailed instructions for and illustrations of the treatment of different kinds of wounds: incised, punctured, lacerated and contused. Jones introduced techniques that are still in use today, including debridement, excision of jagged wounds to convert them into incised wounds and dilating puncture wounds rather than closing them.

Jones heartily criticized some old practices, including the indiscriminate amputation of any limb with a compound fracture. He worked along with other doctors on finding practices that could save the patient's arm or leg from the surgeon's table. His recommendation to like-minded surgeons was that after uncovering the wound, treatment should begin by "removing foreign matter from the wound, and applying soft dry lint to permit free drainage and promote a speedy suppuration. Cautious bleeding, to draw off inflammation was also recommended. If drainage were excessive, amputation should then be considered."[293] Jones admonished the surgeons utilizing his text to always be mindful of the Hippocratic Oath and "as good surgeons, be in the first place well aware of the necessity of the operation before he proceeds to perform it, and secondly he ought to consider whether the patient will in all probability be better for it, or whether he may not be the worse."

Such physicians felt emboldened during this era to shake off old practices and experiment with new treatments. One such case was Dr. Leonard Hopkins of Litchfield, Connecticut, who began his practice in that town in 1776, after apprenticing with Dr. Jarod Potter in Hallingford and then Dr. Seth Bird, the latter a well-respected local practitioner. He served briefly as a volunteer surgeon with the militia but became better known, as Dr. Maurice Bear Gorden tells us, for his "cooling treatment of fevers, in the puerperal especially, and wine in fevers since called typhus—methods which were then thought madness, and some of his cases became the subject of much newspaper discussion." Dr. Hopkins's specialty came to be tuberculosis, and his two treatises on the subject "revealed a knowledge far ahead of his time and prove Hopkins to be a rival with Rush for honors in treating the great white plague."[294]

Historian Gillett is correct in her assessment that the experiences of the Hospital Department in the war led to better understanding of administrative needs. During the war, one of the more successful and innovative administrators was Dr. James Tilton. Tilton first entered the army as a surgeon of the Delaware Regiment in 1776. He was sent to Dumfries, Virginia, that year to supervise the inoculation of Continental soldiers there. He would later serve at hospitals in Long Island and White Plains, New York, as well as in New Jersey and North Carolina, before being promoted to hospital surgeon.

On the reorganization of the Hospital Department in 1780, Tilton was appointed senior hospital physician and surgeon. Throughout his service, Tilton became known for his efforts to reform the army's medical organization. He sought to end the use of overcrowded hospitals and for ways in which to better supply the camps for soldiers in the field. As medical historian Dr. Maurice Bear Gordon summarizes:

> *Tilton successfully tackled the problem of caring for those poor sick souls who were underfed, packed together like sardines, and receiving a poor quality of medical treatment. While commanding hospitals at Trenton and New Windsor, he radically moderated the entire hospital system by subdividing the large hospitals and dividing the sick into small groups, each group being kept in a well-ventilated individual hut.*[295]

Tilton experimented with various treatments as well as the physical aspects of military hospitalization. He advocated for the use of tent hospitals where the climate and season permitted, and in the colder regions and during winter, he advocated for the use of his huts. After the war, Dr. Tilton published his thoughts on improvement and reform in the form of his *Economical Observations on Military Hospitals*, which became highly regarded and led to his appointment as physician of the army during the War of 1812.

Other medical innovations were brought back to community practices after the war, and education in the medical arts, once believed only to be obtainable in Europe, now flourished at American institutions. As Gillett notes, however, the use of vaccinations and an understanding of the biological causes of some diseases were still at least a generation away. In the meantime, medical care still relied on the experiences of practitioners and their wide-ranging use of treatments. Old practices such as bleeding a patient still persisted, and sick veterans of the war still relied on or sought out homeopathic cures in their own communities. Much as surgery had advanced, medical historian William C. Wigglesworth concludes,

> *During the Revolutionary War, as in all wars, great strides were made in treating wounds of the abdomen and chest, but subsequent infection precluded any real improvement in post-operative mortality and morbidity. Surgeons had gone about as far as they could without understanding the nature of infection and without anesthesia.*

The war against infection and the spread of diseases had consumed the efforts of those doctors who enlisted as surgeons, faced the conditions in the overcrowded hospitals and sought ways to alleviate the high mortality rate throughout the revolution. In the years following the American Revolution, they would continue their struggle against known and unknown diseases with limited success. Those who proffered the most advanced treatments for disease found it difficult to move even the greatest of men to a belief in science that went beyond those practices and prescriptions for cures that had scarcely improved over the past century.

CHAPTER 10

ELUSIVE CURES

The Medical Travails of the Commander in Chief and a Common Soldier After the Revolutionary War

Despite the eight stressful years of his leadership during the revolution, Commander in Chief General George Washington remained remarkably healthy during the course of the war.[296] At age fifty-two, he returned to his plantation at Mount Vernon in anticipation of retirement in December 1783. While he rested at home, occasional concerns for his health flared up: bouts of misery from dental procedures and an increased discomfort from what we would acknowledge today as rheumatoid arthritis.

His "retirement" would last but a few short years, for in 1787, he somewhat reluctantly agreed to become a Virginia delegate to the Constitutional Convention in Philadelphia—a call to duty that would eventually result in his unanimous election by the delegates to the presidency, the highest office in the newly formed government of the United States. Washington's family was reluctant to leave Mount Vernon, but as she did his calling, Martha Washington also respected what she clearly saw as her call to support her husband and dutifully packed up her belongings, along with two grandchildren then in her care and seven slaves from the plantation, who traveled in an entourage to Philadelphia, where Washington was inaugurated on April 30, 1789.[297]

During the early days of his presidency, Washington became critically ill when an inflamed tumor, or "malignant carbuncle," developed on his inner thigh. Mistakenly diagnosed as a cutaneous form of anthrax, the tumor developed into a fast-growing abscess that plagued the president for some three months before it was painfully excised by his physician, Dr. Samuel Bard. Washington languished in recovery, having to lie in bed for six weeks

Engraving of Mount Vernon. *Wikipedia Commons.*

on one side to avoid discomfort from the surgery and troubled by intermittent fevers that caused physicians and his family to, at times, fear for his life. Absolute quiet was recommended for the benefit of his healing, and during these weeks of convalescence, carriages were barred from traveling the street outside the executive mansion.[298] When he had recovered sufficiently to resume carriage rides through the city, his coach was remodeled so that he could lie on his side in the carriage as well. For several weeks, he was carried from his room and placed in the coach to drive around town for an hour or more every day with Mrs. Washington.[299]

Washington generally maintained a regimen of exercise, walking briskly through the capital's streets with secretaries in tow. In winter, he is said to have worn a black suit and strolled on the sunlit side of the street. In July, the president wrote, "I have my health restored, but a feebleness still hangs upon me."

That fall, after a visit to Massachusetts, he contracted pleurisy, which turned out to be part of an influenza epidemic that swept through New England that season. He quickly recovered, and by the end of the year, Martha Washington was able to report, "The President's health is quite reestablished."

The following spring, however, brought on yet another bout with serious illness. On May 9, 1790, the president recorded in his diary that he was "indisposed with a bad cold, and at home all day writing letters on private business." He was soon seriously ill with what was likely pneumonia, for by May 15, members of the Senate were calling at the mansion to pay their respects to the stricken leader. Senator William Maclay of Pennsylvania recorded that during his visit, "Every eye full of tears. His life despaired of. Dr. MacKnight told me he would trifle neither with his own character nor the public expectation; his danger was imminent, and every reason to expect that the event of this disorder would be unfortunate."[300]

More physicians were called to his bedside, to little avail. Cabinet members were, understandably, alarmed as well. Vice President Adams fretted that the young country might very well be rent of what unity was held together by the near mythical stature of its first president. Jefferson wrote that Washington had been "pronounced by two of the three physicians present to be in the act of death....You cannot conceive of the public alarm on this occasion. It proves how much depends on his life."[301]

The crisis passed, and by early June, Washington had recuperated enough to enjoy a fishing trip at Sandy Hook, Long Island, in the company of Jefferson and Hamilton on the latter's private sloop. A local newspaper reported on June 10 that during the president's visit, "The weather proved remarkably fine, which, together with the salubrity of the air and wholesome exercise, rendered this little voyage extremely agreeable, and cannot fail, we hope of being very serviceable to a speedy and complete restoration to health."[302]

The president resumed recording in his diary on June 24, with the explanation that

> *a severe illness with which I was seized...and which left me in a convalescent state for several weeks after the violence of it had passed; and little inclination to do more than what duty to the public required at my hands occasioned the suspension of this diary.*[303]

He spent much of the summer convalescing in Newport, Rhode Island, likely at the Vernon house where he had spent time with Rochambeau after the arrival of the French in the portside city a decade before. It was still the finest house in the city, as the once prosperous community had been heavily damaged by the war. In fact, the estates and mansion houses that had been repaired were largely done by the French during their residency, so poor was the town for years after the war.

The president's trip was ostensibly in honor of the smallest state finally ratifying the Constitution, and he was feted about town at celebratory events. Reportedly, President Washington had his good and bad days while convalescing, and his illness seems to have been kept as secret as possible, lest the public know the true nature of the president's condition.[304]

That year, 1790, the Congress had finally settled on Philadelphia for the new nation's capital. Secretary Lear returned to New York to settle accounts while Martha packed up the house for the move. Washington eagerly returned to Mount Vernon, where he began an even more rigorous exercise regimen, riding horseback from five to seven o'clock each morning and taking extensive tours of the plantation as he had for so many years.

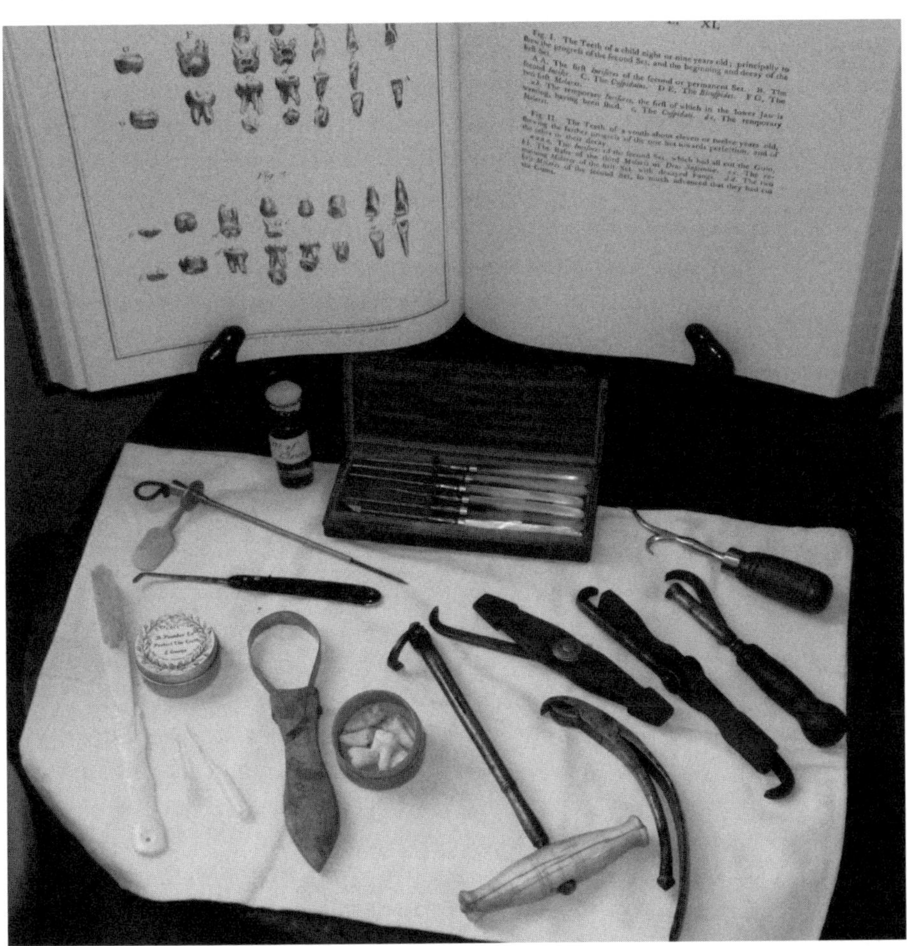

Colonial dental equipment. *Courtesy of Dan Newman.*

The president arrived in the new capital in late November, when he appears to have regained much of his energy. Indeed, he seemed eager to arrive in Philadelphia, writing to Lear that he hoped to take residence "before the weather became 'cold and intemperate,'" and the secretary struggled to get the chosen house in readiness.[305] But while the president had recovered, it appears carrying out the duties of the office after such a serious illness had taken its toll. Early in 1791, Senator Maclay, who had relayed the grim scene the spring before when Washington was near death, wrote that even now, the president seemed to move slowly, with a "pale...almost cadaverous" appearance.[306] He was apparently discomforted by his dentures as well, a now old and recurring misery.

More challenges were to come in the new capital, both politically and medically, for the president. On August 25, 1793, Washington recorded in his diary, "We are well at present, but the city is very sickly and numbers dying daily." A few days later, newspapers proclaimed that an epidemic of yellow fever had overtaken the city and published a column of suggested preventative measures those not yet afflicted could take. Among these were the sprinkling of vinegar and camphor throughout the house and the burning of gunpowder so that the smoke would kill any contagion.

Despite his recent bout with serious illness, Washington seemed surprisingly unalarmed.[307] But after Hamilton and then his wife fell seriously ill, as scores continued to die daily, the president ordered all cabinet members and clerks to remain at home.

The grim state of the capital at this time is hauntingly described by historian James Thomas Flexner in the final volume of his study of Washington and his times:

> *By now, Washington's house was (as he later wrote) "in a manner, blockaded by the disorder...every day becoming more and more fatal... when the President looked out the window, he saw the usually bustling streets virtually deserted. Many Philadelphians had fled and those still in the city cowered behind closed door. The occasional pedestrian flitted rapidly along in the middle of the street, holding against his nose a wad of gauze. If he met another walker, he would maneuver to get to the windward."*

As African Americans were said to be immune to the disease, those free Black people in the city were given the grim task of driving carts through the city "upon which were sprawled several corpses that had been unceremoniously dumped there for further dumping in the pits that had superseded graveyards."[308]

The government had, in effect, evacuated the city by September and moved to Germantown. It was only with the coming of winter that the disease seemed to abate. Martha Washington wrote that while she had little concern of the return of the fever while the weather remained cold, "some people seems to anticipate its return in the summer." Mrs. Washington then wrote of the toll that the disease had taken on the city, how its people "had suffered so much that it cannot be got over soon….Almost every family has lost some of their friends…and black seems to be general dress in the city."[309] The cold season of 1793–94 was particularly harsh and "upon the whole…a very unhealthy winter."

As his sixty-third birthday approached in 1794,

> *Washington was profoundly depressed….According to an ancient belief, the years, known as "climactics" that divided the ages of man were designated by multiplying the various odd numbers-three-five-seven-nine by seven. At thrice times seven you became an adult, nine time seven was the grand "climatric"—the threshold of old age.*[310]

A natural decline began thereafter and "[made] its appearance in a variety of ways."

In the spring, an epidemic of smallpox scoured Virginia, and while Washington was unaffected, he would suffer from two bouts of malaria during the course of the year. That spring, he also sprained his back during a near accident while riding horseback. The president continued his regimen of riding despite the setback and the obvious discomfort. His wife would express her worry a couple of weeks after the mishap:

> *The President arrived her*[e] *on Monday a good deal fatigued with his ride—I fear he got some cold, it rained all day on satterday and he rode in the rain and was wet….I very much fear that it will be a troublesome complaint to him for some time or perhaps as long as he lives he will feel it at times.*[311]

Washington, perhaps at his wife's urging, also finally had a physician examine a long-tolerated lesion, or, as the president expressed it, "An irritable spot on my right cheek which had for years been increasing in pricking and disagreeable sensations." By June, he had procured the services of Dr. James

Tate, whose administrations cured the lesion in two months. So grateful were the president and Mrs. Washington that in October she wrote to the wife of the American ambassador in London to recommend Dr. Tate, who was fortunate to be "possessed of the valuable secret of curing cancerous complaints."[312]

The following months would bring the stress of long-term and long-distance negotiations between Washington's administration, Congress and Great Britain over the Jay Treaty and its provisions, which would also take its toll on the president. One telling sign of this, which was used as fodder by his opponents, was that Washington, for the first time in his presidency, failed to act decisively. Congress had settled on the issue of provisions and forwarded its approval of the treaty to Washington's desk on June 24. The president consulted with his cabinet and sought clarity, as the Senate's intentions on one article had still not been fully decided, despite its recommendation that he sign the treaty. Washington requested that all opinions on the matter be sent in writing—but collecting such correspondence would have meant weeks of delay. The majority of the cabinet assured the president that he need not confer with Congress again; however, his secretary of state, John Randolph, favored holding off on signing the treaty. Washington wavered. The Senate had opposed the publication of the proposed treaty, but as it was about to adjourn for the summer, the president expressed the desire to have the treaty published so that "public opinion could now be heard upon the subject." Before the president's wishes could be addressed, however, a leaked copy of the document was published in an opposition newspaper, under the guise of giving information to the public that Washington and his government had wanted to keep from the American people.

Public outcry would only grow in the coming weeks. Riots occurred in Boston and in the capital, as well. The French protested that the treaty had been printed, and Congress, too, reacted, as members felt slighted by the fact that the president's administration had failed to inform them of the negotiated terms of the treaty. The backlash brought on sleepless nights and the constant worry that negotiations would fall apart completely amid the turmoil. Historian Flexner describes the mood of the president during this period:

> *Washington was an aging man who sustained much suspense and lived through many crises. There is no indication in his writings as to how much anxiety tore at him as the weeks moved by. He was able to make a very quick trip to Mount Vernon—he left Philadelphia April 14, 1795, and returned May 2. His back having healed, he went part of the way on horseback.*[313]

Portrait of Washington and his family by Edward Savage. *Wikipedia Commons.*

Indeed, the stress brought on by his presidential responsibilities had clearly tired Washington. He wrote to John Jay, in contemplation of entering his name for a third term: "The troubles and perplexities…added to the weight of years which have passed over me, have worn away my mind more than my body, and renders ease and retirement indispensably necessary to both."[314]

Washington shared a draft of his farewell address with Alexander Hamilton as early as April 1796, hoping to have it published in the papers before Congress adjourned for that year and to make his intentions clear amid the swirl of rumors that he favored a third term and threatened to turn the republic back toward a monarchy. The president left for Mount Vernon in mid-June for what he hoped would be ten weeks of rest from the political squabbles that continued to plague the government.

Even there, in the relative peace and tranquility of home, the president became agitated over what the newspapers printed about his affairs. He grew particularly perturbed by an ongoing story that began by reporting that Washington was to leave Mount Vernon and return to Philadelphia for the July Fourth celebrations. The president had expressed no such plans, yet when he did not show, the papers erroneously reported that his absence was due to a serious carriage accident.

Hamilton, to the president's annoyance, also counseled delay in publishing his farewell address to the American people, believing that the president should remain noncommitted and that the letter could wait to be published as late as two months before the national election. Washington likely knew, as John Marshall believed, that if his name was entered for a third term, no one would dare oppose him.

The secretary sent a completed draft to Mount Vernon on July 30, and the president studied both his and Hamilton's drafts through several "serious and attentive readings" before rewriting the final document in his own hand. It must have provided the president a great deal of relief to lay the quill down after penning the final lines of his farewell. Now there was retirement at his beloved home to look forward to in the coming year.

Amid preparing for incoming president John Adams's inauguration, those around Washington were kept busy packing items for Mount Vernon, settling the accounts of the house in Philadelphia and selling unwanted belongings from the presidential mansion. While Congress had authorized some funding to furnish the house at the start of Washington's presidency, most items had to be replaced by the second term, at the president's own expense. He hired a sloop to transport their belongings and, when that was full, hired a carriage to transport the rest, along with himself and two guests: Lafayette's young son, whom the president held in favor as he would a grandson of his own family, and the young man's tutor. The drive was apparently laborious, with numerous stops along the way, so that he did not reach his home until March 15, 1797.

Washington luxuriated in leaving behind the political climate in the capital, which was, he wrote, "little more than vanity and vexation," for the calm hillside above the Potomac, where, much like Jefferson at Monticello, he could bask "in the calm lights of mild philosophy."[315] But relaxation was not in Washington's nature. Rather than indulge in such leisure, the former president kept up a rigid routine as a slew of workmen arrived to set about repairing the neglected estate. After rising at dawn to examine the repairs being undertaken, he returned for breakfast a little after seven o'clock each morning.

> *This over, I mount my horse and ride around my farms, which employs me until it is time to dress for dinner, at which I rarely seeing strange faces, come, as they say, out of respect for me....The usual time of sitting at a table, a walk, and tea, brings me within the dawn of candlelight.*

If he was not hampered by company, Washington would retire to his writing desk "as soon as the glimmering taper supplies the place of the great illuminary," where he recorded the day's entry in his diary and attended to correspondence until grown "tired and disinclined to engage in this work, conceiving that the next night will do as well."

On the evening of December 12, 1799, Washington recorded, "Morning cloudy, wind to northwest and mercury 33. A large circle round the moon last night. At ten o'clock it began to snow, soon after to hail, and then to a settled cold rain."[316] The storm had begun just as Washington set out to inspect his farms, as he normally did between ten in the morning and three o'clock in the afternoon. His secretary Tobias Lear noted that while the president had worn his customary tricorne hat and a greatcoat in the storm, some dampness had formed upon his collar, and "snow was hanging from his hair." As it was close to dinnertime when Washington returned, he did not change his clothing, as was customary after his ride.

The next morning, the former president felt some discomfort from a sore throat but made little of it. Still, he stayed inside that day, as it remained stormy. He recorded that night, December 13, that the morning's snow was "about three inches deep. Wind at northwest and mercury at 30. Continued snowing till one o'clock, about four it became perfectly clear." Taking advantage of the break in the weather, he traversed the lawn between the piazza and the river, marking trees to be removed.[317] By evening, his voice had grown hoarse, though Washington read aloud interesting articles from the newspapers that had arrived that day to his wife, Martha, and secretary Lear. He retired to bed that night after brushing aside Lear's suggestion that he might take some medicine. Believing it was no more than a cold, he thought it best to let nature run its course.

The first alarm came when Washington awoke at about three o'clock in the morning and declared himself unwell but protested his wife's summoning a doctor at that hour. By dawn, when an enslaved woman came to light the bedroom fire, she was told to send someone for a doctor and to bring the overseer, who normally tended to the enslaved when they fell ill on the plantation. Washington wished to be bled before the doctor arrived, and after some hesitation, the overseer performed the task. A concoction of molasses, butter and vinegar was given, but he could not swallow it down. Much to Martha's distress, the president asked to be bled of another half pint of blood before his doctor appeared. Secretary Lear applied warming poultices and soaked the patient's feet in warm water.

The president's longtime physician Dr. Craik arrived and bled Washington again, as well as applying a blister to the affected throat. His attempts to have the patient gargle a blend of sage tea and vinegar brought the same discomfort as before. When Craik's administrations had little effect, he summoned two colleagues, Dr. Elisha Cullen Dick of Alexandria and Dr. Gustavas Richard Brown of Port Tobacco. Craik and Brown both diagnosed the former president with quinsy, an extreme form of tonsillitis. They recommended additional bleeding, blisters and purging the body. Dr. Dick, the younger physician among them, was alarmed at what he perceived to be "a violent inflammation of the membranes of the throat," which had almost closed and which, "if not immediately arrested, would result in death." He urged an immediate tracheotomy, a dangerous procedure rarely performed in this era of medicine. Largely for this reason, the two other physicians remained committed to their chosen course of treatment, and despite Dr. Dick's protestations, Washington was bled for the fourth time that day. When he briefly recovered his ability to swallow, the patient was given camphor and other purgatives.

Dr. Craik later recorded that Washington was prepared to die and that "he was fully impressed at the beginning of his complaint…that its conclusion would be mortal, submitting to the several exertions made for his recovery, rather as a duty, than from any expectation of their efficacy."

Now, propped up in bed with poultices on his legs and feet, Washington attempted with some difficulty to plead with those attending that he be allowed to die in peace. Sometime around four o'clock in the afternoon, he asked his wife to retrieve two copies of his will from the writing desk and requested of his secretary that he "arrange my accounts and settle my books as you know more about them than anyone else."

Washington never uttered a complaint or voiced despair, according to those present. Only once did he express to Lear the well-held fear of being buried alive and procured a promise from Lear that his body would not be placed in the vault "in less than three days after he expired."

With that, the vigil began: his wife, Martha; Dr. Craik; and the former president's body servant Christopher Sheels lingered by his bedside.[318] Near midnight, Washington lifted his hand to feel his own pulse and then let it fall limply back on the bed. Dr. Craik came to the bedside, placed his hand over the president's eyes to close them and announced that the end had come.

Historian Jeanne E. Abrams writes,

> *Of the many discussions of the cause of Washington's final illness, the explanation offered by Dr. Michael Cheatham…in the light of what we*

> *know from a contemporary vantage point* [has concluded that]...*an initial strep or staph throat infection led to adult acute epiglottitis which resulted in near suffocation, and that repeated bleedings—over half of Washington's circulating blood—and other heroic measures led to septic shock, ultimately causing his death.*[319]

Like other medical historians, she notes the irony that a man so physically strong and regimented to a life in retirement that most of us today would find harsh and uncomfortable could succumb to what is, in the modern age, a minor illness, curable in most forms by a dose of antibiotics.

The nation grieved Washington, as did those, especially, who knew him best. First Lady Abigail Adams wrote, "No Man ever lived, more deservedly loved and Respected."

Of less stature but no less respected and loved by his family and friends was Sergeant Noah Robinson, the young man whose journal was introduced in the earlier pages of this narrative. In 1781, after a last stint aboard a privateer that sailed to the Caribbean and returned to Salem, he came home to find the community of Attleborough Falls little changed. The community along the Ten Mile River was still largely agrarian, as industry, beyond the necessary sawmills, fulling mills and gristmills of rural settlements, would not come to the town until 1790.

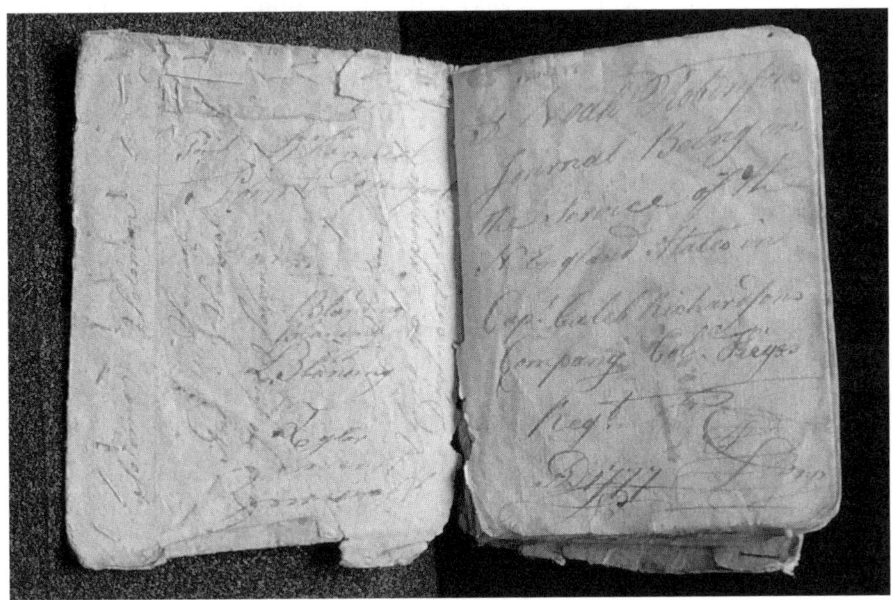

The diary of Noah Robinson. *Courtesy of the Rhode Island Historical Society.*

Noah Robinson was the grandson of his namesake, Lieutenant Noah Robinson (1702–1788), a local hero during the French and Indian War. He was born on March 22, 1758, to Zephaniah Robinson and Deborah Stanley Robinson. A younger brother named Philip was born on November 20, 1760.

Robinson served in several companies of the Attleborough militia during periods between 1777 and 1779, called to duty in Rhode Island at Warwick Neck, Tiverton and Warren, as well as to service in Fall River and at the encampment at Horseneck in Swansea, Massachusetts. In 1780, he signed on a vessel shipping timber from New Hampshire to Salem and on to St. Eustice before returning to Boston.

On his return to Attleborough in May 1781, the young Robinson reunited with his large circle of family and friends in town, including veterans with whom he had served in the war. On one of his first visits back in the community, he went to hear Joel Read, one of the original minutemen of the town, speak on a Sunday before attending a local religious meeting. This may have been one of Read's early forays into local politics. He would go on to serve as a state representative and on the board of one of the town's first large manufacturers built along the river in the nineteenth century. Read was also married to Robinson's cousin Chloe Stanley.

Another veteran and seasoned officeholder in Attleborough was the farmer Elisha May, who had served in the militia, commissioned as a lieutenant in Colonel Jabez Ellis's company. At the outbreak of the war, he was serving on the local committee of correspondence. His service during the Revolutionary War included stints as captain in John Dagget's regiment, in which Noah had served, as well as major, lieutenant colonel and colonel in Isaac Dean's Fourth Regiment of Bristol County. One member of the committee of safety had actually paid Robinson to take his place on the roster in 1779, a common practice during the drafts held in colonial towns. John Daman was likely relieved that he could find a ready substitute in Robinson, rather than leave his wife, Hannah Hunting Daman, and three daughters behind, the youngest having been born barely three years before. Noah had previously enlisted on behalf of his forty-five year old uncle Jonathan Stanley.

The town sent roughly 40 percent of its militia into Rhode Island over the first five years of the war. When the British left Newport, after nearly three years of occupation, in October 1779, the threat of raids along the coastlines decreased significantly, and Rhode Island was able to rely on its own militia once again.

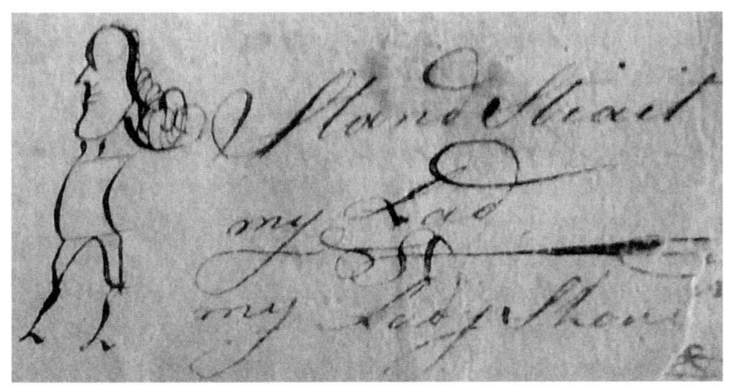

Drawing from Noah Robinson's diary. *Courtesy of the Rhode Island Historical Society.*

Like his grandfather before him, many in Robinson's family, descendants of George Robinson, one of the founders of the town in 1696, served with him in the American Revolution. His uncle Deacon Enoch Robinson served as second lieutenant with Captain Jabez Ellis's company of the Attleborough militiamen who marched from town toward Boston on April 19, 1775. His distinguished career included service as first lieutenant in Captains Elisha May and Abiel Clapp's companies and a final term as captain in Colonel Isaac Dean's company at Tiverton, Rhode Island, in July 1780.

Robinson's cousin Obed (Ebed) Robinson is listed on the April 1775 muster roll and later served as a drummer in the Continental line. Caleb Robinson served from April through August 1775 in Caleb Richardson's company of Walker's Regiment. George Robinson Jr. served in the same company and later returned to become a prosperous button manufacturer in town.

Robinson's relations on his mother Deborah Stanley Robinson's side also served in the war. Most often mentioned in his wartime journal is his cousin Rial (or Royal) Stanley, who initially served as a fifer in Captain Jacob Ides's company of Daggett's regiment. Their paths crossed frequently during the war, and they spent a good deal of time together on leave.

Noah's brother Philip also served, enlisting as a private in Captain Moses Wilmarth's company of Daggett's Regiment and spending two months and twenty-five days, from January to March 1778, in Rhode Island. He later served as sergeant in Caleb Richardson's company before serious illness in the spring of 1779 seems to have brought an end to his service.

Noah's family lived around one of the town's earliest settlements, at what was the simply called the Falls, later known as Falls Village, for the nearby falls of the Ten Mile River. Within twenty years of his return, the river began to provide power for the first manufacturing factories in town, but in 1781, little had changed since before the Revolution.

The close of the war brought hardship to Attleborough, as it did to the economies of outlying communities. Many veterans of the war faced uncertainty; some would eventually leave to take advantage of the land Congress gave out West in exchange for salaries and interest owed to hard-suffered veterans.

Noah seems to have had a clear vision of his own future. In the closing pages of his military journal, it is clear that he has tired of the carnal life of a militiaman and intends to return to his roots of faith and diligence in the care of one's soul, even viewing his journal as an exercise in vanity. He wrote on January 3, 1779:

> *Caution, Let not man think his purse and clothes will give eternal happiness or continual contentment and promotion. But each one walk in peaceably and contentedly on his allotment and not be led by Pride and the Devil who are the destruction of many in this world, and that which is to come.*

He did not cast so grim a light, however, on the countenance of Miss Abigail Draper, a young woman who first stirred his interest during his last term of service. She is almost certainly the woman he dreamt of just two days before Christmas 1778 after mimicking an ancient ritual involving a coin, the stars and love.

> *Took the quarter off my Right Leg, and went out doors & named three stars. Winding the quarter round my left thumb once at each name then un drest and put the quarter under my head & went to bed backwards with out any discourse until I had counted twenty backwards & forwards....*
>
> *I dreamed about one of the names I gave to the stars.*

After spending Christmas and the days following mostly occupied with the tedious task of finishing payroll for the expectant troops, he was released with his regiment on December 29 and headed home. The young Robinson was welcomed at once by his community: the next morning after breakfast, "a number of my acquaintances came to our house and walked with me to meeting, where I heard Mr. Welds preach." That solemn duty past, he spent the remainder of the day at Daggetts tavern and then went home again before joining his cousin Rial and others at the schoolhouse, where they "spent the evening in singing tunes and fiddle dancing."

The following day was spent largely at his uncle's and the homes of other Stanley relatives, ending after dinner in the house of William Stanley, "where we had a fiddler and fiddle gentlemen and Ladies, then the evening passed in jollity." He returned home after nine o'clock.

On New Year's Day, while he "spent the day Chiefly at home…Mrs Milly Draper and Naby came in to our house." Robinson accompanied them on a visit to a Mr. Pullen's and then went home and, later, on a circuitous route of visits: "Walked with W. Daggett up to Daniel S's from thence to Mr. Hds. And then to Mr. Orms, from thence to Mr. Maxey, and drank with my friends from thence I went up the [?] to [?] where I found AD in her room alone and…thus passed the night."

After that night, Abigail seems to have remained his sweetheart, for the day after his arrival home on Monday, May 1781, he recorded, "I was at Mr. Mann's and saw many of my acquaintences.…In the evening, I had the happiness of being at [?] where I spent the evening with Miss Draper."

Noah Robinson married Abigail Draper on March 28, 1782. They had a daughter the following year, named Nabby Robinson. An infant son was born on September 18, 1785; he would not live out his first year. This

The Maxey-Hatch Tavern. *Photo by author.*

chapter of Noah's life, however, is missing for the historian to review. It may be, as Noah came to see the keeping of a journal as a vanity at the end of his service, that no journal was kept during these active years of early marriage and family life. It may well be, also, that a journal was kept, as with the later entries we find in the collection, but that these most personal pages were kept within the family.

What we can construe, however, is that Noah did not return to his previous occupation as a schoolmaster; it's likely that a growing family caused him to seek more gainful employment. The economic hardships that faced the colonies in those years, however, reached across a wide swath of the region. It may well be that Robinson sought work in shipping once again, but by 1787, he seems to have been helping manage the business affairs of his father-in-law in Providence, Rhode Island. There is strong evidence, as well, that Robinson and his family lived in and ran the lodging house that sat on the east side of Benefit Street near what was then known as King's Chapel.

Noah Robinson's surviving journal resumes again in 1787, nearly eight years after he had left the war. His entry for Thursday, August 2, 1787, from what appears to be Westerly, Rhode Island, is telling in several ways.

> *Rested well last night—Lousy weather this morning. Drank my juice as yesterday at 9 o'clock wind at southward, sun shin*[ing]*—went a gunning, no success, dug some root in the afternoon, took a ride on the beach, I took a fine sea breeze.*

Robinson's health appears to have been in peril. He references drinking juice, which was not then the ordinary practice at breakfast that it is today, and the digging of root, for presumably medicinal purposes. He rode to take in "a fine sea breeze"—a common prescription at the time for a number of ailments. The setting of Westerly also has possible connections with Indigenous medicine, which we will explore later.

Robinson left for home the following morning after breakfast, accompanied by his brother Philip and Samuel Perry as far as Little Rest, where they stopped to have a milk punch and then parted. Robinson continued on what would be the Post Road, reaching Allen's tavern for dinner at four o'clock, and then on to Arnold's Tavern on Main Street in East Greenwich, where he stayed the night. In the morning he continued to Warwick and from there to his home, apparently without stopping further, arriving sometime in the afternoon.

Robinson remained active into September, setting off for Wrentham on September 16 and arriving at the familiar Maxey-Hatch tavern, now run by a Mr. Brown, where he spent the night. This was a place the younger Robinson had visited many times while a soldier and likely after. The following morning, after riding five or six miles on the road to Mendon, he "fell in company with Mr. & Mrs. Fairbanks." He seems to have already been acquainted with Laban Fairbanks, who also served in the war, first as a private in Isaac Warren's company with Bailey's Second Massachusetts regiment. He later had the distinction of serving in Washington's Guard from March 1778 at Valley Forge through the Battle of Monmouth in June. He was discharged in June 1780, nearly a year before Robinson's return.

Fairbanks had married Mary Wheelock, and the couple had a young daughter at the time of their meeting Robinson on the road. Robinson accompanied them to their house for tea and spent the night. The lodging was likely the "Old Fairbanks House" (circa 1636) in Dedham, which was, for a long time, the oldest house in the county inhabited by descendants of the original builder. Noah's wife, Abigail, was related to the Fairbankses through marriage, as her uncle Joshua had married Abigail Fairbanks. Her sister Millie, after losing her sweetheart in an accident at sea, married her cousin Samuel, son of Joshua and Abigail.

Robinson rode to Mendon the following morning, even though it was "lousy weather," and returned to the Fairbankses' home in the afternoon, followed by a visit from Dr. Draper and his wife. Dr. Draper of Mendon was a relation to the Drapers of Attleboro and others in the region. He was a physician as well, so we do not know whether this was a social visit alone or a social visit paired with a discreet medical consultation.

With rain continuing into the following day, Robinson stayed on with the Fairbankses, but he left the following morning, despite "Lousy, windy weather," and rode to Mendon, where he dined at a Mr. Torrey's while his horse had a shoe repaired. Noah spent the afternoon and evening at Dr. Draper's house. On Friday, he took advantage of the "pleasant morning" and began another active day:

> *Set off from Mendon over hills & Rocks to Grafton, Oated* [my horse] *and put on to Worcester, a very pleasant place. Dined on Beef and Lamb Pyes and Medallions.…At 3 o'clock set off & came to Captain Samuel Watsons in Lester* [Leicester] *& put up for ye night.*

On Saturday, he pressed on, setting off in the afternoon, after rain had passed, to Captain Draper's residence in Sheniar, where he took lodging for the night. He rose to a pleasant Sunday morning, but as he rode out to attend meeting, he had to turn back due to a pain in his side that made riding unbearable. He rested the remainder of that day, spending some time in the afternoon with another Draper relation who was lodging at the captain's house, and by Tuesday morning, he felt well enough to return home. He rode back to Leicester, fortified himself with a glass of wine at Hinkley's establishment and put on to Worcester. There, he dined at a place called Mowers and then continued on to Grafton, where he "put up at Bicknall's, very thick & noisy. Saw men & women traveling from ye four quarters of the world."

While in Grafton, either during his earlier visit or this one, he consulted with a local healer. The town had been widely populated with Indigenous people of the Nipmuc tribe since their return to the area of their original praying town of Hassanamesit. This is borne out by a torn piece of paper inserted into Robinson's diary, later referred to as a recipe obtained "from the old woman in Grafton." The text reads as follows: "Roots Sassparella, White Soloman Seal, P[an]srey, made into syrup in spring water turning from ye north." This would indicate that Robinson may have been suffering from lung disease or been in the early stages of tuberculosis, called consumption in those times, as the herbs listed in the prescription were all remedies for respiratory conditions, with the added stipulation that water for the syrup be collected from springs flowing from the north—presumably colder and healthier water than that from the wells of southern New England. His earlier visit to Westerly, Rhode Island, and his recording of digging roots there may also indicate a similar cure prescribed by a healer of the Narragansett community. It was not uncommon for people of Robinson's generation to seek out a cure from homeopathic or Indigenous recipes after advice and treatment from a consulting physician failed to bring recovery.

Robinson felt well enough to travel the next morning and ate a hearty breakfast before putting on for Mendon, where he again stayed with Dr. Draper. The company dined on broiled chicken that night, and while he writes that he "dined heartily," the pain in his right side began to return.

On Thursday, September 27, he set off again in bad weather for Wrentham. He reached Brown's tavern and stayed there into the following morning, when he set off for his father's home in Attleborough.

Gravestones of Noah Robinson and his infant son. *Photo by author.*

A few days later, on Monday, October 1, Robinson records that he "rode to Mr. Joel Reed after some Roots. My Father imployed himself for the Day in gathering Roots and herbs for a syrup according to the [prescription] given from the old woman in Grafton."

Robinson resumed active travel during the following days, riding to Providence to check on his affairs, taking his daughter and wife to "Father Draper's" and visiting Colonel Elisha May. He visited Dr. Mann in town as well as Stephen Draper before lodging at his father's house.

Robinson returned to Providence but needed a second bottle of syrup from his father by October 15. In the months that followed, his condition worsened, and though no pages exist to tell us of the progression of the disease or the suffering and desperation his family went through in those months of illness, we know that Robinson died on June 30, 1788. Noah Robinson was buried in the cemetery of the Attleborough church where he and his children had been baptized, his gravestone shouldering above the smaller memorial to his infant son, who had died just two years before.

APPENDIX A

A List of the Names, Time of Commitment and Discharge of the Prisoners of War Committed to Providence Gaol Since the Commencement of the Present War to 5th Day of September AD 1777

John Johnston committed October 8th 1775 and discharged January 12, 1776

James Galloway, James Wadson, Peter Dugens, committed October 24th, discharged January 12, 1776

John Robinson a midshipman belonging to Aska Heugh [?] Donegall & Jonathan Fords committed October 28 and discharged February the 8th…

John Smith & James Wilson committed November 16th and discharged March 3rd

Capt. Stanhope & Matthew Scalion, a midshipman belonging to the Glascow, committed December 2nd and discharged the 6th

Thomas Katon, Michael Wilson, Daniel Munrow and Thomas Connor committed January 3rd 1776 and discharged March 3rd

Henry Stevenson a midshipman belonging to the Rose, James Griendrod and William McDonald committed January 7th—James Griendrod discharged February 18th and William McDonald March 3rd…

James Westcott committed February 9th and discharged April the 14th

Daniel Welton, Robert Cooper, John Thompson, John Hudson, James Robonson, Joseph Hudson, William Deacon, Phillimon Mountecou, Edward Rick, and James Wadson committed March 23rd and discharged June 6th—

John Wallace, a Lieutenant belonging to the Rose—committed April 12th

Christopher Masterman, Chutterbuck [?] a midshipman, William Marsh, a midshipman, Joseph Dallany, Thomas Broseton, William Weekes, Daniel Sutherland, Thompston Cunningham, James Moffatt, Joseph Blake, Thomas Sossink [?], Edward Bourke, John Marsh, John Williams, William Sarcy, Edward Poigmone, John Aguiys [?], James Robinson, James Ware, Edward Neills, James Nesbitt, Thomas Boway, and John Barnes committed April 21 and discharged May the 17: all except Clutterbuck and Marsh—

Frank Cassey, George Robinson, Peter Brown and Robert Abet committed May 23rd and discharged June 27th

John Fires [?], John McDonald, James Caster, & John McDougall committed October 3rd and discharged November 6th—

George Doughtey, John Cladenboule, William Sadler, John Taylor, David Harty, John Martin, David Smith, Robert Morgains, Henry Dove, George Staner, Edward Ward, David Gordlet, Alesander Lindsley, Charles Mullen, Isaac Nicholson, committed December 2nd and discharged January 6th 1777

William Parsons, William Aeler [?], James Henry, Lawrence Murphy, John Gameo, Henry Linnes, John Little, and Robert Sharpe committed January 11th and discharged March 9th except William Parsons and John Little who was discharged February 14th…

APPENDIX B

Providence, November 19, 1777: A List of Prisoners to Be Sent in a Carteal [to] *Rhode Island to Be Exchanged*

Martiner Hay
John Watson
John Morsey
James Robinson
Edmund Lee

Above were seamen taken on Prudence

Jacob Collins
John Clark
William Robbins
William Smith
Richard Clark
Richard Stear [?]
Thomas Stanhope
John Smith (boy)
Richard Goff
Reap Aitenson
Edward Todd
John Gordon
William Pessmore
William Hodge (boy)
Allick Annes (cook)
John Hussy
William Sonderson
Edward Pain
Edward Dody
Donkin Mark Mollen
Edward Williams
James Edwards
Henry Hambleton
Robert Mac Clintuck
John White
John Parke
John Steward
Hugh Toola
John Borg
Richard Bell
Thomas Haws
Varnum Mac Markmaster

Charles Barney
James Dempsey
John Brown
Samuel Renshaw
John Fish
Thomas Sopp
Robert Burrey
James Mac Cave
John Taylor
John Harvey
Hew Brown
Thomas Arnot
Daniel Rogers

William Rilley
William Sandres
Michael Ramsy
John Haslinton
James Dobbins
James Woolspring
Henry Luke
David Calder
Cappell Fowler
James Louder
John Waters
Joseph Hull
John Allen

John Scoffin—midshipman, Francis Vintries third midshipman

Capt. Peleg Bardin
Capt. Samuel Lawton

APPENDIX C

A List of Prisoners Sent to Sir Peter Parker
the 11th December 1777

Seamen belonging to the Syren Frigate

John White
John Destman
Hugh McClarren
John Arnold
James Bull
John McArthur
Thomas Adams
Michael Thomas
Edmund Paterson
William Batten
John Ludlow
Christopher Tucker
Thomas Winder
Stephen Trumbeith
John Primus
Thomas Bugel
John McLean
Henry Cosby
Peter Luman
John Smith
David Hulton

Marines

Edward Lumbard
George Turner
George Maver
Thomas Field
Thomas Drew
John Little
Thomas Winter
Hugh Little John
James Spence[r]
William Spencer
Joseph Greenfield
John Wallais
Thomas Radford
Charles Smith
John Cooper
John White
Hugh Freeman
John Noon
James Rey
Edward Thompson
Joseph Mendes [?]

William Sier
Workman Hoskins
John Curry

Thomas Egleton
Albert Hurn
Samuel Eames
Devereaux Goodwin
John Parot
Thomas Roper

John Davison a marine on board the Kingfisher
John Sellers—seaman belonging to the Kingfisher
Thomas Wed [?] marine on board the Kingfisher

Richard Hardy—midshipman on board the Lark
Andrew Naum—surgeons mate
Richard Hutchings—boatswain
Archibalb McIntire—Gunner
William Wright—Masters mate
Henry Faseil—Capt. Steward

Providence Dec. 11, 1777
MSS 9003 V.3, page 31

APPENDIX D

Gen. Hospital Providence: List of Patients, Diseases, and Treatments

Book 1, 1777

Aug. 8th John Gonsolve
Capt. Garzia's co. of Eliot's Reg.
Veneral
Low Diet

John Starbuck [?] Prisoner
Veneral
Low Diet

Both men treated with Calomel, antiveneral comp., vesper, lotion…

Ward No. 1

Field Dayley, Capt. Cole's Co.
Col. Greene's Reg.
Fractured leg

Sept. 4th
James Luelch, prisoner taken on Prudence
Wounded in hindarm with a musket ball
Belonging to Juno, Frigate of 32 guns

Aug. 13th
Robert Clarkson, Capt. Garzia's co. of Eliot's Reg.
Veneral
Low Diet

Sept 28th
Edward Pierce, Capt. Garzia's Co. of Eliot's Reg.
Veneral

Ward No. 2

Aug. 15th

Thomas Walker, Capt Garzia's co. of Eliot's Reg.
Veneral
Low Diet—discharged Sept. 5th

Archibold Forbes, Col Rives reg.
Convalescing
Stephen Collins, came from Newport on Carteal

Sept. 20th
Robert Gilley—Capt. Earles Co. of Col [?] Reg.

Sept. 10th
John Forbes Sergeant, Col Rieves reg
Veneral [?]
Low Diet

Sept. 12th
William Shay, Capt. Hoppins Co. Col. Stanton's Reg.
Cattarh

Sept. 27th
John Babcock, Capt. Barton's Co. of Col. Sherburne's Reg.

Nov. 4th
James Kelsey, Col. Sherburne's Reg. Capt. Bartn'e Co.
Fever

Aug. 12th
John McCloud, Capt. Adam's Co. Col Eliot's Reg.
Fractured arm, powder burns

Ward No. 2

Thomas Peggin, Capt. Hammit's Co. Col. Stanton's Reg.
Fractured leg

John Kennedy of Col. Eliot's reg. Capt. Garzia's Co.
Diarrhea

Sept. 25th
Thomas Jones, Capt. Earl's Co. Col Krupps Reg.
Measles

John Strait, prisoner,
Diarrhea

Ward No. 6

Aug 29th
John Holbrook, Capt. Wilson's Co. Col. Thayer's reg.
Dysentery

Aug. 25th
Continental Troops came from Coventry Hosp. belong to Col. Greene's Reg. and Col. Angell's reg.:

Nathan Brown
Veneral

Job Smith
Itch & ulcers

William Biddle
Inflammation of eye & itch

Israel Bryent
Ulcer on hip & rheumatism

Samuel Cushing
Convalescent

Daniel Maxfield
Inflammation of eyes

Joseph Manchester
Inflammation of Eye

Peter Sampson
Veneral

Edward Anthony
[?]

Fortune Sailes
Fever

Continental troops came from Coventry Hosp. belonging to Col. Angell's Reg, Sept. 1, 1777

Benjamin Thorn
Inflammation of Eye

John Ranford [?]
Convalescent

John Saunders
Hooping cough

Nicholas Wilson
Veneral

James Mitchell
Scrophulous

Elias Betts

Jonathan Dolbey
Hooping cough

Richard Hinds
Rheumetism

Asel Bennet
Convalescent

Sam Marintine (of Greene's reg.)

William Gilbert

Nicholas Wilson
Veneral

Amos Torry
Dysentery

Richard Thurber

APPENDIX E

A List of the Sick Sent from Warren to Providence Sept. 4, 1778

Whites

Josh Payne—gone to join his Reg.
George Hopkins—do
John Davis
Wm. Shriggs
Stephen Day
George Popple
Patrick Hickney
John Bushbee
Edward Harvard
Increase Sterns
Daniel Wilkins
Webster Symptom
Elijah Molton
Ruebin Moor
John Pearce
Josh Emmens
Wm Goff
Ebenezer Whitney
Elmather Boardman
Richard Butler
Eli Cooke
Isaac Warner

Canterbury Barns
Elias Seymore
Daniel Gardener
Josh Stapple
Benj. Holley
John Scilly
David Hastings
Sam Whalbier
Peter Smith
Labulan Wilcott
Vasal White
Stanton Luther
John Mosely—left at Warren
Johnston Spiers
Wm Dempsey
Fran [?] Laburran
Timothy Dutton
David Inman
Alex Arshkins
Andrew Springger
Benjamin Branch

Blacks

Thomas Amos
Dominic Earl
Primus Train
Cato Chace & Black wife

Total: 44 men

[submitted by] R. Rogerson, Surgeon

APPENDIX F

A Return of Officers and Nurses in Gen. Hospital at Providence April 23, 1779

Rhode Island Historical Society MSS 673 B4, F67, S10

Name	Station
D. Townsend	Senior Surgeon
Stephen Harding	Jr. Surgeon
Henry Stephens	Jr. Surgeon
Joseph Bowen	Surgeon's Mate
Samuel Thurber	Hospital Comm.
Seth Wheaton	Steward
Alfred Arnold	Clerk
Alise [?] Sheldon	Comm. Clerk
George Stainor	Ward Master

Nurses

Sarah Stainor	Matron
Rosanah Saymor	Nurse
Elizabeth Jenkes	Ditto
Nancy Brown	Ditto
Isabel McMillion	Ditto
Anna Barnes	Ditto
Mariam Burch	Ditto

NOTES

Preface

1. Mary C. Gillett, *The Army Medical Department 1775–1818* (Center of Military History, 1979), 3.

Chapter 1

2. Merrill Lindsey, *The New England Gun: The First Two Hundred Years* (New Haven Colony Historical Society and David McKay Company, 1975), 33.
3. Lindsey, *New England Gun*, 12.
4. Lindsey, *New England Gun*, 12.
5. Michael Bellesiles, *Arming America: The Origins of a National Gun Culture* (Knopf, 2000), 445.
6. Abbott Lowell Cummings, *Rural Household Inventories 1675–1775* (Society for the Preservation of New England Antiquities, 1964), 167.
7. Cummings, *Rural Household Inventories*, 258, 260.
8. William Love Deloss, *Samson Occom and the Christian Indians of New England* (Pilgrim Press, 1899), 355–67.
9. Robert A. Geake and Lorén Spears, *From Slaves to Soldiers: The First Rhode Island Regiment in the American Revolution* (Westholme, 2016), 35.
10. J. Franklin Jameson, *The American Revolution Considered as a Social Movement* (Princeton University Press, 1926), 88.
11. Edward Field, *State of Rhode Island and Providence Plantations at the End of the Century* (Mason Publishing, 1902), 225.
12. William Achtermeier, *Rhode Island Arms Makers & Gunsmiths 1643–1888* (Man at Arms Magazine, 1980), 19.

13. Rob Orrison, "The Colonial Response to the Intolerable Acts," American Battlefield Trust, https://www.battlefields.org.
14. Harold Peterson, *The Book of the Continental Soldier* (Promontory Press, 1975), 30.
15. What is now downtown Pawtucket was long the border between North Providence, Rhode Island, and Attleboro, Massachusetts. The site of the falls represents the beginning of the Seekonk River, which flows southeast to merge with the Providence River at Fox Point. See Robert Geake, *A History of the Providence River* (The History Press, 2014), 28.
16. Achtermeier, *Rhode Island Arms Makers*, 20.
17. For a full account of the Salem raid, I highly recommend Charles Peter Hoffer's *Prelude to Revolution: The Salem Gunpowder Raid of 1775* (Johns Hopkins University Press, 2013).
18. Peter Charles Hoffer, *Prelude to Revolution* (Johns Hopkins University Press, 2013), 48.
19. Field, *State of Rhode Island*, 230.
20. Louis Arthur Norton, "A Wartime Visit to the Enemy's Capital," Journal of the American Revolution, February 28, 2023, https://allthingsliberty.com.
21. Achtermeier, *Rhode Island Arms Makers*, 49.
22. The later location of the "Turk's Head" building.
23. Rhode Island Historical Society Collections, MSS 9001 B, Box 1.
24. RIHS, MSS 9001 B, Box 1.
25. As Jane Lancaster has written, "Providence was flourishing as 1775 began....Some two hundred tradespeople and artisans representing over thirty-five different trades operated local industries and supplied goods and services for Providence and surrounding areas. Among them were housewrights and carpenters, chaise and shay makers, coopers, shipwrights, blacksmiths, butchers, tailors, hatters, barbers, pewterers, silversmiths, and watch and clock makers." *Rhode Island History*, vol. 5 (August 1976).
26. Lancaster, *Rhode Island History*, 19. Bicknell would win a contract from the federal government, in an order of 1798, for "2000 Charleville muskets."
27. Achtermeier, *Rhode Island Arms Makers*, 49.
28. Achtermeier, *Rhode Island Arms Makers*, 49.
29. Peterson, *Continental Soldier*, 30.
30. Peterson, *Continental Soldier*, 32.
31. Lindsey, *New England Gun*, 56, 59.

32. Tew, an old veteran of the French and Indian War, wrote to Thomas Jefferson in 1803 to inquire about land that Great Britain had promised to officers and ask whether a recent law passed by Congress regarding land claims might apply to his case. "I had the Honnour to Command a Company," Tew wrote, "and was Entitiled to 3000 acers [*sic*] of Land." Tew apologized for his boldness but added, "I am growing old and that Land may be Some[thing] to Suport me in my Old Age." See Thomas Tew, letter to Thomas Jefferson, October 30, 1803, Founders Online, https://founders.archives.gov.
33. Peter Charles Hoffer, *Prelude to Revolution* (Johns Hopkins University Press, 2013), 50.
34. Field, *State of Rhode Island*, 232.
35. Weapons were procured from France as early as 1776 through the efforts of secret envoy Congressman Silas Deane and his partnership with Pierre Beaumarchais. It is unclear when exactly the first shipments of arms and munitions began, but it is thought to have been during Deane's first year in Paris. Deane would later be recalled by Congress on suspicion that he had profited from the deal, but he would also be a key negotiator in bringing forward the alliance with France in 1778.
36. Lindsey, *New England Gun*, 4.
37. Achtermeier, *Rhode Island Arms Makers*, xiii.
38. Peterson, *Continental Soldier*, 37.
39. Peterson, *Continental Soldier*, 37.
40. Victor R. Rolando, *200 Years of Soot and Sweat: The History and Archaeology of Vermont's Iron, Charcoal, and Lime Industries* (Vermont Archaeological Society, 2007), 17.
41. Bart Forbes, "Forbes of Iron," Clan Forbes Society, August 1, 2020, https://www.clan-forbes.org/post/forbes-of-iron.
42. Unfortunately, the forge could not deliver. When the contract was forwarded to a Massachusetts forge, it also failed to meet the deadline. See James M. Volo, "Did the Americans Manufacture Their Own Artillery Guns During the Revolutionary War?" Quora, https://www.quora.com.

Chapter 2

43. Jeanne E. Abrams, *Revolutionary Medicine: The Founding Fathers and Mothers in Sickness and in Health* (New York University Press, 2013), 120–22.

44. George Washington, letter to Dr. William Shippen, February 6, 1777, Founders Online, https://founders.archives.gov. See also Janet A. Aker, "Gen. George Washington Ordered Smallpox Inoculations for All Troops," Health.mil, August 16, 2021, https://health.mil.
45. Abrams, *Revolutionary Medicine*, 123.
46. Abrams, *Revolutionary Medicine*, 124.
47. Paul David Nelson, *General Horatio Gates: A Biography* (Louisiana State University Press, 1976), 77.
48. Frederic Kirkland, ed., *Journal of Dr. Lewis Beebe* (Arno Press, 1971), 328.
49. Joseph Plumb Martin, *Private Yankee Doodle: Being a Narrative of Some of the Adventures, Dangers, and Sufferings of a Revolutionary Soldier*, edited by George E. Sheer (Little, Brown, 1962), 65.
50. Martin, *Private Yankee Doodle*, 66.
51. Jennifer L. Galpern, ed., *Excerpts from the Diary of Jean-François-Louis, Comte de Clermont-Crevecour (1752–1824)*, from the collection of the Rhode Island Historical Society, MSS 673, Folder 1.
52. Galpern, ed., *Diary of Jean-François-Louis, Comte de Clermont-Crevecour*, 14.
53. Martin, *Private Yankee Doodle*, 110–11.
54. Johann Conrad Döhla and Bruce E. Burgoyne, *A Hessian Diary of the American Revolution* (University of Oklahoma Press, 1993), 104.
55. Döhla and Burgoyne, *Hessian Diary*, 97. The site was likely the island the Indigenous people called Woonachaset, presently known as Coasters Harbor Island. For many years, a single dwelling that served as a smallpox hospital was the only structure on the island. It remained that way during the Revolutionary War. The Newport Asylum was constructed on the site after the war, in 1822, and later, the Newport Poor Farm also occupied the island. The site of said poor farm became part of the present-day Newport Naval War College.
56. John Russell Bartlett, ed., *Records of the Colony of Rhode Island and Providence Plantations in New England*, vol. 7 (J. Crawford Greene, 1862), 559.
57. Barlett, *Colony of Rhode Island*, vol. 7, 559.
58. Barlett, *Colony of Rhode Island*, vol. 7, 559.
59. Barlett, *Colony of Rhode Island*, vol. 7, 561.
60. *Diary of Jean-François Louis, Comte de Clermont-Crevecoeur, 1780–1783*, Rhode Island Historical Society Men's Diaries, MSS 9001-C.
61. Kirkland, ed., *Journal of Dr. Lewis Beebe*, 332. Journal entry of Wednesday, June 5, 1776.
62. *Diary of Jean-François Louis, Comte de Clermont-Crevecoeur, 1780–1783*.

63. Maurice Bear Gordon, *Aesculapius Comes to the Colonies: The Story of the Early Days of Medicine in the Thirteen Original Colonies* (Ventnor Publishers, 1949), 306.
64. Abrams, *Revolutionary Medicine*, 18.
65. Gordon, *Aesculapius*, 251.
66. Beth Trissel, "Herbs of Colonial Williamsburg and Early America," *One Writer's Way*, May 10, 2012, https://bethtrissel.wordpress.com.
67. Gordon, *Aesculapius*, 287.
68. Gordon, *Aesculapius*, 292.
69. Joshua Sheperd, "Drunk and Disorderly: The Dreadful Havoc of Spirituous Liquors," Journal of the American Revolution, October 27, 2016, https://allthingsliberty.com.
70. James Thacher, *A Military Journal During the American Revolutionary War, from 1775–1783* (Plymouth, 1827), 198.
71. Marquis de Chastellux, *Travels in North America in the Years 1780, 1781, and 1782*, vol. 1, translated by Howard C. Rice Jr. (University of North Carolina Press, 1963), 68.
72. Christian McBurney, "Amazing Letter Discovered from a Black Soldier of the First Rhode Island Regiment—Containing a Shocking Request," *Small State Big History* (blog), February 27, 2021, http://smallstatebighistory.com.
73. From the original letter provided to the author by curator Patrick Donovan of the Varnum Memorial Armory, East Greenwich, Rhode Island. The letter currently is on display at the Museum of the American Revolution, Philadelphia, Pennsylvania.
74. Benjamin Lincoln, letter to George Washington, May 13, 1782, Founders Online, https://founders.archives.gov.
75. McBurney, "Amazing Letter."
76. Marquis de Chastellux, *Travels in North America*, 71–72.

Chapter 3

77. McBurney, "Amazing Letter."
78. Gillett, *Army Medical Department*, 20
79. Bartlett, ed., *Colony of Rhode Island*, vol. 7, 571.
80. Marquis de Chastellux, *Travels in North America*, 22.
81. Marquis de Chastellux, *Travels in North America*, 22.
82. Marquis de Chastellux, *Travels in North America*, 43.

83. He was also favored by Richard Henry Lee, president of the Continental Congress, who seemed fully embroiled in the politics between Morgan and those who supported Shippen, writing to the latter on New Year's Day 1776, "The Congress have lately invested General Washington with complete powers to displace, place, and direct everything relative to the military Hospitals....Let me advise you, to make your immediate application, lay your plan before him, and prove as you have done to me the propriety of adapting it....As for Morgan, the very Air teams with complaints against him." James Curtis Ballagh, ed., *Letters of Richard Henry Lee*, vol. 1 (Macmillan, 1912): 106–07.
84. Ballagh, ed., *Letters of Richard Henry Lee*, vol. 1, 47.
85. Moses Horton is listed as belonging to Captain Thomas Allen's Company in Cooke's Regiment, "doing duty on Rhode Island," as of September 25, 1776. Benjamin Cowell, *Spirit of '76 in Rhode Island* (A.J. Wright, 1850), 53. He is also listed as serving as a corporal through April 1777 and then enlisting in "Col. Smith's regiment for fifteen months April 8, 1777."
86. Cowell, *Spirit of '76*, 124.
87. Gillett, *Army Medical Department*, 56–57.
88. Gordon, *Aesculapius*, 89.
89. Gordon, *Aesculapius*, 89.
90. Gillett, *Army Medical Department*, 56–57.
91. Gillett, *Army Medical Department*, 56–57.
92. Isaac Foster Jr., letter to John Adams, June 14, 1776, Founders Online, https://founders.archives.gov.
93. Foster Jr., letter to John Adams.
94. David R. Starbuck, "The General Hospital on Mount Independence: 18th Century Healthcare at a Revolutionary War Cantonment," *Northeast Historical Archeology* 19, article 2 (1990), https://orb.binghamton.edu.
95. Russell P. Bellico, "The Fort George Hospital During the American Revolution," *Fort George Advice* (Winter 2012): 3–5, https://lakegeorgebattlefield.org/wp-content/uploads/2020/01/Ft-Geo-Hosp-Bellico-article.pdf.
96. Jeannette D. Black and William Greene Roelker, eds., *A Rhode Island Chaplain in the Revolution: Letters of Ebenezer David to Nicholas Brown 1775–1778* (Rhode Island Society of the Cincinnati, 1949), 26–27.
97. Black and Roelker, *Rhode Island Chaplain*, 26–27.
98. Gillett, *Army Medical Department*, 63.

99. Starbuck, "General Hospital."
100. Letter from Surgeon Samuel Wigglesworth to the Committee of Safety of New Hampshire, September 27, 1776, as quoted in Gordon, *Aesculapius*, 118.
101. As quoted in David R. Starbuck, "Military Hospitals on the Frontier of Colonial America," *Expedition* 19, no. 1 (1997).
102. Gillett, *Army Medical Department*, 64.
103. Thacher, *Military Journal*, 81.
104. Nelson, *General Horatio Gates*, 83.
105. Starbuck, "General Hospital," 38–39.
106. Starbuck, "General Hospital," 65.
107. Gillett, *Army Medical Department*, 65.
108. Gillett, *Army Medical Department*, 94.
109. Thacher, *Military Journal*, 91.
110. Thacher, *Military Journal*, 103.
111. Thacher, *Military Journal*, 112.
112. Thacher, *Military Journal*, 80.
113. Gillett, *Army Medical Department*, 87–88.
114. Cowell, *Spirit of '76*, 124–25.
115. Rhode Island Historical Society, Revolutionary War Papers, Gen. Hospital Providence, List of Patients, Diseases, and Treatments Book 1, 1777, MSS 673.
116. Rhode Island Historical Society, Revolutionary War Papers, MSS 673, B3, F222, Sec. 10.
117. Rhode Island Historical Society, Revolutionary War Papers, MSS 673, B4, F222, Sec. 10.

Chapter 4

118. Rhode Island Historical Society, Beriah Brown Papers, B4, F7.
119. See Robert Geake, "In Their Master's Stead: Patriots of Color Who Served for Another," *Cocumscussoc Review*, https://smiths.castle.org.
120. G.T. Cranston, "The Whole History of Rome Point," *Independent*, December 2, 2018, http://independentri.com.
121. Cranston, "Rome Point."
122. John Russell Bartlett, ed., *Records of the Colony of Rhode Island and Providence Plantations*, vol. 3 (J. Crawford Greene, 1858).
123. Cranston, "Rome Point."

124. Mark Boonshoft, "Dispossessing Loyalists and Redistributing Property in Revolutionary New York," New York Public Library blog, September 19, 2016, https://www.nypl.org/blog.
125. Robert M. Calhoon, *A Companion to the American Revolution* (Wiley-Blackwell, 2008), 235.
126. Christian M. McBurney, "The Accidental Killing of Simeon Tucker During the Revolutionary War," unpublished 2014 article sent to author.
127. McBurney, "Simeon Tucker."
128. McBurney, "Simeon Tucker."
129. Norman E. Donoghue II, *Prisoners of Congress: Philadelphia's Quakers in Exile 1777–1778* (Pennsylvania State University Press, 2023), 19.
130. Sarah Crabtree, *Holy Nation: The Transatlantic Quaker Ministry in an Age of Revolution* (University of Chicago Press, 2015), 81.
131. Crabtree, *Holy Nation*, 81.
132. Arthur J. Worrall, *Quakers in the Colonial Northeast* (University Press of New England, 1980), 142.
133. McBurney, "Simeon Tucker."
134. McBurney, "Simeon Tucker."
135. Elizabeth Drinker Crane, ed. *The Diary of Elizabeth Drinker* (Northeastern University Press, 1991), 214–15.
136. Crane, ed., *Elizabeth Drinker*, 222–23.
137. Crane, ed., *Elizabeth Drinker*, 218.
138. Donahue, *Prisoners of Congress*, 56.
139. Crane, ed., *Elizabeth Drinker*, 306.
140. Donahue, *Prisoners of Congress*, 56.
141. Major General Nathanael Greene, "Letter to George Washington, 26 August 1780," Founders Online, https://founders.archives.gov.
142. The author, in his book *New England's Citizen Soldiers: Mariners & Minutemen*, highlights several incidents when enraged officers took the punishment of men accused of desertion into their own hands.
143. Joseph Lee Boyle, "Revolutionary War Desertions," file emailed to author on January 30, 2024.
144. Joseph J. Ellis, *The Cause: The American Revolution and Its Discontents 1773–1783* (Liveright Publishing, 2021), 204.
145. George Washington to Samuel Ward, August 31, 1780. See Ellis, *American Revolution*, 223.
146. George Washington to John Laurens, April 9, 1781, Founders Online, https://founders.archives.gov.
147. Ellis, *American Revolution*, 223.

Chapter 5

148. Louis Clinton Hatch, *The Administration of the American Revolutionary Army* (Longman's Green, 1904), 88.
149. Jackson Turner Main, *The Social Structure of Revolutionary America* (University of Princeton Press, 1965), 23.
150. Allen's men had been sanctioned by Connecticut in April 1775 to attempt to take the fort. Neighboring Massachusetts had granted Benedict Arnold and his men the same in the effort to capture Ticonderoga. The uneasy alliance between the two commanders led to victory but also to a personal conflict between the men, as Arnold immediately called for Allen's dismissal due to the unrestrained plunder and destruction his men wreaked on the community of Skenesborough, New York.
151. Orders of General George Washington, September 8, 1775, Founders Online, https://founders.archives.gov.
152. Thomas A. Desjardin, *Through a Howling Wilderness: Benedict Arnold's March to Quebec, 1775* (St. Martin's Press, 2016), 50.
153. Isaac Senter, *The Journal of Isaac Senter* (Historical Society of Pennsylvania, 1846), 5.
154. Desjardin, *Howling Wilderness*, 25.
155. Senter, *Journal*, 9.
156. Desjardin, *Howling Wilderness*, 67.
157. Senter, *Journal*, 11.
158. Senter, *Journal*, 17. According to Senter's record, this was a six-to-five vote for proceeding: Lieutenant Colonel Greene, Lieutenant Colonel Enos, Major Bigelow and Captains Topham, Thayer and Ward voted to carry on, and Lieutenant Peters, Adjunct Hide and Captains Williams, McCobb and Scott wanted the entirety of the troops to return.
159. Arnold himself and surgeon Isaac Senter were not taken prisoner. Arnold was wounded by a musket ball in the thigh during his first assault and taken back to the hospital where Senter was in charge. For a time, the men waited with pistols drawn, believing that they would be taken, but they and others in the hospital were evacuated safely. Senter returned to Rhode Island, where he played an administrative role in the oversight of the military hospitals there for the remainder of the war.
160. Hatch, *Administration*, 89.
161. Ellis, *American Revolution*, 159.

162. Worthington Chauncey Ford, ed., *Writings of Washington*, vol. 6 (Scribner's, 1900), 395. Letter of March 1, 1778.
163. National Park Service, "The Women Present at Valley Forge," https://www.nps.gov.
164. National Park Service, "Women Present at Valley Forge."
165. Ellis, *American Revolution*, 190–91.
166. Richard K. Showman, ed., *The Papers of General Nathanael Greene*, vol. 2, *1 January 1777–16 October 1778* (University of North Carolina Press, 1980), 288.
167. Showman, ed., *Papers of General Nathanael Greene*, vol. 2, 288.
168. Showman, ed., *Papers of General Nathanael Greene*, vol. 2, 335–36.
169. Gerald M. Carbone, *Nathanael Greene: A Biography of the American Revolution* (MacMillan, 1980), 93.
170. Showman, ed., *Papers of General Nathanael Greene*, vol. 2, 393.
171. Showman, ed., *Papers of General Nathanael Greene*, vol. 2, 393.
172. Showman, ed., *Papers of General Nathanael Greene*, vol. 2, 173.
173. *Orderly Book of the New Hampshire Regiment Raised for the Defense of Rhode Island May 25–August 25, 1778*, from the Collections of the Society of Cincinnati, Institute of the American Revolution (Washington, D.C.).
174. Carbone, *Nathanael Greene*, 105.
175. Carbone, *Nathanael Greene*, 111.
176. After the campaign on Rhode Island, Greene returned home to Coventry and his pregnant wife. Caty Greene had followed him briefly to Tiverton, but the August heat forced her to return home. She was now in the final term of her pregnancy, and Greene attended to his wife and home as much as he could, traveling to Boston at Washington's request to further soothe the offended French officers in John Hancock's elegant home before returning to Coventry on September 23. He set out from Boston in a driving rain, and close to home, he was met by a servant on horseback who informed him that his wife was gravely ill. She had been in the throes of labor for nearly two days. Sometime after nine o'clock, when Greene arrived home soaking wet, he witnessed the birth of their third child.
177. Showman, ed., *Papers of General Nathanael Green*, vol. 2, 541.
178. Anne Bezanson, *Prices and Inflation During the American Revolution, Pennsylvania 1770–1790* (University of Pennsylvania Press, 1951), 83.
179. Bezanson, *Prices and Inflation*, 87–88.
180. Bezanson, *Prices and Inflation*, 89.

181. John Russell Bartlett, ed., *Records of the Colony of Rhode Island and Providence Plantations*, vol. 2 (J. Crawford Greene, 1862), 499.
182. Bezanson, *Prices and Inflation*, 66.
183. Richard K. Showman, ed., *The Papers of General Nathanel Greene*, vol. 3 (University of North Carolina Press, 1980), 347.
184. Showman, ed., *Papers of General Nathanel Greene*, vol. 3, 343.
185. Showman, ed., *Papers of General Nathanel Greene*, vol. 3, 343.
186. Richard K. Showman, ed., *The Papers of General Nathanel Greene*, vol. 4 (University of North Carolina Press, 1980), 247.

Chapter 6

187. As reprinted in William R. Lindsey, "Treatment of American Prisoners of War During the American Revolution," *Emporia State Research Studies* (Kansas State Teachers College) 22, no. 1 (Summer 1973): 6.
188. Lindsey, "Treatment of American Prisoners," 6.
189. Olive Anderson, "The Treatment of Prisoners of War in Britain During the American War of Independence," *Institute of Historical Research Bulletin* 28 (1955): 66.
190. Anderson, "Treatment of Prisoners," 66.
191. Anderson, "Treatment of Prisoners," 8.
192. Anderson, "Treatment of Prisoners," 8.
193. Jeremiah Greenman, *Diary of a Common Soldier in the Revolution 1775–1783*, edited by Robert Bray and Paul Bushnell (Northern Illinois University Press, 1978), 23–24.
194. A foretelling of actual events that would occur in New York in 1779, when starved American prisoners were fed biscuits before their release, most of whom died of the poison ingested before reaching home.
195. Greenman, *Diary*, 26–27.
196. Edwin G. Burroughs, *Forgotten Patriots: The Untold Story of American Prisoners During the Revolutionary War* (Basic Books, 2008), 21.
197. Burroughs, *Forgotten Patriots*, 24.
198. T. Cole Jones, *Captives of Liberty: Prisoners of War and the Politics of Vengeance in the American Revolution* (University of Pennsylvania Press, 2020), 101.
199. James Russell Bartlett, ed., *Colonial Records of Rhode Island*, vol. 8, 1776–1778, 27.
200. Bartlett, ed., *Records of Rhode Island*, vol. 8, 15.

201. Jones, *Captives of Liberty*, 101.
202. Bartlett, ed., *Records of Rhode Island*, vol. 8.
203. Jones, *Captives of Liberty*, 101.
204. Burroughs, *Forgotten Patriots*, 46.
205. Burroughs, *Forgotten Patriots*, 59.
206. Danske Dandridge, *American Prisoners of the Revolution* (privately printed, 1910), 45.
207. Burroughs, *Forgotten Patriots*, 64.
208. Governor Samuel Cooke, letter to General George Washington, February 9, 1777, in Bartlett, ed., *Records of Rhode Island*, vol. 8.
209. Burroughs, *Forgotten Patriots*, 64.
210. Dandridge, *Prisoners of the Revolution*, 67.
211. Burroughs, *Forgotten Patriots*, 53.
212. Cowell, *Spirit of '76*, 163.
213. Carl P. Borick, *Relieve Us of This Burthen: American Prisoners of War in the Revolutionary South 1780–1782* (University of South Carolina Press, 2012), 8.
214. "Wright Families of Georgia," http://homepage.rootsweb.com.
215. Dandridge, *American Prisoners*, 137.
216. Dandridge, *American Prisoners*, 153.
217. As reprinted in Dandridge, *American Prisoners*, 150–53.
218. Dandridge, *American Prisoners*, 100–02.
219. Dandridge, *American Prisoners*, 100–02.
220. Dandridge, *American Prisoners*, 103.

Chapter 7

221. Jones, *Captives of Liberty*, 125.
222. Jones, *Captives of Liberty*, 125.
223. Jones, *Captives of Liberty*, 125.
224. See Johannes Schwalm Historical Association, https://jsha.org.
225. Marcia Green, "O Tannenbaum! Two Ashton Families Lit Cumberland's First Christmas Trees," *Valley Breeze*, December 3, 2015.
226. Jones, *Captives of Liberty*, 127.
227. Jones, *Captives of Liberty*, 135.
228. Jones, *Captives of Liberty*, 148.
229. Jones, *Captives of Liberty*, 151.

230. Ballagh, ed., *Letters of Richard Henry Lee*, vol. 1 (MacMillan, 1912), 350. Letter to George Washington, November 20, 1777.
231. Ballagh, ed., *Letters*, 350.
232. Jones, *Captives of Liberty*, 161.
233. Jones, *Captives of Liberty*, 162.
234. Ballagh, ed., *Letters of Richard Henry Lee*, vol. 1 (MacMillan, 1912), 404. Letter to Arthur Lee, May 12, 1778.
235. Jones, *Captives of Liberty*, 169.
236. Jones, *Captives of Liberty*, 169.
237. Rhode Island Historical Society, MSS 9003 V.3, p. 80.
238. Among the many celebrated stories of the *Ranger* is the following episode, taken from the website Continental Navy: "The ship Ranger again left Portsmouth on 18 June 1779 to cruise in company with the Providence and Queen of France. Cruising again off the Newfoundland Banks during mid-July, the little squadron fell in with the Jamaican fleet of about 150 ships undetected in the dense fog of early morning. Masquerading as British vessels, the three American warships sailed amidst the enemy fleet all day dispatching boarding parties manning small boats. Taking eleven prizes while not firing a shot or raising any alarm, the Continental Navy vessels and their prizes slipped away from the fleet under the cover of night. Eight of the prizes were sent into Boston accompanied by the Providence with their aggregate cargo valued over one million dollars. The ship Ranger again returned to her home port at Portsmouth where yet another re-provisioning was done." Joe, "List of Officers and Men Ship-of-War Ranger's Cruises 2/24/1779–11/23/1779," Continental Navy, January 13, 2019, https://continentalnavy.com.
239. Joe, "List of Officers and Men."
240. John K. Robertson, *Proceedings of the Committee of the Rhode Island General Assembly and the Council of War, 1778–1783* (2019), 97.
241. The Daughters of the American Revolution Patriot List identifies John Greene as having contributed services during the Revolutionary War. He served on the Coventry Town Council during the war as well.
242. The First Rhode Island regiment was stationed on the island at this time, mostly improving the forts they had occupied during the earlier Battle of Rhode Island in 1778; Robertson, *Proceedings*, 382.
243. Bartlett, ed., *Records of the Colony of Rhode Island and Providence Plantations*, vol. 9, *1780–1785* (J. Crawford Greene, 1864), 162–63.

244. Bartlett, ed., *Colony of Rhode Island*, vol. 9, 162–63.
245. Bartlett, ed., *Colony of Rhode Island*, vol. 9, 162–63.
246. Bartlett, ed., *Colony of Rhode Island*, vol. 9, 495.
247. Jones, *Captives of Liberty*, 209–11.
248. Burroughs, *Forgotten Patriots*, 111.
249. Burroughs, *Forgotten Patriots*, 112.
250. Burroughs, *Forgotten Patriots*, 113.

Chapter 8

251. Gerald Carbone, *Nathanael Greene: A Biography of the American Revolution* (Palgrave/Macmillan, 2008), 127.
252. Carbone, *Nathanael Greene*, 130.
253. Bartlett, ed., *Colonial Records*, vol. 9, 46.
254. Bartlett, ed., *Colonial Records*, vol. 9, 286.
255. Howard S. Russell, *A Long Deep Furrow: Three Centuries of Farming in New England*, 222.
256. Hatch, *Administration*, 111.
257. Hatch, *Administration*, 112.
258. Bezanson, *Prices and Inflation*, 322–23.
259. Hatch, *Administration*, 112.
260. Bartlett, ed., *Colonial Records*, vol. 9, 369.
261. Judith Jenks Ray, *Founders and Patriots of the Town of Cumberland, Rhode Island* (Glen Bay Press, 1990), 9.
262. John Buchanan, *The Road to Charlestown: Nathanael Greene and the American Revolution* (University of Virginia Press, 2019), 54.
263. Buchanan, *Road to Charlestown*, 54.
264. Richard K. Showman, ed., *Papers of General Nathanael Greene*, vol. 8, March–July 1781 (University of North Carolina Press, published for the Rhode Island Historical Society, 1980), 207.
265. Buchanan, *Road to Charlestown*, 114.
266. Buchanan, *Road to Charlestown*, 115.
267. Buchanan, *Road to Charlestown*, 115.
268. Buchanan, *Road to Charlestown*, 121–22.
269. Bezanson, *Prices and Inflation*, 323.
270. Russell, *Long Deep Furrow*, 217.
271. Russell, *Long Deep Furrow*, 217.
272. Russell, *Long Deep Furrow*, 218.

Chapter 9

273. Gillett, *Army Medical Department*, 110.
274. Gillett, *Army Medical Department*, 97.
275. Gillett, *Army Medical Department*, 309.
276. Thacher, *Military Journal*, 131.
277. Richard V. Simpson, *Tiverton and Little Compton Rhode Island: Historic Tales of the Outer Plantations* (The History Press, 2012), 90.
278. In May 1780, the Rhode Island Council of War "resolved that Mr. John Innes Clark be requested to proceed with Dr. Craik in Tiverton & Bristol & examine the Barracks in Tiverton and the Buildings on the Estate in Bristol late Belonging to Mr. William Vassal and now improved by Mr. Nathaniel Fales Jr. Under a lease from this state, and if in their opinion they should be suitable and Convenient for the purpose, that they take possession of Part or all of said buildings and apply to the Deputy quartermaster general to have them immediately fitted in the best possible manner for the Reception of said Sick as aforesaid." Robertson, *Proceedings*, 384.
279. Gillett, *Army Medical Department*, 117.
280. Gillett, *Army Medical Department*, 120.
281. Hugh Rankin, *The North Carolina Continentals* (University of North Carolina Press, 1971), 252.
282. Rankin, *North Carolina Continentals*, 253.
283. Gillett, *Army Medical Department*, 118.
284. Gillett, *Army Medical Department*, 119.
285. Galpern, ed., *Excerpts from the Diary*, 120.
286. Galpern, ed., *Excerpts from the Diary*, 122.
287. Galpern, ed., *Excerpts from the Diary*, 122.
288. Galpern, ed., *Excerpts from the Diary*, 124.
289. Daniel M. Popek, *They "…Fought Bravely, but Were Unfortunate:" The True Story of Rhode Island's "Black Regiment" and the Failure of Segregation in Rhode Island's Continental Line, 1777–1783* (Authorhouse, 2015), 533.
290. Popek, *Fought Bravely*, 534.
291. Gillett, *Army Medical Department*, 127.
292. Gillett, *Army Medical Department*, 128.
293. Gillett, *Army Medical Department*, 222.
294. Gillett, *Army Medical Department*, 220.
295. Gordon, *Aesculapius*, 305.

Chapter 10

296. Abrams, *Revolutionary Medicine*, 62.
297. Jesse J. Holland, *The Invisibles: The Untold Story of African American Slaves in the White House* (Rowman & Littlefield, 2016), 27.
298. Holland, *Invisibles*, 63.
299. Stephen Decatur Jr., *Private Affairs of George Washington from the Records and Accounts of Tobias Lear* (Riverside Press, 1933), 36.
300. Decatur, *George Washington*, 133.
301. Abrams, *Revolutionary Medicine*, 66.
302. As reprinted in Decatur, *George Washington*, 133.
303. Decatur, *George Washington*, 133.
304. The trip was touted as a celebration of Rhode Island's ratification of the Constitution earlier that year. Indeed, after his arrival on the *Hannah*, the first two days were taken up with official duties, accompanied by an entourage of officials, including Jefferson; the governor of New York, George Clinton; and several Congressional representatives. Decatur writes, "Arriving in Newport on the morning of the seventeenth, Washington was greeted with the usual salutes and cheering crowds. In the afternoon there was a large banquet in his honor at the Town Hall, with numerous toasts, but most of the day was spent walking about the island enjoying the wonderful views. The next day the party…sailed up Narragansett Bay to Providence. The next day there was another grand dinner at the Court House, when 13 toasts were drank under discharges of cannon." Decatur's notes, based on Secretary Tobias Lear's account, record that Washington left in a packet following the event and returned to New York "after a passage of 24 hours only," but in fact, Washington remained in Newport until September. The public and apparently New Yorkers were told that the president had retreated to Mount Vernon.
305. Decatur, *George Washington*, 158.
306. Abrams, *Revolutionary Medicine*, 68.
307. James Thomas Flexner, *George Washington: Anguish and Farewell (1793–1799)* (Little, Brown, 1972), 85.
308. Flexner, *George Washington*, 86.
309. As quoted in Abrams, *Revolutionary Medicine*, 70.
310. Flexner, *George Washington*, 202.
311. Flexner, *George Washington*, 72.
312. Decatur, *George Washington*, 149.

313. Flexner, *George Washington*, 208; W.W. Abbott, *George Washington Papers*, vol. 34 (University Press of Virginia, 2024), 175.
314. Flexner, *George Washington*, 272.
315. Flexner, *George Washington*, 339.
316. Flexner, *George Washington*, 456.
317. Flexner, *George Washington*, 456.
318. Christopher Sheels replaced Washington's longest-serving slave, William Lee, after Lee became too infirm to continue that job and was relegated to making shoes at Mount Vernon. Sheels soon became a favorite slave of the former president and likely prepared his body for burial as a last service to his master. See Holland, *Invisibles*, 34.
319. Abrams, *Revolutionary Medicine*, 76.

ABOUT THE AUTHOR

The author (*center*) with members of the Second Rhode Island Regiment reenactors. *Photo courtesy of the author.*

Robert A. Geake is a public historian and the author of fifteen books on Rhode Island and New England history, including (with Lorén Spears) *From Slaves to Soldiers: The First Rhode Island Regiment in the American Revolution*. Other books include *A History of the Narragansett Tribe: Keepers of the Bay*; *Native and New Americans*; *New England's Citizen Soldiers: Mariners and Minutemen*; *Fired a Gun at the Rising of the Sun: The Journal of Noah Robinson of Attleboro in the Revolutionary War*; and a work in progress, to be titled *The Battle Off the Field in the American Revolution*.

The author and historian has had the privilege of participating in the symposium at Valley Forge titled "African Americans in the Philadelphia Campaign and the Valley Forge Encampment of 1777–1778," sponsored by the Valley Forge National Park Service (NPS) and the Association for the Study of African American Life and History (ASALH). He has also given his presentation "In League with Liberty: The Persistence of Patriots of Color and the Formation of the Black Regiment in the Continental Line" to libraries and historical societies, including the Institute of the American Revolution in Washington, D.C. Most recently he completed an extensive timeline of the formation and service of the First Rhode Island Regiment for the Battle of Rhode Island Association's website: https://battleofrhodeisland.org/highlights-of-the-timeline-of-the-1st-rhode-island-regiment.

Geake served two terms as president of the Cocumscussoc Association, which maintains Smith's Castle, a historic house museum in North Kingstown, Rhode Island, and continues as chair of the association's Education Committee. During his time as chair, adult educational programs began and were expanded to include the seminars "Roger Was Here" in 2019, which brought scholars on Roger Williams together to discuss his life and legacy, and "Anchored in Rhode Island: The Slave Trade and Reckoning with Our Past," held in 2023. He also serves on the advisory board of the Rhode Island Slave History Medallion project and was responsible for organizing the effort to place a medallion on the grounds of Smith's Castle.

Most recently, he is working with the Battle of Rhode Island Association and other sponsors to produce a series of seminars on "The Underwritten of the American Revolution" over the next few years of the war's anniversary.

As a public historian, Mr. Geake is a contributor to the blog *Small State Big History* (https://smallstatebighistory.com) and, most recently, *The Cocumscussoc Review* on https://www.smithscastle.org. His essay on "Rhode Island and the American Revolution" is among those contributed to EnCompass, a digital resource for the study of Rhode Island history from the Rhode Island Historical Society and the Rhode Island Department of Education.